Developing Language and Literacy 3–8

Ann Browne has taught extensively throughout the 3 to 8 age range. She is currently the programme leader for the Early Years PCGE at the University of East Anglia. She has contributed numerous articles to *Reading* and *Language and Learning*. Her previous book, *Helping Children to Write*, was published by Paul Chapman in 1993.

Developing Language and Literacy 3–8

Ann Browne

P·C·P
Paul Chapman
Publishing Ltd

Paul Chapman Publishing Ltd
144 Liverpool Road
London
N1 1LA

British Library Cataloguing-in-Publication Data

Browne, Ann
    Developing language and literacy 3–8
    1. English language – Study and teaching (Elementary)
    I. Title
    372.6'044

    ISBN 1 85396 282 1

Typeset by Dorwyn Ltd, Rowlands Castle, Hants
Printed and bound in Great Britain

A B C D E F G H   9 8 7 6

Contents

Introduction

The intention in writing this book was to provide an informative, up-to-date guide about good practice in language and literacy for all those who work with young children. I hope that the book does this by providing practical guidance on implementing an English curriculum for 3–8-year-olds.

English has always been an area rich in debate, research and new ideas which have led to frequent evaluation of practices, but the past ten years in particular have seen many major changes. The National Curriculum, the National Writing Project, the National Oracy Project and the LINC (Language in the National Curriculum) Project have been powerful agents for curriculum change in schools and nurseries, have affected teachers' thinking about how English is learned and taught and have influenced practices in school. This book reflects many of these ideas and developments.

The approach and practices suggested in this book are in keeping with the traditions of good early-years education and draw from a number of established educational principles. Educators recognize that children learn best when they actively engage with their learning and when they are given real and relevant reasons for learning. They know that children construct and test hypotheses about new experiences and that taking risks and making mistakes are a valuable part of the learning process. Early-years educators relate what is being taught to what children already know. In order to extend each child's learning they support and guide children through each new stage of learning. They know that the abilities and attitudes that young children develop in the early years are an important part of a life-long learning journey during which children will need to acquire all the language skills necessary to interpret, manipulate, control and organize language for their own present and future purposes.

Devising an effective English curriculum which takes account of the principles of early-years education calls for committed and knowledgeable professionals. Thoughtful and effective practitioners do not just know what to do, they also understand the reasons for their actions. In order to achieve their aim of developing children's learning in the best way possible they are aware of the issues and are willing to reflect on practice. For these reasons each chapter contains references to research and makes suggestions for further reading as well as describing good practice.

I would like to thank all the children, students and teachers who have provided me with many opportunities to reflect on language learning and learners, to consider an appropriate language curriculum for young children and made it possible for me to collect the examples that are included in this book.

I hope that this book recognizes the expertise and importance of all who contribute to the education of young children, acknowledges the willingness and curiosity that children bring to learning and that it contributes to the quality of teaching and learning in the early years.

Ann Browne
August 1995

Chapter 1

Speaking and listening

Introduction

The development and understanding of speaking and listening is of vital importance to those concerned with educating the young child, for a number of reasons: first, that the majority of young children learn to speak easily and fluently in their home language by about the age of 4 signals children's capacity to learn. Secondly, speaking and listening are themselves a means of learning at school and in the world beyond school. Finally every adult is concerned to develop children's oral abilities further so that they become confident and competent communicators with a range of people and in a variety of situations.

This chapter begins by examining the development of children's early language before they enter the more formal settings of the nursery or first school and by describing how and why children learn to talk. Standard English and received pronunciation, two important issues for teachers concerned with developing their pupils' communicative competence, are considered. The next sections are primarily concerned with language development at school and include speaking and listening across the curriculum, strategies for extending children's oral competence and activities that can be included in a the curriculum for speaking and listening.

Children as learners of oral language

By the time that children are 4 or 5 virtually all of them have achieved an amazing competence in at least one language dialect. Studies of the vocabulary development of young children have shown that the average 5-year-old knows at least 2,000 words and may know over 10,000 (Crystal, 1987). The number of words that are understood is thought to be far in excess of either of these figures. As part of the process of gathering this extensive vocabulary, the majority of young children have also mastered most of the phonemes or sound units of the speech used in their home or community. Research has also indicated that on entry to school the bulk of children's speech is grammatically correct and children from English-speaking homes use all the basic sentence patterns of English in their speech (Strickland, 1962; Loban, 1976). Although some children may make grammatical errors, saying, for example, 'she bringed it' rather than 'she brought it', such mistakes are usually the result of the overgeneraliz-ation of a grammatical rule, in this case an awareness of how past-tense verbs are often formed, rather than a random mistake. As well as being competent speakers young children are also expert listeners. It is their ability to listen that has enabled them to join in with the speech of adults from the time that they were a few months old. Listening has given them clues about the sounds and sound combinations which are used to form acceptable words and has provided children with an understanding of how sentences are formed.

By the age of 3 or 4 months children are actively developing as partici-pants in oral communication. Babies respond to the talk of others with smiles, movements and sounds. They discover their own voices and gurgle with pleasure as adults speak to them. As children begin to experi-ment with producing sounds themselves they gain greater control over their throat and mouth muscles and begin to engage in turn-taking be-haviour, characteristic of spoken dialogue, waiting for a pause in the speech of others before producing their own sounds. This stage in lan-guage development, known as babbling, gives very young children the opportunity to experiment with and imitate the sound patterns of their community language. By about 5 or 6 months babies may begin inten-tionally to use their voices to attract attention and to initiate social ex-changes. During the next few months babies start to establish a range of sounds some of which are wordlike. These might include sounds such as 'ba-ba', 'da-da' and 'ma-ma'. Adults are often delighted with the emer-gence of sounds that resemble familiar words and attribute meaning to these. They respond to children by repeating and expanding those words that they recognize, saying such things as, 'Da-da, yes, what a clever girl. Here's daddy now. Daddy is coming'. With encouragement such as this children gradually begin to attach meaning to particular groups of sounds and words hearing, for example, that 'da-da' can become the word 'daddy'. Adult responses encourage babies to experiment more and the way in which they shape their responses provides a basis on which children can build a vocabulary that sounds increasingly like that of adult speakers. From the age of about 15 months onwards, children begin, with increasing accuracy, to imitate the articulation of sounds that they hear others use. They demonstrate their wish to join in communicative acts with others, signalling their intentions through their actions, gestures and the tone and nature of their utterances. Their communications in-creasingly resemble the words and phrases used by the adults around them. At about 2 years of age children's speech is characterized by abbre-viated utterances that transmit meaning (Brown and Belugi, 1966). They produce correctly ordered groups of content words that can be understood by others. For example a young child may say, 'Mummy gone shops'. The typical adult response to an utterance of this sort is to acknowledge the meaning, praise the utterance and expand what was said by giving the child the 'correct' adult version by replying 'Yes, that's right. Mummy has gone to the shops, hasn't she?'. These sorts of responses provide children with models of the extended grammatical structure of language which they incorporate into their own speech. From about the age of 3 years most children begin to construct longer, more complex sentence and are able to use a number of tenses and voices. Their development as speakers and listeners continues until, by the time they start school, the majority of children are accomplished communicators with a large vocabulary, a command of a range of sentence types and a clear sense of grammatical correctness.

Children's purposes for learning to talk

When teachers are constructing a curriculum for oracy in school with the intention of extending what children have already learned, they need to take account of what children need to learn about oral language, to be aware of how children's competence in oral language has developed between birth and starting school and to understand why children develop so rapidly as speakers and listeners.

The vast majority of children develop their capacity to speak and to listen without any direct instruction or teaching. The way in which children do this reveals a great deal about them as learners in a general sense as well as about them as language learners. This tells adults a great deal about the sorts of strategies that enable children to learn and to learn about all aspects of language.

Babies are learners from the moment of their birth. The first cry that they utter as they are born, as with their later cries and sounds, results in attention and responses from those around them. From the start adults respond to children's facial expressions and the sounds that they make with encouragement, praise and an expectation that the child's communication has meaning. At the same time as babies are learning that producing sounds enables their needs to be met, the adults who surround them are demonstrating the nature and use of speaking and listening. Care givers assume that even very young babies are potential conversation partners and as they interact with babies they speak to them in a way that assumes that the baby is listening, may understand and has the potential to respond. Children overhear a great deal of conversation between those who surround them and are exposed to a great deal of conversation that is addressed directly to them. Adults interpret, repeat, support, extend and provide models of speech for children as they communicate with them. They do not limit their language or the child's learning but rather expose the child to the full range of purposes and models of language that are used in the child's environment. It is as children are exposed to more and more language and supported in their production that they become increasingly proficient in their language use.

Initially babies may use language for functional reasons, to express their needs and to get others to do things for them. At an early stage they may also see the social purposes of language – the attention of others is usually pleasurable and the production of sounds and language is one way for them to sustain interactions. Babies seem to enjoy producing sounds and at times produce endless repetitions of similar sounds as they babble and gurgle and later experiment with real and nonsense words. Finally children seem to develop language because they are cognitive beings and active explorers of their worlds. Language is one method of finding out about the world that they live in. It enables them to widen their understanding by questioning, commenting, suggesting reasons, drawing upon previous experience and receiving information from others.

Standard English and received pronunciation

Standard English

Debate has always surrounded the issue of standard English and this area is now receiving more attention as a result of the present National Curriculum Orders for English (DfE, 1995a), where the ability to speak and write in standard English is presented as a significant feature of English teaching in school. As standard English comes under scrutiny again there is a danger that the issue will be misunderstood and that dialects that differ from standard English will be rated as second class, sloppy and ineffective, and that children who enter school fluent in the language spoken in their homes and communities but who are used to communicating in ways that are different from the language used and valued in school, often standard English, will be classed as having 'no language' or an impoverished form of language.

Standard English is one dialect of English. Like other dialects it is a systematic form of language that has accepted rules and conventions. The difference between standard English and other dialect forms is that standard English is the form of language used for 'non-regional public communication' (Whitehead, 1990), and because of its public and official use is often felt to be the most socially prestigious dialect form of English.

The National Curriculum Council consultation report on English in the National Curriculum (NCC, 1993) states that when defining standard English it should be noted that:

- Standard English comprises **vocabulary** as found in dictionaries, and agreed conventions of **spelling** and **grammar**.
- Speech varies according to the degree of formality.
- Core grammatical features of Standard English include subject verb agreement, correct and consistent use of verb tenses, correct use of pronouns, adverbs and adjectives. In spoken Standard English significant

features are standard forms of irregular verbs; agreement between person, case and number (especially with the verb 'to be'); the correct use of pronouns.
- The aim should be to equip young people with the ability to use Standard English when circumstances require it . . . It is important to encourage pupils' ability to extend their speaking . . . repertoires: to make their language 'fit' the context.

(*Ibid.*, p. 16)

The document acknowledges the richness and variety of dialectical difference in England and Wales and suggests that as pupils progress through Key Stages 1 and 2 they should use the vocabulary and grammar of standard English with increasing fluency and proficiency in those circumstances that require it.

English in the National Curriculum (DfE, 1995a) repeats many of the ideas and explanations used in the consultation document, such as 'Pupils should be encouraged to develop confidence in their ability to adapt what they say to their listeners and to the circumstances, beginning to recognize how language differs, *eg the vocabulary of standard English and that of dialects, how their choice of language varies in different situations*' (*ibid.*, p. 5); and at Key Stage 2 the document states that pupils should be given opportunities to, 'investigate how language varies according to context and purpose and between standard and dialect forms' (*ibid.*, p. 12).

As long as these references to standard English are not interpreted to mean that it is superior to any other dialect used by pupils, few would disagree with the suggestion that all speakers of English should be given the opportunity to express themselves in a range of dialects, including standard English, when it is appropriate. Standard English gives speakers of English access to a world language that is appropriate in formal or serious situations such as interviews, communicative situations beyond the home and with people outside one's immediate family or peer group. All children have the right to feel confident when speaking to a range of people and in a variety of circumstances. But is also important to remember, first, that language is closely allied to one's identity and any denigration of a child's normal dialect may be seen as a criticism of the child, his family and his environment and, secondly, that it is not necessary to use standard English all the time. When communicating with friends or colleagues we can all use jargon and incomplete or irregularly constructed sentences. It is also worth considering that, when they start school, the majority of children living in the twentieth century are probably well aware of the standard dialect form of English through exposure to the language used on television and radio broadcasts such as story telling, news and documentary programmes. They are also likely to be implicitly aware of numerous other dialect versions of English as viewers of and listeners to *Coronation Street*, *EastEnders*, *Brookside* and *Neighbours*. They are well able to code switch as they listen to and understand these very different varieties of English and as with the development of their early language, their ability to listen is the basis from which the production of language will emerge. It is likely that as children see the need to use different varieties of English their language use will change and develop to meet new needs and audiences as long as they are exposed to different models and to situations which demand the use of different dialects. In this way they will be able to judge the power, use and limitations of standard English and set it alongside their home dialect as yet another speech option.

One way in which teachers may encourage all children to use standard English may be through reading and writing. Standard English is the dialect most commonly found in books and the one that we all need and aspire to when writing for others. Book language provides a model of complete and grammatically exact language for children to listen to and respond to. As children themselves begin to write for audiences beyond themselves they will come to see the need for extended and clear communication that draws on a vocabulary and grammar that is shared by all potential readers. Sensitive intervention in children's writing will lead to the discussion of the different varieties of English that exist, the reasons for their existence and provide opportunities for children to use standard English purposefully.

Received pronunciation

Standard English and received pronunciation are often thought of as synonymous; this is not the case. Standard English is a dialect and refers to regular grammatical patterns and a distinctive set of vocabulary. Received pronunciation does not refer to grammar or vocabulary; instead it refers to pronunciation or accent. Most accents reveal the speaker's geographical origins, but received pronunciation is a regionless accent used by a minority of English speakers. It is not used as the model of English pronunciation in British schools and indeed speakers should be 'rightly proud of their regional pronunciation which identifies where they come from' (DES, 1988a, p. 14). In short, 'spoken standard English is not the same as received pronunciation and can be expressed in a variety of accents' (DfE, 1995a, p. 3).

Perhaps the role of the school in relation to accents in general is to counter negative attitudes to them, since these can affect self-esteem and identity. A distinctive regional accent may identify a new entrant to school as coming from a different place, or being an outsider and impede the child's acceptance as a member of a new local community. Some people manifest hostile attitudes to English spoken, for example, with an Asian accent. If this occurs the teacher, drawing on her own knowledge and awareness of language, needs to discuss this with the pupils stressing the need to respect one's own language and that of others. Relationships in the classroom between adults and children and between the pupils themselves are often established through talk. Good relationships leading to feelings of self-worth and acceptance are essential for all learning and especially for the development of oral language. The teacher's own attitude to the language the children use is crucial for the development of children's personal confidence and their willingness to take the risks that will be necessary as they extend their language repertoire in response to new situations and new audiences.

Speaking, listening and learning across the whole curriculum

Children's language development is associated with their exploration and greater understanding of the world they inhabit. Through listening, questioning, formulating hypotheses and statements about what they understand and interpreting the responses they receive they have learned a great deal. Language aids children's cognitive development by providing them with a tool to make discoveries, giving them a mechanism to make sense of new experiences and offering them a means of making connections between the new and what is already known.

The abilities to listen and to speak are of paramount importance if children are to succeed both inside and outside school. Speaking and listening occupy more time than reading and writing in the lives of most people and enable life-long learning and social interaction to occur. In school a developing facility with oral language is crucial for learning. In the early years a great deal of teaching and assessment is carried out through through talk as the teacher explains, describes and elicits the children's understanding of the learning activities she has provided in the classroom. Learning to read and to write are founded upon children's oral language competence, their unconscious expectation that written language, like oral language, contains meaning, follows a particular structure and comprises sentences, words and parts of words. As children progress through the education system knowledge and information is increasingly transmitted and recorded through reading and writing. Pupils' learning depends on a growing competence in a language mode that grows out of their ability to speak and listen. Perhaps the most important reason for developing children's oral language is that all learning depends on the ability to question, reason, formulate ideas, pose hypotheses and exchange ideas with others. These are not just oral language skills, they are also thinking skills. As Donaldson (1978, pp. 88–89) wrote,

> What is going to be required for success in our educational system is that [children] should learn to turn language and thought in upon themselves . . . He must be able not just to talk, but to choose what he will say, not just to interpret but to weigh possible interpretations. His conceptual system must expand in the direction of increasing ability to represent itself.

Consequently, all teachers are rightly concerned with widening the vocabulary, form and function of the oral language repertoire of all the pupils that they teach.

English is never a discrete subject area in the curriculum, it draws its content from other subject areas and is used as a tool in all aspects of life in and out of school. It is always cross-curricular in its application and can be developed in every area of the early-years curriculum.

What can oracy do?

In and out of school and in all areas of the curriculum speaking and listening can be used to • act on and give instructions • act on and make suggestions • ask and answer questions • challenge • clarify • converse • describe • discuss • evaluate • exchange ideas • explain • explore understanding • express emotion • give and act on instructions • give orders • hypothesize • imagine • initiate action or change • investigate • make oneself understood • negotiate • participate • persuade • plan • reason • reflect • rehearse roles or experience • report • request • reshape what is known or thought • share opinions, experiences and emotions • speculate • state opinions • summarize • tell and listen to stories • think aloud • understand ideas • understand others. Readers might want to add to or modify this list as they examine their own purposes for speaking and listening.

The following extract shows the potential language has to be a powerful tool for learning across and beyond the early-years curriculum. Three Year 1 children, Suki, Martin and Thomas, were working together in the art area. They had been asked to print a large area of sky as part of a background for a display relating to the story *Charlie's House* (Schermbrucker, 1992). The teacher had asked the children to work together to complete the activity. They had to decide on the colour they would use for the sky and then decide what equipment they would use for the printing:

S: Blue . . . This sky is blue.
M: Like, like . . . the sky in the book.
T: Is it? . . . I mean . . . just . . .
S: Course it is . . . the sky in South Africa's always blue, like the sun is always shining.
M: Doesn't.
S: Does . . . What do you mean?
M: Has to rain sometimes . . . that's why, that's how they got the mud . . . and in the winter . . .
S: Yeah, I remember it rained.
T: They got paint pots to get the water.
M: But its not in the book.
[M goes to find the book and brings it to show the others] . . .
M: Look . . . nowhere . . . nowhere blue.

This extract shows children using talk to focus carefully on the activity and to do it well. They are using talk for a number of purposes and in a number of ways. Through their talk they are reflecting on a previous learning experience which occurred when they listened to the story, and integrating this with their own knowledge and understanding of hot climates. Although they had seen the pictures in the book, they had not realized the significance of the grey skies in relation to the climate. As they talk they listen carefully to one and other, give each other time, check out Martin's suggestion and seem happy to adjust their thinking in the light of what has been said and the evidence contained in the book. Exchanging ideas has given them the opportunity to re-evaluate what they had seen and to extend and amend their previous knowledge. Had the children been working at this task singly or with an adult who was directing them, it is unlikely that this learning and reflection would have taken place. In this extract the conversation emerging from a collaborative activity has been a valuable way of exchanging opinions, sharing knowledge, justifying ideas, reflecting on previous experiences and accepting new learning.

The aims of a speaking and listening curriculum in the early years

Although children will enter the nursery or reception class as competent users of oral language they will still lack experience of using language in certain ways. Teachers of young children will identify what children can already do and those aspects of language that should be developed in school. Their aims for oracy will build on what children can already do and may include extending children's competence as oral language users in the following areas:

- Taking account of the needs of listeners. Assessing the listener's understanding and knowledge; needing to be more explicit in certain situations and with certain audiences.
- Talking in front of large audiences.
- Waiting their turn to speak in large groups.
- Understanding and answering the teacher's questions.
- Participating purposefully, using reasoning and discussion, in collaborative classroom tasks.
- Using different styles and forms of language appropriate to particular situations, such as telling jokes, participating in a debate or giving reasons and step-by-step explanations.
- Being able to organize what is said.
- Acquiring and using a more extensive repertoire of words.

Having aims such as these will help early-years practitioners to devise oracy activities and to organize the children, resources, activities and their own interactions to enable children to gain experience in these areas.

The problem with talk

Given that talk can make a valid contribution to learning, why does it get squeezed out of the curriculum? When comparing children's language at home and at school, Wells (1986) found that at school children speak less with adults, and in the conversations that they do have, get fewer turns, express a narrower range of meanings and use grammatically less complex utterances. They also ask fewer questions, make fewer requests and initiate a smaller proportion of conversations. In comparison with parents, teachers dominated conversational exchanges giving children far fewer opportunities to speak in class than at home. Wells (*ibid.*, p. 87) concluded that 'For *no* child was the language experience of the classroom richer than that of the home'. This is an important message for educators who need to see children's talk as important and valuable in its own right if they are to foster the growth of children's learning and language learning. Whilst listening may be an essential part of the oracy curriculum, the opportunity for children to develop their own meanings through talk is a vital part of learning.

During the school day teachers plan and prioritize pupils' learning. There are a great many competing demands on the time available for learning and teaching. Because children do talk and listen at school it is easy for some teachers to overlook the oracy curriculum. Some teachers do not understand the value of talk, they can be dismissive of talk and they may see planning for productive talk as an organizational headache.

Not understanding the value of talk

It is easy for adults to place most emphasis on work that is regularly recorded, that can be seen and can be assessed easily. Talk is none of these things. How do we tell if children have made a real effort to listen or to speak? How do we justify talk to others if there is no visible product? If teachers view talk as an inferior means of demonstrating learning and emphasize the more visible parts of the curriculum such as writing and recording, productive talk is unlikely to happen. The pressure to cover the statutory curriculum has encouraged some teachers to resort to a more didactic style of teaching, a style that is concerned with the transmission of facts rather than the exploration of ideas. This approach to teaching reduces the opportunities and necessity for discussion and the language interaction that does occur is more likely to be concerned with eliciting and giving correct answers rather than using oral language for any of its other purposes. In some teachers' minds the sound of children talking signals that children are not working and may prompt them to say, 'Stop talking and get on with your work'. They may fear that talk will develop into noisy and undisciplined behaviour. Teachers who do not understand the place of talk in learning, who do not value talk at school and who feel insecure about noise in the classroom will influence their pupils' perceptions of talk. Children taught by teachers like those described above will not see speaking and listening as work, and when they are given opportunities to speak will tend to use talk socially rather than as a means of learning.

The problem of organizing

Routines and rules about quiet or silence while the teacher marks the register, while children move from the classroom for PE, lunch, playtime and assemblies and silent periods for reading, PE and stories reduce the time available for talk in the school day. Too many rules about times when children's talk is not allowed can also transmit negative messages about the importance of talking and listening. Some teachers can find the prospect of organizing purposeful talk for the whole class daunting. Whole-class discussion times are rarely productive even during discussion times after a story or registration. The majority of children are usually silent while one child or the adult speaks, very few children get the opportunity to contribute and any interaction between the children is rare. Some adults believe that if children are allowed to talk while they are working they will talk purposefully and that this is sufficient to develop their oral language. Permitting quiet talking during an activity is not the same as children talking about an activity and using talk to exchange ideas, to question, to solve problems and to explain. Collaborative activities that demand discussion between pupils need to be consciously organized by the teacher even if they do not always find this easy.

The teacher's role in the development of speaking and listening

Teachers, and other adults in school, can play an important part in extending the oral development of young children. The effectiveness of their role is related to

- their own understanding of the value of talk
- their attitude to talk
- their organization for talk
- their own use of language
- their awareness of strategies and activities that encourage speaking and listening.

Understanding the value of talk

This chapter contains a strong case for the learning potential of talk. By learning to speak children demonstrate that they are active learners and constructors of their own knowledge and as adults support the development and use of children's speech they enable children to articulate and satisfy their curiosity. As teachers extend pupils' learning experiences, children need to become more reflectively aware of what they know and of what they need to know, so that they can gradually take over more and more responsibility for their own learning. The teacher's willingness to explore topics collaboratively with pupils allowing them to negotiate meanings and extend their understanding through talk is the key to developing children's learning. This means that teachers have to allow time for children to talk to adults and to each other about tasks that are undertaken and new ideas that they meet. Allocating time for discussion during the school day necessitates the recognition of the value of the activity.

Attitude to talk

Children will feel confident and comfortable in speaking if the teacher shows a positive respect for and interest in their language and gives status to the different varieties of language used by the children in her care. If this is not the case then they are less likely to contribute confidently and fluently to discussions and conversations. Children also need to receive the message that talk is valued at school, that it is not second best to reading and writing as a measure of ability, but that it has a place in developing shared understandings, sorting out one's own thoughts and passing on information. The teacher should make time to praise positively good examples of talk in the classroom and allocate time to it during the school day.

Organization for talk

At school children need the opportunity to experiment with different ways of talking for different purposes and different audiences in order to experiment with and extend their choice of words, accent, grammar and style. Talking with their peers in a variety of groupings will help pupils to talk freely, creatively and clearly. There may be a greater need for children to explain and clarify their thoughts with equivalent users of language than there is during interactions with teachers who, children often think, know the answers already. Speaking and listening should take place in purposeful contexts, where it is important to communicate something that is known, to ask about something that one wants to know and most of all to speak when one has a real interest in or knowledge about a subject and others are interested in listening. This is not always the case at school where children's own experiences, interests, questions and conversational initiatives may be ignored as activities devised by the teacher are pursued.

The teacher as the organizer for speaking and listening will specifically plan for a range of opportunities and situations in which children explore and share ideas, arranging the learning environment so that it supports children's discussions with one another as well as supporting discussions between the pupils and the teacher. She will provide resources and information, giving children opportunities to tape record rather than write their responses to activities, encouraging all children to participate in talk exchanges, sometimes changing groups for talk activities to ensure that children encourage each other, are stimulated by and listen to each other's language, ideas and enthusiasms and provide real purposes and audiences for talk. She will also observe children as they talk to see whether the arrangements are successful or whether changes will be necessary in order to enable talk to occur more productively.

The teacher will also share her role as an organizer with the pupils by involving them in decisions about the composition of groups, the role to be assumed by each group member and the specific tasks that the group takes upon itself. For example a group of children working on the class theme of 'Food' may decide that they want to make an information book about different kinds of bread. Will each child in the group research one type of bread, its ingredients, how it is made and where it is most commonly eaten? Will any of the children be able to bring different sorts of bread to school? Will the children ask the classroom assistant to help them make different sorts of bread? What will their information book look like? Who will make it? Who will illustrate it? What headings will they use to record their findings? How will they make all their decisions? The teacher will encourage the children to consult each other as they plan the format of their task and the allocation of roles.

The teacher will also share the role of expert. In the example given above the teacher will encourage the children to take as much responsibility as possible for their project. She may help the children to establish some initial ground rules for their work but she will also be helping the children to identify each other as experts and to access information from other people or from books. As the task proceeds or once the task has been completed the group may report their findings to the class. At this point the teacher could share the role of questioner with other members of the class rather than being the initiator of the questions and the focus for the group report.

Children also need to be given the opportunity to reflect on talk in order for them to improve as users of talk. By positively commenting on the way in which children use talk and discussing ways of improving it the teacher will be treating talk like other areas of the curriculum and raise its status in the eyes of the class.

The teacher's use of language

Young children are strongly influenced by the models of talk presented to them by the adults who are important in their lives. Teachers are significant adults and as such can present a powerful model of language use to children. But how often do teachers present children with a model of talk used for speculation, enquiry or debate, or demonstrate that they too are exploratory users of language (NCC, 1989)? Very often the teacher's talk is perceived by children as being mainly about management, the teacher tells, commands, or judges when she speaks to children and very often her questions give children too little time to respond and elicit only minimal answers . Wells (1986) suggests that in order to encourage children to use talk as a means of learning teachers need to be good listeners. They need to give children their full attention when listening thereby indicating that what children say has value. They need to be supportive and encouraging to children in their use of language and intervene in children's talk only when it is appropriate. Their questions should be real questions asked because they truly want to know the child's opinion or thoughts, not asked merely to check that the child knows what the teacher wants him to know. As teachers speak to children in the classroom, they need

- To treat what the child has to say as worthy of careful attention.
- To do one's best to understand what he or she means.
- To take the child's meaning as the basis of what one says next.
- In selecting and encoding one's message, to take account of the child's ability to understand – that is, to construct an appropriate interpretation.

(Ibid., p. 218)

Teachers also need to have high expectations of children's abilities to engage in conversation. Wells found that where teachers had high expectations they were more likely to encourage children to express their ideas at length, but that when they held low expectations of children as speakers and listeners, they gave children few opportunities to sustain a topic of conversation and the teacher's own style of language almost totally comprised simple questions.

In order to support children's learning through talk the teacher can act as a respondent and a prompt to children's thinking, making it possible for them to understand what they may not have understood without the intervention of an adult. As a support the teacher does not take over the children's exploration, and merely telling them the answer or what to do next; instead she guides their thinking as she responds to their needs. This process is known as scaffolding (Wood, Bruner and Ross, 1976). The significant features of interacting with children in this way are to:

- listen to what the child says as he identifies the problem
- summarize what the child has found out so far and what the difficulties now appear to be
- orientate the child's attention to the significant aspects of the difficulty
- believe that the child can work out the answer
- help the child sequence his enquiry
- give the child time to continue to grapple with the problem
- ask a limited number of genuine questions about the problem or about the child's approach
- respond as one would in a discussion with an equal
- use tentative talk, such as 'I was wondering' or 'Perhaps if . . .'

- hold back and let the child do most of the talking as he continues to work out a solution
- leave the child once he has resumed work but offer to provide support again if required.

This approach enables children to retain control of their learning and because the child remains actively involved, he is more likely to remember and understand what he has achieved. It also give the teacher the opportunity to identify children's achievements and needs in relation both to speaking and listening and learning in a more general sense.

Adults who engage children in meaningful oral exchanges manifest the following characteristics as they interact with them. They

- attend to and support the speaker only responding to what is said after having carefully followed and listened to the speaker's words and meaning;
- engage in dialogue during and about shared activities, thus creating a shared experience and a shared reason for talk;
- create meaningful social, functional and communicative situations for talking in which speaking and listening can be used for a variety of purposes and with a genuine audience. Where there are real things to do and new problems to solve children are provided with a challenge that should stimulate their involvement with the task and their need to talk;
- spend time with children giving them experience and models of conversations;
- pose open questions and explore issues which are of interest to all the participants;
- demonstrate an interest in language, in the way in which it is used and the way in which words sound, are chosen, are interesting and are fun, thus extending children's vocabulary through encouraging their interest in words;
- assume that children have something important to say;
- view speaking and listening as an equal partnership and expect the child to contribute to this partnership; and
- provide an atmosphere of safety in which children feel confident enough to voice or rehearse opinions and venture questions.

Confident talk develops in a climate where:

- children feel able to make mistakes, be tentative and 'think aloud' without being judged;
- their own language, way of talking (and right to be silent) are respected and where their opinions are taken seriously;
- teachers listen to pupils and offer their own views rather than questions;
- the physical environment and the organisation of learning encourage collaborative talk and there is occasionally time for talk to develop beyond the immediate task in hand.

(Baddeley, 1992, p. 142)

Strategies to develop speaking and listening

Effective talk will be produced and developed if appropriate experiences that include using speaking and listening are planned and included in the daily working pattern of the class. The planned activities need to be organized with the intention of extending particular aspects of children's language and in a way that maximizes the possibility of productive inter-action between children.

Resources and experiences

If the teacher is to plan experiences and create contexts for talk in the classroom, she needs to make sure that the classroom contains a num-ber of resources that can be used by the children. The list that follows contains some suggestions: ● tape recorders and lots of tapes ● telephones ● dressing-up-clothes ● puppets ● story props ● a quotation board labelled 'Things We've Heard!' ● visitors who use various accents, dialects, languages and who provide the children with the opportunity to engage in talk for different purposes ● lots of prac-tical activities ● using children's questions as starting points for inves-tigations, topics and themes ● planning carefully for speaking and listening when devising the English scheme of work ● magnet board and figures ● games ● support for the use of home languages ● role-play areas ● a listening area ● interest areas and interactive displays ● a carpeted meeting area ● play equipment ● careful ar-rangement of tables. Well chosen resources are important but the teacher also needs actively to demonstrate their use to the children. The following example shows the importance of not only providing children with the appropriate resources but also the need for the teacher to organize the activity, participate in the activity and support the activity in order to achieve the aims she has previously identified.

In the nursery the home corner had been transformed into a building site. The usual furniture and equipment had been moved and stored elsewhere and large blocks and plastic bricks had been placed there. There was also a selection of hard hats in the area. The preparation for building-site role play had included a display of tools and materials, reading *Miss Brick the Builder's Baby* (Ahlberg, 1981b) and *Charlie's House* (Schermbrucker, 1992) and a walk around the locality to look at small and large building projects and repairs that were taking place. The first group of children to work in the building site were asked to build a number of walls to divide the area into different rooms in a flat. Each child worked on his or her own wall and there was very little exchange of conversation except to negotiate the use of the materials for each individual project. When the teacher observed this she decided to become one of the builders and accompany the next set of children into the building site. She model-led the language used by construction workers and organized the group of three children to work together and with her as they planned and built one wall. At the end of the day she reread *Miss Brick the Builder's Baby* to the class and discussed the work that had taken place in the construction site. The children described how they had worked and gave examples of the type of language they had used. Further examples of building workers' language and behaviour were considered and rehearsed. As the week continued the teacher provided more resources such as Wellingtons, mugs and milk bottles and at sharing times the children participated in short role plays associated with building sites. Some children made safety notices for the area and others made orange and white streamers to mark out the site. From time to time adults participated in the play and guided the children's language and actions. By the end of the week not only had a set of walls containing windows and doors been constructed but the children had also really begun to experiment with the vocabulary and language forms that might be found on a building site, one of the original aims for the activity. After a disappointing beginning this became a very successful activity. The teacher's clear focus and the support she offered to the children enabled them to get into role and to widen their understanding and experience of language in a new situation.

Teachers can use everyday classroom routines and occurrences as times to foster speaking and listening. Introducing slightly different activities at story times and varying the way children listen to stories can be a productive way of encouraging children to listen. The teacher can announce that as she reads the story she is going to make a deliberate mistake and she can ask the children to listen carefully and to put up their hands when they hear the mistake. The teacher may choose to read a story containing a refrain such as 'but my cat likes to hide in boxes' (Sutton, 1973) and the class can be invited to join in with this. The class can be asked to listen out for particular words in stories, such as the children's names in *On The Way Home* (Murphy, 1982). After the story reading they might try to recall all the names of the children in the book. The teacher could ask the children to help her with a story-telling session. The teacher might begin the story and then ask the children to contribute sentences as the story develops. The teacher can keep the story focused by beginning sentences for the children using phrases such as 'One day . . . , On the way . . . , Then . . . , At last . . .' Using a wordless picture book that the children are familiar with at story time is an opportunity to invite the children to tell the story. Each child can be asked to volunteer a sentence as the pages are turned. This activity can be repeated and the class asked to identify the differences between each version. Games such as 'Simon or Sarah says' and word games such as 'Odd One Out' encourage children to listen and give them a reason for listening.

Most activities at school offer children opportunities for speaking and listening, but only if teachers focus on their talk potential. As teachers plan their work they might ask themselves which activities can be organized in a way that encourages or necessitates speaking and listening for

Table 1.1　Activities to develop speaking and listening

Activity	Purpose	Audience	Setting	Numbers	Language development (range and key skills)
Debate an issue	Solve a classroom issue, e.g. how to organize the writing area	Other members of the class	Carpet area of the classroom	Whole class	Ask questions Evaluate Exchange ideas Initiate action or change Negotiate Plan Reason
Making a board game	Make a resource for the classroom	Initially each other then report to the whole class	Table in the classroom	Two to four children	State opinions Act on suggestions Clarify Exchange ideas Make oneself understood Negotiate Plan Report
Carrying out an experiment	To discover something new	Initially each other then report to the teacher and class	Table in the classroom	Two to four children	Act on instructions Ask questions Exchange ideas Explain Give instructions Plan Reason Report Summarize
Discuss a piece of writing	To improve their writing	Response partner	The writing area	Two children	Clarify Evaluate Reflect State opinions Think aloud

Table 1.1 *Continued*

Activity	Purpose	Audience	Setting	Numbers	Language development (range and key skills)
Interviewing a visitor	To find out information	The visitor	Carpet area in the classroom	Whole class working together after working in twos initially to think of questions	Ask questions Exchange ideas Participate Request information Understand others
Response partners	To discuss writing	Partner	Quiet space	Two children	Listening Evaluating what is heard Giving opinions Turn taking Responding appropriately Clarifying Discussing ideas
Role play	To extend language range	Other members of the group	Play area	Up to four children	Adapting speech to situation Using a widening vocabulary Thinking about how one communicates
Oral book reviews	To familiarize others with books in school	Other members of the class	The carpet/classroom	One child	Listening Evaluating what is heard Expressing an opinion Confidence Audibility Explaining opinion Giving reasons Questioning

different purposes and different audiences. Activities such as problem-solving, maths investigations, technology, experiments and writing and telling stories can incorporate a talk dimension if carefully planned. Table 1.1 gives an organizational framework for some common classroom activities and illustrates the different sorts of language that may emerge from them.

Organizing for talk

For many years the part of the school day allocated to developing children's skills in speaking and listening was news time or a show and tell session, often occurring at the start of the day. Many practitioners have questioned the value of these times. During these sessions there is no extended conversation or dialogue, the child either says very little, relies on giving brief answers to the teacher's questions or speaks without pausing for a prolonged time as the remainder of the class become increasingly restless. Organizing a prolonged interaction between an individual child and the teacher and demonstrating real interest in what the child is saying is usually difficult and the sessions often result in a series of brief questions and answers which do little to extend children's capabilities as speakers and listeners.

Fortunately it is no longer necessary to limit discussions and the sharing of children's ideas and experiences in this way, and many different ways of organizing for extended speaking and listening are now known. The following structures for group work that encourage children to share ideas and listen to others have been gathered from a number of sources including the work of the National Oracy Project members (Baddeley, 1992) and class teachers skilled in promoting talk in the classroom. All demand clear explanations from the teacher about their structure and purpose and they may require a few trial runs before they work smoothly. However it is well worth persevering with them since their value lies in the way in which they encourage children to communicate with each other rather than directing their thoughts and questions to the teacher. They also provide all children with someone who will listen and respond to them straight away. For classes unused to working in these ways it is best to begin with groups of two children and to introduce some of the more unfamiliar group structures slowly when the children have gained some experience at discussion, listening and speaking in small groups.

Talk partners

Talk partners can be identified by linking children's names on a large sheet of sugar paper or they can just be the child sitting next to them at the time. Pupils use their talk partner to • consult • to try out an idea • formulate a response • discuss a point • raise questions • explain a point • share an anecdote from their own experience for a limited period and with a useful outcome. As an example, partner A might report B's idea to the whole class or to another group; B might do the same for A. This is a good alternative to news time. The paired discussion with a talk partner might be used to provide a starting point for writing a story or the children may use their talk partners as response partners to talk through an idea or a piece of writing as part of the composing or editing process.

Snowballing

This is an extension of the first strategy and can be used for the same ends. Individuals' ideas are shared with talk partners then shared in a group of four and finally reported to the whole class.

Brainstorming

This can be done with talk partners, in small or large groups or with the whole class. The children quickly contribute and record their ideas about an issue, topic or question. All contributions are listed without comment. If necessary the lists can be collated and the children use these as a starting point for their work. If the children are not able to write easily the teacher can act as a scribe for whole-class contributions during this activity.

Buzz groups

The children use the person sitting next to them or their talk partner to

- remember what they were doing during the last session;
- talk through the teacher's instructions before they begin on the task that has been set; and
- talk through someone's presentation, to pick out the ideas they found most interesting and to raise questions.

Hotseating

Individual pupils take on the role of a character from a book or someone with a particular viewpoint on an issue, to answer questions from the rest of the class. The class works in pairs or small groups to generate ideas and prepare their questions.

Sharing sessions

The whole class sits in a circle. Small groups or pairs who have prepared a contribution share this with the rest of the class and chair the subsequent discussion. For example four young children share their news with each other and choose one child's contribution to relate to the whole class. The child who shares his news takes three questions about it from the whole class before handing back to the teacher.

Visiting listener

One person (teacher or pupil) visits each discussion group and notes good ideas or examples of supportive listening or speaking and reports these to the whole class during a whole-class discussion time. What is to be looked for can be discussed with the class before the listener begins his visits thus drawing the children's attention to good features of talking and listening.

Rainbowing

After working on a topic, each member of each group is allocated a number or a colour. Then each child with the same number or colour meet together in new groups to share ideas, to report on their research or to compare what their original group did.

Jigsawing

The class is organized into groups of about four to six children to investigate one aspect of a theme that has been introduced to the class. Each member of this group is allocated one specific aspect of their mini-topic to find out about and is designated as an expert on this. The next step is for all those who were designated experts in their original groups to meet together and discuss what they have discovered. Each expert then returns to his original group to report on his part of the group investigation. The original group then works together to finish its task or to plan a report to the rest of the class incorporating all the information they have gained.

Envoying

If a group needs to check or obtain information, one child, who has previously been nominated as the envoy, can be sent to the teacher or to the book corner or library to find out what the group needs and then report back to the group. This is a very useful strategy for the teacher to use to prevent too many children asking for her attention at any one time.

Listening triads

The children work in threes and take on the roles of speaker, listener or recorder. The roles should change each time the group meets. The speaker explains or comments on an issue or activity. The questioner prompts or seeks clarification. The recorder gives a report of the conversation to the other two. This gives all children the opportunity to take on responsibility for supporting, sharing and summarizing ideas.

Circle times

The whole class may sit on the carpet in a circle. Only the child or adult who is holding an object such as a ball or an imaginary magic microphone can speak. This time is used for affirmation statements, 'Cuong always helps me on the computer . . .', to express opinions, 'I think . . .' or feelings, 'Today I feel happy because . . .', or for games such as 'I Went to Market . . .'

A speaking and listening project

Undertaking a project on speaking and listening can be a good starting point for raising the status of talk, encouraging children to reflect on their own use of language and as a preparation for introducing collaborative group work. Such a project might start by making a collection of words to describe talk. In the following example the words were contributed by the children over a period of a week. They consulted dictionaries and asked adults at home for their suggestions. All the words were written by the children on a large chart.

How Many Words can we Find to Describe Talk?
speak, converse, discuss, gossip, instruct, address, babble, persuade, lecture, mean, suggest, express, declare, say, shout, yell, natter, jabber, voice, swear, state, rap, assert, cry, announce, call out, comment, argue, report, tell, chatter, communicate, announce, whisper, murmur, garble, exclaim, gabble, gab, name, lie, pronounce, mutter, utter, interrupt, ad-lib, mention, question, answer, think out loud, chat, gossip, negotiate, greet, joke, mumble, inform, advise, threaten, insist, challenge, flatter, translate, explain, waffle, share, ask, listen, enquire, agree, disagree, interrupt, jeer.

Using this as a starting point, the children could

- match rhyming pairs of words, e.g. 'flatter' and 'natter'
- match opposites, e.g. 'whisper' and 'shout'
- consider when they use different types of talk
- act out different ways of using talk
- illustrate different ways of using talk
- look for examples of talk written in books
- alphabetically order the talk words
- add speech bubbles to illustrations
- construct their own talk history
- list the kinds of talk they find difficult and easy
- use talk in different role-play settings, for example as a café owner and customer, TV interviewer and interviewee, adult and child
- find words for talk in different languages
- begin to consider what makes a good talker and a good listener.

These activities would provide children with the opportunity to gain many of the experiences outlined in the Programme of Study for Speaking and Listening (DfE, 1995a). At Key Stage 1 these include:

- Considering how talk is influenced by the purpose and the intended audience (range, 1b).
- Participating in drama activities, improvisations and performances of varying kinds, using language appropriate to a role or situation (range, 1d).
- Considering their own speech and how they communicate with others (standard English and language study, 3a).
- Recognizing how language differs, e.g. how their choice of language varies in different situations (standard English and language study, 3a).
- Exploring

  - the meanings of words
  - words with similar and opposite meanings
  - words associated with specific occasions (standard English and language study, 3b).

- At Key Stage 2, reflecting on how speakers adapt their vocabulary, tone, pace and style (range, 1a); evaluating their own talk and reflect on how it varies (key skills, 2a); developing their understanding of the similarities and differences between the written and spoken forms of standard English, and investigating how language varies according to context and purpose (standard English and language study, 3a).
- Using an increasingly varied vocabulary, and focusing on words and their meanings, including

  - discussion of more imaginative and adventurous choices of words
  - consideration of groups of words (standard English and language study, 3b).

Conclusion

Children's ability to learn language without any direct instruction or teaching signifies their impressive capacity for learning and this is truly a lesson for all adults who have responsibility for the care and education of children in the early years. However, it is not sufficient to assume that because children are competent users of oral language their competence will continue to develop without special provision. Speaking and listening are powerful tools, both for their own sakes and for learning, and as such they need to be nurtured and developed by all those who have an interest in children's learning. In order for children to become confident, articulate and sensitive users of language, speaking and listening needs to be an important part of the English curriculum in the early years.

Suggestions for further reading

Norman, K. (1990) *Teaching Talking and Learning in Key Stage One*, NCC, York.
Wells, G. (1986) *The Meaning Makers*, Heinemann Educational, Portsmouth, NH.

Chapter 2

Reading

Introduction

It is unlikely that there will ever be a fixed body of knowledge or total agreement about the best approaches to learning and teaching. Teachers change their approach as they learn from their own experience, from colleagues and from courses. They are constantly looking for ways to make learning easier, more meaningful, more relevant and more enduring for pupils. This is particularly true in the area of reading and it is right that, as more is understood about the process of learning to read, reading practices are examined and adapted so that they are efficient and relevant to the immediate and future needs of young children.

The majority of children do learn to read but teachers and researchers hope that a fuller understanding of reading and the use of teaching approaches that match this understanding will enable children to learn to read with ease and enthusiasm. Teachers need a reasoned understanding of the reading process and up-to-date information about the teaching of reading in order to teach children well. Those who do not understand the reasoning behind their own practice and other approaches are in danger of reinventing the wheel or of losing their sense of direction as they respond to the latest dictate (often an uninformed summons to return to the past) or jump on to the latest bandwagon (sometimes a reworking of what is already known). Offering children a 'pick and mix' reading curriculum, containing elements from every approach in the hope that some of these will meet some of the needs of most children, is too simplistic. Using a mixture of methods and teaching discrete reading skills can obscure the children's and the teacher's understanding of the purposes for reading. This may prevent some children from learning to read and others from seeing reading as a valuable long-term pursuit. Every teacher needs to know what strategies readers need, why they need them and when to teach them if they are to succeed in teaching children to read easily, pleasurably and with lasting results: 'Teachers should recognise that reading is a complex but unitary process and not a set of discrete skills which can be taught separately in turn and, ultimately, bolted to-gether' (DES, 1988b, para. 9.7). Learning to read frequently attracts a great deal of attention from educators and outsiders. To view it as an area of controversy and to argue about methods and materials diminishes the activity and the considerable knowledge that professionals have about this significant area of the curriculum. Our aim as informed professionals should be to use the best of current thinking and practice to ensure children's development as readers in both the short and long term. To do this it is necessary to reflect on past and current thinking about reading.

Children's literacy development needs to be seen as part of a con-tinuum, where each stage is built upon earlier experiences and provides the foundation for later ones. Traditionally the period between 5 and 7 has been seen as the time when a firm foundation for reading is estab-lished, but the process begins before this and continues after it. Children encounter different literacy experiences in their homes and communities before and during their school life and they mature and develop at dif-ferent rates. Their progress as readers and learners is individual and sometimes idiosyncratic. Learning to read does not necessarily begin at 5; neither does it end at 8. Some 8-year-olds may still need more supported experiences with books and all readers will need more practice at reading an increasing variety of texts for different purposes before they are fluent.

This chapter begins with a survey of reading research and methods and considers what they offer to early-years teachers in the 1990s. This section concludes with suggestions about formulating one's own approach to reading. The next part of the chapter focuses on planning a reading curriculum and considers practices, opportunities, resources and organ-ization for reading.

What is known about reading and learning to read

Early approaches to reading

At the beginning of this century, and for the next 50 years or so, reading was seen as a skills-based activity which required the reader to analyse a text into letters and words and to match these with their oral equivalents. It was assumed that children started school with no knowledge of read-ing and that they would need to be taught translation and decoding skills by their teachers. This view of reading resulted in teaching methods that emphasized learning grapho-phonic correspondences and remembering a sight vocabulary of words.

Phonics

The phonics approach was used from the middle of the nineteenth cen-tury and, although it became less significant during the 1950s, it has continued to influence practice in schools. In this method the relationship between letter shapes and letter sounds is used to teach children to read. The 44 sounds of English are represented by 26 letters of the alphabet. Because there are more sounds (phonemes) than symbols (graphemes) one grapheme may represent more than one phoneme. For example the letter C may be sounded as *c, s* or it may be silent, as in 'science'. This is one of the difficulties with teaching phonics. Many irregular or different grapho-phonic correspondences occur in words which readers encounter in early texts. For example, the sound represented by the symbol *a* is different in '*all*', '*hat*' and '*make*'. Despite the difficulties with phonics there are links between letter symbols and sounds and, when used in conjunction with other reading strategies, some phonic knowledge can be helpful to readers.

Morris (1974) suggested that teaching children about the sound and symbol correspondences which occur in letter strings such as 'uff' and 'ought' can be valuable and less confusing for young readers, as these are less likely to vary than individual letter sounds. Recently the work of Goswami and Bryant (1990) has indicated that children who are aware of the phonological structure of language, that is that words contain groups of sounds, are at an advantage when learning to read.

A totally phonic approach to reading would now be considered very limiting by most teachers. Instead phonic awareness, particularly of initial sounds and letter strings, is seen as one of a number of strategies that can be drawn upon by readers when they are confronted with an unfamiliar word. To attach too much significance to the teaching of phonics could be unwise, particularly as, in 1993, HMI noted that 'This year a higher proportion of time than previously was spent teaching phonic skills . . . This increase in the time and attention given to phonics, however did not guarantee either a high quality of teaching or of learning phonic skills' (HMI, 1993, p. 7, para. 6). They went on to suggest that children do not need a discrete phonics programme in order to become competent readers; instead they recommended that phonics should be taught 'within a balanced programme of reading', a view that is repeated in English in the National Curriculum (DfE, 1995a).

Being aware that there is a relationship between letters and sounds is helpful to readers, but it does not need to be taught as a phonic programme. Teaching phonics effectively and relevantly can take place after reading sessions and through some of the texts that the teacher presents to the class. Teaching about letter sounds can be introduced and applied after a child has read with the teacher. Words, the letters they contain and the sounds of these letters can be discussed when they are relevant to the learner's needs and when they help with recognizing the actual words that are being read. Teaching phonics in this way is purposeful and is reinforced by being applied immediately or when the child next reads. Teachers may also share texts with children which contain simple rhymes, repetition and word games. By drawing children's attention to the aural and visual patterns and play on words in books, teachers will be developing children's familiarity with the sounds of language. Texts such as *Dr Seuss's ABC* (Seuss, 1963), *Each Peach Pear Plum* (Ahlberg and Ahlberg, 1978), *The Streetwise Kid* (Simeon, 1989) and nursery rhymes, action rhymes, alphabet books and advertising slogans all offer children lessons about phonics. In these texts the emphasis on sounds does not dominate the content but is integral to it, and the teaching of phonics is part of reading not separate from it, as HMI and the DfE suggest.

Sight vocabularies

Whole-word methods began to be used in the 1940s and 1950s. With this approach children were expected to learn all the words contained in each reading-scheme book before the book was read. These were often learned from a set of cards known as flash cards. Each card was looked at and the word written there was said aloud. The words that were selected for learning in this way were those that occurred most often in children's reading material and could be distinguished from one another easily because of their distinctive shape. For example the word *aeroplane* is visually quite different from the word *girl*. It was thought that children would find learning complete words more motivating than learning letter sound correspondences and that scheme books containing interesting, rather than phonically regular words, would appeal to children. This approach gained enormous popularity through the publication of the Ladybird Books (McNally and Murray, 1968), although it was criticized at the time for not providing children with independent strategies for reading unfamiliar material, encouraging rote learning and creating dependency on the teacher.

It is true that some words are more easily remembered than others including those with distinctive shapes such as *bicycle*, those that are important to children such as their names or words such as *dinosaur* or those that are seen frequently such as *street*. But many words that occur regularly in books for young children have similar visual features. Function words such as *there*, *their* and *here*, and *him*, *his*, *her* and *has* fall into this category. Function words are also unlikely to have an important meaning for individuals and this can make them difficult to remember out of context. Learning large numbers of words by rote can also place considerable strain on young children's memories. The reading materials that supported this approach often contained a limited number of frequently repeated words which limited the interest and the development of stories in the early books. Although a pure whole-word approach is rare now, some people still think that it is important for children to memorize a reading vocabulary. Many of the books for beginning readers in modern reading schemes continue to reflect this belief and contain only a limited number of words.

The automatic recognition of words can be very helpful to readers. When they recognize words quickly they are free to concentrate on the meaning of the text. Mature readers build up a large sight vocabulary through their experiences with books and print and use automatic word recognition as one of their reading strategies (Stanovich, 1980; Raynor and Pollatsek, 1989). But beginning readers who have had far fewer reading experiences than fluent readers will not have had the opportunities to build up a large store of automatically recognizable words. Having a large sight vocabulary is a result of being a good reader rather than the cause. Practising with flash cards and words in word tins is more likely to produce boredom and misunderstandings about reading than to create fluent and enthusiastic readers.

More recent thinking about reading

Over the past 30 years there has been a great deal of research into a great many aspects of literacy by educationalists, psychologists, sociologists and linguists. The results of this work have significantly altered teachers' perceptions about reading and learning to read. Reading is now seen as a multifaceted process, and readers are now known to call upon their understanding of the process and to employ a number of strategies in order to read well. It is no longer considered to be a simple activity relying on skills and memory.

The relationship between oral and written language

The relationship that exists between oral and written language has always been considered important for reading. This was the basis for the phonic and the whole-word approaches. However this relationship is now seen as something more complex and more helpful than realizing that printed letters and words have oral equivalents. Ashton-Warner (1963), Goddard (1974) and the Breakthrough to Literacy team (Mackay, Thompson and Schaub, 1970) made this clear when they suggested that children's own spoken language should be written down and used as their first reading material. They were suggesting that if what the child said was written down as it was said, the child would be able to see the relationship between oral and written language. If the child was then asked to read what had been written the structure of the sentences and the use of familiar words would help him to recognize the written equivalents of what he had said. As he had composed the text, he would remember what it was about and would be able to predict the words that it contained. The language experience approach to reading demonstrated that sentence structure, context and the prediction of meaning, all of which are aspects of oral language use and processing, as well as sounds can be used when reading.

Using the children's own language to create personal and relevant reading materials and encouraging inexperienced readers to use a number of strategies when reading were an important development. However this approach also had some limitations. Despite the relationship between oral and written language there are also differences. The written language that is encountered in books is usually distant from its author, draws on a particular set of conventions, is tightly structured and is more formal than oral language (Smith, 1977; Rubin, 1980). If children only read what they themselves write, they will not gain the experience of the syntax and style of written language or widen their reading vocabulary beyond the words they use in everyday speech. Critics of language experience suggested that the daily writing and reading of the child's own news could result in a reading diet that might constrain children's reading development (Reid, 1974). However, the principle of children reading texts that they dictate to the teacher or compose independently is an important one. It demonstrates the relationship between oral and written language and encourages children to apply oral language-processing strategies to print. It enables them to explore concepts about print, to work with known texts, to look carefully at words and it can be highly motivating.

The wider aspects of the shared processes used to compose and understand oral and written language became and continue to be the subject of much attention. Readers who approach text knowing that reading is a communicative activity and who expect and wish to understand what is being communicated are able to draw upon their existing oral language-processing strategies when they read. Goodman (1972) suggested that fluent readers apply three aspects of knowledge about language when they read. These are knowledge about syntax (the way that words are ordered and organized), semantic expectation (the meaning of words and the meanings created by words) and grapho-phonic awareness (the relationship between symbols and sounds).

Syntax is an important device in language. The order in which words are placed in sentences follows rules which all language users know and use when they construct and understand language. Applying this knowledge is of great assistance when reading as it often enables the reader to anticipate the sorts of words that follow the ones that have just been read. In English we expect sentences which are organized in the following ways:

- The cat chased the mouse *not* The chased cat the mouse.
- The black cat chased the grey mouse *not* The cat chased black the mouse grey.

Reading the first sentence in each of these pairs is straightforward, but reading the second one, where the word order is muddled, is more difficult.

Semantics is used to describe meaning in language. Readers expect to understand the meaning of words that they read and the sense of what is conveyed in a text. If they encounter words or passages which do not make sense to them, they hesitate and reread what has been read in order to help them understand. If what they are reading makes sense they will read more easily. Reading the two passages that follow may help readers to appreciate how semantic strategies are employed:

From The Turn of the Screw *by Henry James*
The story had held us, round the fire, sufficiently breathless, but except the obvious remark that it was gruesome, as, on Christmas Eve in an old house, a strange tale should essentially be, I remember no comment uttered till somebody happened to say that it was the only case he had met in which such a visitation had fallen on a child.

Nomral reading
Nomral reading is a knid of high spede geussuing game, which explians why we find it difficult to proof raed. The raeding process is incredibly flexilbe and can cope with all kinds of worng infromation, such as revresed letters, missprimts, punchation errers and chainges in teip font, eny of witch wood compeltely fox a computre. But so long as sence is comming over the I bounds on. What does hold up the porcess are unfamiliar language constructions, as a when of juggled the about are all sentence words the brian gets into an awful staet tyring to recnocile a snesible anticipated messaeg and the ronsensical messaeg which was actually recived.

Readers may have found both of these texts difficult to read because they were, in quite different ways, difficult to understand. Experienced readers often have to read and reread both as they pursue the meaning. It is not usually the muddled spelling in 'Nomral reading' that distracts readers but the loss of meaning when the semantic and syntactic supports are taken away part way through the text, since meaning is both an enabling strategy and the purpose for reading.

At times readers use grapho-phonic strategies, that is, the ability to match the visual elements of print with their oral equivalents, either as individual letters, syllables or whole words. If a sentence reads, 'The man was walking the dog', but the reader does not recognize the word *walking*, but does recognize that the unknown word begins with *w*, he can limit his guesses of this word to those that are syntactically and semantically appropriate and begin with *w*. In this way an awareness of word shape and letter sounds is helpful as they can reduce the number of possibilities when readers encounter an unfamiliar word.

Through their experience as speakers and listeners children are familiar with syntactic, semantic and phonic strategies as ways of processing language when they learn to read. So by making the communicative aspects of reading clear to children, showing them that reading is about the recreation of meaning and providing them with experiences of books, stories and writing which allow them to see the connections, children can be introduced to reading positively and easily.

This suggestion about helping children to begin to read by extending their existing language strategies is supported by our understanding of how children learn to speak. They do not learn to speak by being taught sounds, or by being taught a predetermined set of words which they then practise. Their oral language learning takes place in a context of talk, where they witness demonstrations of the purpose and use of talk, where they receive responses and encouragement from experienced speakers, where they are treated as speakers and where there is every expectation of success. Children are not expected to speak perfectly from the start, nor do they have to wait until they have perfect control over spoken language before they are allowed to speak. Inexperienced speakers are permitted and encouraged to practise as they learn. Their utterances take place in real situations, have meaning from the start and concern things they are interested in. It is now thought that learning to read may be easier and more relevant to children if teachers work with children on reading in ways that are similar to those that have successfully supported the development of oral language. Applying these favourable conditions for learning oral language to learning to read has resulted in an approach where children are met, from the start, by positive expectations about their ability to read. They are placed in situations where they are surrounded by books and demonstrations of reading and the role of the adult is to support and extend what the child tries to do as complete texts are read together.

Children as active learners

Early-years educators now accept that, through actively engaging with the world around them and generating and testing their hypotheses about their experiences and observations, young children bring a great deal of knowledge and a number of established and productive learning strategies to school. It is now known that 'children do not sit passively waiting to be told what they should learn . . . They learn by having a go, by trying things out. Early childhood is a continual process of experimentation, risk taking and negotiation, in purposeful, intentional ways' (Wray, Bloom and Hall, 1989, p. 61). It is also accepted that young children understand a great deal about literacy before they are able to read. As they grow up they see print in their homes, in their communities and even on their clothes and they observe others reading and reacting to print. These experiences have usually led them to discover that writing has meaning and that the activity of reading is a linguistic, social and psychological event (Ferreiro and Teberosky, 1983).

Older approaches to reading did not take account of how young children learn or of what they might know about literacy. They did not capitalize on their innate capacity for learning and their own learning strategies. Teachers can now do both of these. They can make learning to read part of a continuum of language learning when they work with what children can do and accept that each child will know different things about literacy. They can reject reading programmes and sequenced skills teaching that are based on the view of the child as a passive learner and necessitate giving every child the same experiences in the same way. Teachers can now decide to teach by reacting to the active learning that they see and responding 'to the problems that children face at crucial points in their development' (Ferreiro, 1986).

Studies of preschool literacy learning

Research into the preschool language and literacy experiences of children who were able to read before starting school have revealed a number of factors that help children to make a successful start to reading (Clark, 1976; Clay, 1979; Wells, 1982; Brice-Heath, 1983). Their findings have indicated that IQ, father's occupation or the duration of care givers' schooling were not significant factors. Instead, it was the children's understanding of stories and books and their exposure to models of reading which contributed to their success. Many of the experiences which they identified have now been incorporated into the early reading curriculum of schools so that all children will receive the experiences which will enable them to make a positive and successful start to reading. These are to understand and be aware of ● how a book is held and read ● the directional rules of writing ● that print not illustrations carry the un-varying message ● that print is composed of words ● that words con-tain letters ● that punctuation helps the reader to understand what has been written ● that stories usually have a particular structure ● that people do read and that they read for different purposes. This knowledge does not need to be taught in a decontextualized way in school, it will arise as stories and books are shared, discussed and used with children.

The purposes for reading

Investigations into the reasons that adults have for reading and the pur-poses for reading that children can identify seem to have been prompted by two factors. First there is increasing concern about the number of children who can read but seem not to have any reason to read and so choose not to and, secondly, the recognition that when children identify their own purposes for learning they learn more easily and more actively.

For adults, reading is a purposeful activity which often has an outcome. Literacy helps them to fulfil their roles in many different areas of their lives. In the home they read recipes, instructions, suggestions about DIY, news from school, information, letters, cards and postcards from friends and rela-tives. Textbooks, articles, advertisements, and magazines are read for em-ployment and educational purposes. People are helped to fulfil their roles as members of the community when they read bills, election leaflets, tax forms and newspapers. As consumers, adults read advertisements, catalogues, credit-card statements, shopping lists and special offers. They can use read-ing for entertainment when they consult holiday brochures, knitting pat-terns, magazines, maps, the *TV Times* and *RadioTimes* and when they choose to read books. Adult readers read a range of writing, in a variety of situations and for many different reasons, but their reading is always purposeful.

When teachers and other adults are asked why children learn to read, their answers often fall into two categories: for the pleasure that reading can bring and for the information that reading can give them. These are valid and positive reasons, but there are sometimes other reasons for the reading that is done in school. Practice at reading is often undertaken in order to help children to improve their reading ability and teachers know that children's ability to read will affect how they progress through the education system. Sometimes improvement becomes the main reason for reading. When this happens children may develop a very limited picture of purposes for reading. They may be learning that reading is an important activity that gains adult approval but they may not be learning about how to use and enjoy reading. It has been suggested that materials and approaches influence children's perceptions of the uses of reading and reflect teachers' priorities about reading. Reading schemes, the teaching of skills and short, frequent periods of reading aloud to the teacher are often associated with success, competition and academic need, rather than the wider purposes for reading.

The list of adult reasons for reading shows that being able to read gives individuals the opportunity to become more autonomous, to make choices, to evaluate different points of view, to analyse information, to make informed decisions and to gain access to new ideas and opinions. The ability to read places people in a powerful position. It enables individuals to decide what they read and what their purposes for reading will be. To be literate does not only include knowing how to read and write but also the place and value of these activities in one's life. Because reading is so important, it is not enough for early-years teachers to be enthusiastic about reading because they believe that it is a pleasurable and worthwhile activity that will be useful in later stages of education. Teachers need to recognize how children can and will use this ability and let this determine their aims for teaching reading. To teach reading because it is fun, it is useful and because legally we have to is not sufficient. The most important aim for teaching children to read is to empower them as individuals now and for the future. As far as possible it is important to offer young children a wide reading curriculum which demonstrates the opportunities that reading can offer to them in the here and now. Children need to understand that reading is enjoyable and informative and relevant to their present lives.

Models of reading behaviour

Models of reading are used to represent what is regarded as important in the different approaches to reading that exist. They can be used to identify starting points and the sequence in which processes need to be learned and applied. They illustrate what young children need to know as they learn to read.

The bottom-up model

The bottom-up model represents a skills-based view of learning to read. Here, reading involves the translation of printed symbols, letters, clusters of letters and words into their oral equivalents. The letter and word recognition skills that are required are taught by the adult to the learner. Teachers who consider that children learn to read by learning the skills of reading have been influenced by this model. Following this model would involve

> the development of readiness; the acquisition of a sight vocabulary of words which occur frequently in children's reading and spoken vocabulary; the development of independent reading by the use of phonic analysis and synthesis and other word recognition techniques; the development of speedy, relaxed silent reading for content, ideas and pleasure.
>
> (Tansley, 1967, p. 28)

The bottom-up model, identified by Singer and Ruddell (1985) suggests that readers read by looking at print, identifying letters, matching phonemes and graphemes, blending letter sounds together, recognizing some words using their sight vocabulary, pronouncing words aloud, and after working through the stages, finally recover the meaning of the text.

The bottom-up model does not explain the full extent of reading behaviour as it is now understood. Reading is not usually a letter-by-letter or word-by-word activity, but one that calls for the use of a variety strategies. The work on the nature of reading that has taken place over the past 30 years suggests that rather than simplifying the process the bottom-up approach may make it more difficult for young children to learn to read. With a bottom-up approach, reading skills tend to be taught outside the context of a sentence or a story. This denies children the opportunity to draw upon what they already know about reading. They are unable to use their expectation and experience of meaning in print, books and stories to help them understand what they are reading and to recognize unfamiliar written words. The books that accompany these approaches have generally been written to provide practice in the skills that children have been taught. This can make them artificially repetitive and devoid of meaning or feeling. The unnaturally simple sentences hinder children's attempts to match the language of books with their experience and use of language and often make it difficult for them to apply semantic, syntactic and bibliographic cues.

The following examples may help to demonstrate why the bottom-up model is now considered by many to be unsatisfactory. As you read the first story consider how, despite the impossibility of decoding it letter by letter or word by word, you are able to read and understand what has been written:

The Man Who Kept House
Once — – t– th-r- —- – woodman who th–ght th– no o– w-rked – h-rd – – did. O– ev— wh– – c— h-m- fr– w-rk, – s–d to h– w-f-, 'Wh– – y– d- all d-y wh-l- I – aw-y c— w–d'?

'I k–p h–se,' re—– –– w-f-, 'and k—– h—– – h–d w–k.'
'H–– w—–!' said the —––. 'Y– d–'t k–w wh– h–– w—– –! Y– sh—– tr- c—– w—–!'
'-'- be glad to,' —– –– w—–.
'Why d–'t y– do m- w–k s–– d-y? I'– st– – h-m- –– k–p h—–,' —– –– —––.
'If y– st– h—– –– do —– w-rk. y–'ll h—– to m—– butt-r, c-rry w-t-r- fr- —– w—–,
w-sh —– cl—––, cl—– –– h–se, —– l–k aft– —– b-by,' —– –– w-f-.

As they prepared to read this passage readers may have found that the title, the organization of the text, the punctuation and their experience of stories (bibliographic cues) led them to have certain expectations about what the text might contain. As they read they are unlikely to have mentally inserted every missing letter in the text. They were probably able to read the story by drawing on their understanding of how language is organized (syntax), for example the three opening words of the text. They might have used some grapho-phonic strategies – recognizing letters such as *h* and *w* at the beginning of words may have suggested that *hard work* was about to be repeated. However for the majority of readers the main strategy that is used is that of continually checking and pursuing meaning (semantics) and drawing on other cues to ensure that their understanding is correct.

Most readers experience no difficulty with reading the next text and answering the questions which follow, but very few are satisfied when they have read it. As you are reading you might consider why this is the case:

The Wuggen and the Tor
Onz upon a pime a wuggen zonked into the grabbet. Ze was grolling for poft because ze was blongby.

The wuggen grolled and grolled until ze motte a tor.

Ze blind to the tor, 'Ik am blongby and grolling for poft. Do yum noff rem ik can gine some poft?'

'Kex,' glind ze tor, 'Klom with ne wuggen. Ik have lodz of poft in ni bove.'

Now answer these questions:

Where did the wuggen zonk?
What was s/he grolling for?
Why was s/he grolling for poft?
Who did s/he meet?
What on earth was this about?

Most readers express dissatisfaction with this text because it does not make sense to them. Despite being able to sound out the letters and put them together to form words (phonics) and recognize some words quickly (whole-word recognition), it is impossible to understand what has been written. Most readers agree that because they have not understood, they have not really been able to read the passage.

From these examples it is possible to see that readers actively pursue the author's meaning using a variety of strategies. Phonics and word recognition are not always used when reading and that when they are used they may not be sufficient to truly read, that is to read with understanding. As was written in *English for Ages 5 to 16*, 'Reading is much more than the decoding of black marks upon a page: it is a quest for meaning and one which requires the reader to be an active participant' (DES, 1989a, Chap. 16.2).

The top-down model

Since the bottom-up model does not take account of all the strategies that readers need in order to read, an alternative model of the reading process was constructed. This is known as the top-down model. Here reading begins in the reader's mind. Before sampling the words in the text the reader hypothesizes about the meaning of what he or she is about to read using non-linguistic cues, such as experience of the world, expectations about the book and the information conveyed by the illustrations. The reader's desire to recreate the meaning contained in the text is at the centre of this model. Reading viewed in this way does not demand that every letter or word is examined or translated into its oral equivalent. It entails the selective use of semantic, syntactic, bibliographic and graphophonic cues as the reader makes predictions about the meaning contained in the text. As these predictions are confirmed or rejected, using meaning as the check, the reader uses fewer or more of all the cues that are available.

The interactive model

The most recent model, known as the interactive model (Rumelhart, 1985), integrates elements of the previous models with current research and practice. It takes account of how children learn to speak, their competence as learners, their knowledge about reading, the strategies used by fluent readers and the interaction between the reader and the text. It describes reading as resulting from the reader's use of the features of language and the application of the reader's own experience and expectations of text. The following quotation, taken from *Becoming a Nation of Readers*, describes this model:

> Reading can be compared to the performance of a symphony orchestra. This analogy illustrates three points. First, like the performance of the symphony, reading is a holistic act. In other words, while reading can be analyzed into subskills such as discriminating letters and identifying words, performing the subskills one at a time does not constitute reading. Reading can be said to take place only when the parts are put together in a smooth, integrated performance. Second, success in reading comes from practice over long periods of time, like skill in playing musical instruments. Indeed, it is a lifelong endeavor. Third, as with a musical score, there may

be more than one interpretation of a text. The interpretation depends upon the background of the reader, the purpose for reading, and the context in which reading occurs.

(Anderson, Hiebert and Wilkinson, 1985, p. 7)

In the interactive model of reading the reader uses the features of text, letters, words, headings, title, illustrations, structure and content in combination with his own resources for reading, such as previous experiences of print, expectations of books, knowledge of the subject matter, knowledge about language, the ability to predict, and an expectation of meaning, in order to read.

Personal models

All teachers of young children know a great deal about reading and readers. They have learned about reading during initial teacher education courses, and continue to update their knowledge by participating in INSET courses and staff development days. Any discussion of learning in school will almost always include some reference to reading. Teachers are aware of the debates and controversies surrounding practices and resources. They know that standards in reading are prominent in the minds of parents, governors, headteachers, Ofsted, future employers and the media. As teachers of young children they will spend a great many teaching hours every week helping children to learn to read using a set of practices that seems to work for them and for the pupils they teach.

Despite policies, guidelines and team planning the implementation of any curriculum in school will vary from class to class. Planning the curriculum begins with the teachers' personal convictions about the purpose of education. Is it to prepare children for the world of work? To enable them to become good citizens? To enrich their lives? To place them in a better position to make choices about their lives? Whatever view one holds will influence the content of what is planned, the priorities that are established and the organization of the curriculum. These will also be affected by teachers' assumptions about how children learn. Do children learn by being told? Do they learn through experience? Is learning only valid when it is directed by the teacher? How much do children learn outside school? From each other? By themselves?

Teachers also have beliefs about the value and use of reading. They are readers. They are aware of the value which society places on reading. They know how reading is applied outside school. They know that a major part of their role is to have a class filled with successful, developing readers and they know that their own aims for reading, even if they are achieved, will form only a part of the long-term development of each child's reading.

As the teacher plans her termly, weekly and daily reading programme she will be drawing on her beliefs about the purposes of education, learners and learning and the uses of reading, as well as her understanding of the

reading process and her knowledge and awareness of practices and resources related to reading. Each individual will have his or her own model
of reading which is related to his or her own definition of teaching and
learning. One's own beliefs, knowledge and teaching style are a major
influence on the content and organization of the reading curriculum which
is planned and implemented. The list which follows, which should be read
from the bottom to the top, illustrates how a reading curriculum is set
within a wider framework of each individual's view of education:

A personal model of reading

- Actual classroom practices (teacher's role, choice of resources, pri-
orities, allocation of time, organization).
- Planning the reading curriculum.
- Teacher behaviour and teaching style.
- Principles for learning to read.
- Understanding of the reading process.
- The teacher's personal understanding of teaching.
- Short and long-term goals for teaching.
- Beliefs about what reading is for.
- Beliefs about how learners learn.
- Beliefs about the purposes of education.

Planning and implementing a reading curriculum

The suggestions and practices which are described in this section make
use of the findings from the research described in the previous section.
The individual principles which underpin these suggestions for a reading
programme are as follows:

- Learning to read does not just begin when the child starts school.
- Any teaching should be offered to children in a way that enables them
to make connections with what they know and understand already.
- Children need to see reading as relevant to and important in their
present lives.
- Children need to develop positive attitudes towards reading and establish their own purposes for reading if they are to become readers.
- Reading is reinforced and extended when it develops in conjunction
with other language areas.
- Children are active learners who learn most effectively by participating
in reading with the guidance of an experienced adult.
- Children need to be able to make use of all the strategies and cues that
are available when they read.
- Good teaching is coherent and is planned by someone who understands what they are doing and why they are doing it.

When devising a reading programme it is necessary to consider the context in which reading is developed as well as the activities, practices,

opportunities for reading with children, resources and ways of organization that are available. The context consists of what children need to know
about reading, the environment for reading in the school and the class,
supporting reading through the development of writing and the demonstrations of literate behaviour that are provided for children.

The context for reading

What developing readers need to know

In order to give children the experiences they need to become readers it is
important to be aware of what they know about reading, what they can
do as readers and what their experiences of reading are to date, both
inside and outside school. Children need to know that

- they will learn to read
- reading is a communicative activity
- reading is purposeful
- books draw upon the reader's own knowledge and experience of the
  world
- books use a set of conventions
- stories often have a particular structure and style
- the meanings contained in books can be retrieved through using syntactic, semantic, grapho-phonic and automatic word-recognition strategies.

If there are any gaps in what children know about reading, teachers can
then provide the opportunities for children to gain all the knowledge and
experiences that are needed to make the learning to read easier.

The environment for reading

All classrooms should be rich and dynamic literacy environments, providing children with opportunities to read, to write and to learn more
about the nature and purpose of literacy. They should have a writing
area, a listening area and a library area. Everyone in the class should
contribute to displays of writing which illustrate the nature, variety and
uses of print. Children should be immersed in the sounds of written
language as stories, poems, rhymes, information books and letters home
are shared with them. There should be frequent story-reading and story-
telling sessions with opportunities for children to listen to and read
known stories and rhymes for themselves in the listening area. Children
should have access to books to read in class and to take home, as well as
ready access to resources for writing. From the first day children enter
school there should be an expectation that every child will read and write.

The atmosphere throughout the school and in the class should be conducive to risk taking and independent learning. The teacher might make
explicit the expectation that children should make attempts to work things

out for themselves before asking for help. In an environment where the process and effort of learning are valued it is be easier to encourage children to read in a way that allows them to take risks. Children who believe that reading is primarily about accuracy are likely to read deliberately and slowly and to rely on adults for help, rather than using their own capacity for problem solving and meaning making. Children gain less practice at reading when they read slowly and rely on others.

For many children imaginative play activities, drawing and games provide them with the opportunity to explore and experiment with literacy and it is in these situations that the beginnings of literacy frequently appear. Often it is in the context of play that children make up their first stories as they create and enact their own dramatic narratives either alone or with others. If play activities are equipped with resources for reading and writing, literacy will become more accessible to young children. During play they are able to explore the roles and activities of people who read and write and the uses of reading and writing. As they play at being readers and writers and play with the materials of reading and writing they will be gaining familiarity with the tools and activities of literacy, learning what reading and writing are and what they can do with them. During play children are in control, they can feel confident, powerful and free to take risks.

Children need easy physical access to play areas and need to be actively encouraged to make use of the literacy materials that they contain. Such materials may include notepads, memo boards, telephone pads, calendars, diaries, telephone directories, recipe books, the *RadioTimes*, newspapers, books, magazines, cards, postcards, letters, bills, pens and pencils. If given the resources and opportunities, even children who cannot yet read or write in the formal sense will often behave as readers and writers.

The relationship between reading and writing

There is a mutually supportive relationship between learning to read and learning to write as both involve understanding and using written symbols. Writing supports reading by reinforcing the visual aspects of language. When writing children are encouraged to use their knowledge of the writing system, of what words look like and of how they are spelt. Developmental writing, in particular, encourages children to think about the sound and sight of words as they write, and children who learn to write in this way 'demonstrate greater phonological awareness than children who are used to copying under teachers' writing' (Barrs and Thomas, 1991). If, as part of the combined literacy curriculum, time with groups and individuals is given to looking at words and spelling patterns, 'their growing knowledge of how words are constructed will support their reading' (*ibid.*, p. 73).

Models of literate behaviour

As Clark (1976) and Clay (1979) both found, children learn from and are motivated by seeing models and demonstrations of literacy and literate behaviour. So it is important that in school and in the classroom they see the teacher and other adults read stories, take the register, write captions for displays, refer to and use books for information, write letters or notes for children to take home, engage in literacy activities alongside the children and provide demonstrations of literacy through shared writing and reading. Displays, discussions and examinations of packaging and other print in the school and local environment may also show children how reading is used.

The reading programme

Activities and practices

Most children enter the nursery or reception class with a range of physical and cognitive abilities. They are able to run, jump, walk, talk and play. Most children will have had opportunities to use pens, pencils, construction and other toys as well as experiences of books and stories. However, one still sees young children at school engaged in activities that have been designed to foster physical skills such as hand-eye co-ordination, directionality, aural discrimination and visual discrimination as a preparation for reading and writing. Given what we now know about children's capabilities in language and their awareness of literacy it now seems unnecessary for them to engage in practising tracing, colouring and handwriting patterns rather than engaging in the actual pursuit of literacy. Early literacy activities should provide children with the opportunity to extend what they already know by enabling them to explore, experiment, take risks and reflect in ways that are immediately connected to print, books and stories.

The reading programme for a class should contain a number of regular practices centred around a varied selection of carefully chosen texts. In addition it should contain other activities which are used from time to time to enrich the programme and extend children's learning about particular aspects of reading. The practices and activities that follow are all connected to print and reading and are suitable for all young children, from 3 to 8, although some procedures may become less frequent as children become more proficient at reading on their own. For example, shared reading might be a daily occurrence in nursery and reception classes and a weekly event with Year 2 children.

Shared reading with enlarged texts

Introducing and extending reading in this way was first suggested by Holdaway (1979). It involves the use of commercially produced, teacher-made or children-produced books with enlarged texts and illustrations, popularly known as 'big books', which are shared with groups or classes of children. As the children become familiar with the books they are encouraged to join in reading them with the teacher. This supportive, collaborative activity is helpful to all readers, giving them practice in and models of reading.

The book is positioned on an easel or book rest so that all the children can see the illustrations and the text clearly. Before reading the book the teacher discusses the book with the children, asking questions such as: What is this book going to be about? How do we know? What is it called? Who wrote it? Who published it? Who illustrated it? Have we read any other books by this author or illustrator?

Beginning with the title page the whole book is read straight through, with the adult pointing to each word as it is read. The book is read with the class frequently so that it becomes well known to them. The children should have the opportunity of reading the book without the teacher, either in its large form or in a smaller version which may have an accompanying tape. Smaller versions of familiar, enlarged texts are often among the first books that children share with adults during individual reading sessions. Once the children are familiar with the text they can take turns in reading it aloud to the class or individuals can take on the voices of the characters in the story. Sharing books in this way increases children's awareness of the layout of books, the narrative structure of stories, what is available to read as well as the pleasures and purposes of reading. The teacher may follow the reading by drawing the children's attention to words, letters, phonic blends, rhyming words, punctuation and other features of print. If the teacher wishes to focus on a particular letter or word in the text, she can write the letter or word on the flip chart, and ask for contributions from the children to compile collections of words beginning with that letter or to make a lists of words that look and sound like the one she has chosen.

Books that are used for shared reading need to ● contain language suited to being read aloud ● encourage prediction ● encourage response ● have a clear narrative structure ● include illustrations that support the narrative ● refer to situations with which readers can empathize ● contain texts which have rhythm, rhyme or repetition.

The use of enlarged texts is very useful to early bilingual learners of English since shared reading provides a visual and oral demonstration of reading. Community-language or dual-language texts used in this way can be very helpful in supporting biliteracy, since when children see, hear and join in reading these, they will be receiving the same experiences and insights about reading as their monolingual English-speaking peers. Dual-language books generally need to be made in school but a list of publishers of enlarged texts is given at the end of this chapter.

Apprenticeship reading

The apprenticeship approach became well known after the publication of *Read With Me* (Waterland, 1988), although a similar approach had been written about earlier by Bennett (1979) and Meek (1982). As the word 'approach' signals, it comprises a particular form of organization, ethos and choice of resources. Reading aloud and sharing books takes place alongside other co-operative and developmental literacy activities. In the apprenticeship approach the teacher works with each child individually as they read and discuss a book together. The process is undertaken in the spirit of genuine collaboration with the child. The adult's role is one of expert participant rather than expert instructor. She is there to provide the child with support and access to the text until the child is ready to take over. The focus of her interventions is to indicate how the child can enjoy the book more efficiently and independently rather than to judge progress or correct errors. Depending on the experience and fluency of the reader, sharing books in this way involves the following elements:

- Reading a complete text to ensure a meaningful experience for the child.
- Discussing the title, author and possible content of the story, if the text is unfamiliar to the child, before the book is shared.
- The teacher reading to the child who follows the text so that the child becomes familiar with the story.
- The child retelling the story using the illustrations and text to guide him.
- The child joining in with the reading when he feels able to do so.
- The teacher and the child reading in unison.
- The child gradually taking over the reading until he is reading alone.
- The adult supporting the child by prompting or supplying words so that the meaning is not lost.
- A discussion about the child's response to the book.
- The child discussing the book with the teacher after reading it silently.

Initially the majority of books that are shared are familiar to the child from story sessions, big-book sessions and previous readings with adults. At this point the child is using his memory of the story to join in with and retell the story. He is learning about print through behaving as a reader and, very importantly, he is establishing his belief in himself as a reader and gaining sufficient confidence to risk joining in with and taking over from the adult's reading. Gradually the child is able to approach more new texts with less preparation and to read with less support from the adult. But whatever stage the child has reached the teacher must tolerate hesitations and meaningful miscues, giving the child opportunities to self-correct, as she listens to and supports the child's reading. This approach places a great deal of emphasis on the quality of the texts that are shared in order to ensure that the child derives pleasure and meaning from the reading, to enable the child to use all the reading cues that are available and to sustain interest as the texts are returned to and read again. As quality is most frequently found in story books this approach is sometimes called the 'real books' approach. This is misleading as the emphasis is as much on philosophy as on the resources.

Shared writing

During shared-writing sessions the adult models writing for a large group or for the class. Because this activity concerns a demonstration of writing it gives children insights into many aspects of texts and reading including words, letters, style and structure. As the children are concentrating on the content while the teacher transcribes, they have the opportunity to read and reread what is being written.

For shared writing the teacher should have a number of large sheets of paper clipped to an easel and she should write with a large felt-tip so that all the children can see what and how she writes. Before writing the teacher and the children should discuss what is to be written as well as the purpose, audience and style of the writing.

Topics for shared writing may include ● retelling a familiar story ● making up a new version of a known story ● making up a new story ● writing a story in another language ● writing a rhyme or a poem ● recording a visit ● writing instructions ● recording information ● recording songs ● writing a letter ● making a list.

As she writes, the teacher will demonstrate and may draw the children's attention to any of the following teaching points that she wishes to emphasize: ● where the writing starts ● word spacing ● punctuation ● grammar ● spellings ● patterns in words ● the sequencing of ideas ● drafting ● developing the plot ● styles of writing ● choice of words.

During a second reading of the text, the children discuss any changes that they would like to make to the content, order and detail of what has been written as well as changes to spelling and presentation. If the text is to be illustrated the children can then work on these while the teacher writes out the text in best. Shared-writing sessions are often used to write enlarged texts to be used in shared-reading sessions. Big books that are produced as a result of shared-writing sessions can be provided with texts in languages other than English with the help of older children or adults.

Writing and making books

Making books and writing stories is highly motivating for children. Through authorship they learn more about the format, features and purpose of books and print. Books can be read in assemblies and put in the school or class library. They can be added to the class stock and if appropriate can be photocopied and produced in multiple copies for use as group readers. Book making is one way of providing texts that are relevant to the particular community within which the school is located. Books can be written that reflect the locality, feature the children in the class as central characters and be produced as dual texts with heritage languages appropriate to the school.

In the process of book making children can find out how books work. They can investigate how different kinds of books are organized. Some books have an index, a list of contents, chapters, notes about the author, summaries, dedications and reviews. The children may reproduce these features in the books that they write. In addition when writing the book the children will have to plan, draft, revise and produce a best copy either on the word processor or by hand so they will be carefully rereading what has been written as they aim to produce publishable material.

In order to produce books children will need access to a variety of materials, probably all those available in the writing area. Sometimes books can be ready made but it is valuable for the children to make their own books and decide on their own choice of design and format. This can be a useful technology and maths exercise for pupils. Teachers might like to display instructions about ways of making books in the writing area. Two stimulating sources of book-making techniques for teachers and children are *Making Books* (Chapman and Robson, 1991) and *Developing Literacy through Making Books* (Johnson, 1990).

Using story props

Story props are pictures of the central characters and objects from a story. They are made by the teacher or by the children and are usually mounted on to a small magnet so that they can be used on a magnet board, but Blu-tack is also effective if a magnet board is not available. When the story is told or read to the class the props are placed on to the board as they appear in the narrative. The figures are then moved around as the story develops. Words and key phrases from the text may be placed alongside the pictures. Once the children have seen the story props in use they can be kept in the listening area with the book and an accompanying tape for the children to use when they read the book again.

Names

Making a collection of children's names can be a rich starting point for examining words and letters. Names can be sorted and matched according to initial letters, number of syllables and length. They can be arranged in alphabetical order and may be used to make an alphabet frieze or poster for the class. Children can experiment with writing their names in various colours and sizes using a variety of tools and materials. The sounds, names, shapes and formation of all the letters contained in the names can be discussed and compared during the activities and later when the poster or the frieze is referred to. Similar activities may also arise from an examination of food packaging and labels or environmental print in and around the school. The children may may make an alphabetically ordered book recording words that they see around them.

Signing in

Instead of calling the register the teacher can institute a large signing-in sheet on which children can write their name each day. This could be read by the whole class at the start of the morning and might illustrate the uses of reading and writing for keeping records and providing information.

Collections

Collections of words that begin with the same letter or that contain the same letter strings can be started and added to over the course of a week. Each time something is added the sounds and names of letters can be discussed and the words read by the class.

Rhymes and games

Nursery and other rhymes as well as advertising slogans and jingles can be sung and recited together. Other oral language games such as 'I Spy' and 'Odd One Out' can be played with and by the children. These activities provide relevant introductions to grapho-phonic knowledge and awareness as well as helping children to see the fun and use of literacy.

Sequencing

Sequencing activities develop children's familiarity with stories, story structure and narrative language. Pictures and words taken from a book or photographs and sentences recounting an activity the children have undertaken are given to pairs of children. The activities might include an experiment, a school event, an outing, a cooking activity or a science activity. Working together the children are asked to arrange the pictures and or sentences in order. When engaged in this activity the children are practising the oral and written language of the story or the activity. By doing this activity collaboratively they are negotiating meaning, recalling past experiences and sharing ideas as well as listening to one another. After the children have sequenced the cards they can use them as the framework for narrating a story or event to other children or to an adult. The children can also make their own cards for this activity based on their own favourite books or class events.

Themes

All themes provide opportunities for children to read books and other material and to write in a variety of styles. As teachers plan their themes they may like to consider the particular literacy opportunities which will arise during all the activities in all areas of the curriculum. At times a theme which focuses particularly on books or language may be selected by the teacher. This will be a rich opportunity for extending reading. Examples of literacy and language themes are provided in Chapters 5 and 6.

Opportunities for reading

The practice of listening to young children read aloud for a few minutes each day, two or three times a week, is a common one in early-years classrooms. It became standard practice because it gives the teacher the opportunity to • assess progress and keep track of development • provide help for individual needs • check the child's developing use of reading strategies • give every child individual contact time • demonstrate her interest in reading • give each child time to read • become aware of difficulties.

In recent years, however, this practice has been questioned, for although the aims listed above are valid ones, critics doubt that listening to reading for short periods achieves these aims effectively. It rarely provides quality individual contact time either at a personal or educational level, since most reading sessions last between two and three minutes and the average interruption-free time is about 30 seconds (Southgate, Arnold and Johnson, 1981). HMI (1993) were critical of this brevity. They commented that the value of reading to the teacher lies in the quality of preparation and follow-up work in which the individual reading session is embedded. A few minutes of interrupted time make HMI's suggestions for good practice very difficult to implement and give very little time for diagnosis and help, or for sharing enjoyment and interest in reading. If children are to make progress in reading and learn to enjoy books they will need more practice at reading than 10 minutes of individual reading to the teacher each week can provide. Working in this way individual children may receive very little reading time but the teacher will have spent a large proportion of her week, at least five hours or almost a whole school day each week, on this one aspect of reading. Moon (1988, pp. 185–86) sees the practice not only as inefficient but also as one which may actively damage children's reading development: 'reading aloud might be the best way to prevent children becoming readers because it slows down reading and forces the reader to concentrate on surface features and intonation at the expense of comprehension.'

In a situation where teachers are conscious of time, are half focusing on other children and are most alert to the reader's hesitations, they may provide unfamiliar words too quickly, giving children the message that reading is about accuracy rather than meaning. In such a short period it would be unlikely for sufficient text to have been read for the teacher to seek the child's response to the book and check understanding.

Most children make progress in reading because reading aloud from a book to an adult in school is not the only practice in reading that they receive. They read to others at home and in school. In class they read computer screens, worksheets, instructions, their own writing, the teacher's writing, as well as hearing stories and engaging in oral and written language games (Farquhar, 1987). Reading non-book material gives the teacher the opportunity to provide additional feedback about reading to the child (Campbell, 1992).

However, an interested adult who spends time on reading with individuals and who provides encouragement, enthusiasm and resources is crucial to children's reading development (Clark, 1976). So how might the teacher use reading time more efficiently? Both Southgate, Arnold and Johnson (1981) and Arnold (1982) have suggested that teachers should spend longer, less frequent periods of time with children in order to provide a real opportunity for teaching and learning. Reading sessions should be long enough for the child to read a whole story or episode and discuss this with the teacher, as in the apprenticeship approach.

Reading conferences

Reading conferences are one way of spending extended periods of time with children. During a reading conference the child reads aloud to the teacher. The teacher attends to the child's confidence, independence and interests as a reader. She notes the range of strategies the child employs and the child's knowledge and understanding of print and books, as well as encouraging the child to reflect on and enjoy reading. During the reading the teacher responds to any difficulties that the child demonstrates in a way that causes least disruption to the reading. She limits her interventions to those miscues which detract from the child's understanding of the text. If the child substitutes an inappropriate word the teacher might say 'no' and read part of the sentence which led up to the miscued word, using rising intonation to invite the child to reconsider what she has read. If the child makes no attempt at the word the teacher might employ the previous strategy, provide the word, or draw the child's attention to the initial letter of the word. In order to maintain the flow of the reading she might provide the unknown word but return to it and discuss it with the child after the reading has been completed. The teacher's interventions signal to the child the sort of cues that might be used when reading. She will want to indicate that using syntactic and semantic cues through rereading and reading on are helpful and provide the context for the use of grapho-phonic cues. Spending time with children in this way gives the teacher the opportunity to monitor progress, discuss the child's response to the book, his general reading interests and his difficulties and make suggestions about ways forward for the child.

The allocation of time for reading conferences depends on good classroom organization (Campbell, 1990). The class needs to be engaged on activities which match their capabilities, the children need to know what to do if they finish an activity and they need to know that they do not interrupt reading periods. The normal classroom routines must support pupil autonomy and independence.

The reading conference is not the only time that the child spends on reading each week. Children receive practice at reading through all the literacy activities that occur during a normal school day including shared reading of enlarged texts and reading and listening to stories in the reading area as well as engaging in other activities that necessitate the use of literacy. They may also read during periods of shared reading, prepared reading, group reading, quiet or silent reading and paired reading. These are described below.

Prepared reading: This is a way of using teacher time efficiently with more experienced readers. With this approach the child reads the text silently before discussing the story and reading a little of the text, maybe the final page, aloud to the teacher. The book may have been read at home or at school. Prior to the discussion and reading with the teacher the child may need to refresh his memory of the text and should spend a few minutes reading the book again quietly. The discussion of the book will focus on the child's response to the text, the parts of the book that he enjoyed or did not enjoy and why and what he might like to read next. The teacher and the child might talk about any difficulties the child encountered when he read the book. The teacher might suggest ways of dealing with these difficulties or work with the child on examining particular words, letter strings or sounds.

Group reading: Here four to six children grouped according to ability or experience take turns in reading a page at a time aloud from the same book; those who are not reading aloud listen and read the page silently. The books that are used are often drawn from the core-books collection and with more experienced readers sets of plays can be read. If an adult is part of the group she too should read a page in turn thus providing a model of literacy involvement. After the book has been read the children discuss the story and any difficulties they had as they read. This strategy enables a whole text to be read and discussed by a number of children in one reading session. All the class may be organized for group reading at the same time with adults reading with some of the groups, or group reading can be included as one of the planned activities for the day.

Silent reading: The large-scale implementation of this practice grew in response to a suggestion from the *Extending Beginning Reading* Project (Southgate, Arnold and Johnson, 1981) which found that children's reading in school was often too limited in length for them to develop their experience and enjoyment of books. Periods of silent reading in class give children the opportunity for a sustained read from a book of their choice, enable them to see adults enjoying reading and enhance the status of reading for its own sake. The guidelines for organizing silent reading were first described by McCracken (1971). He suggested that

- a regular time should be allocated for silent reading each day
- each child should have a personally selected book ready before the start of the session
- the teacher should also read a book during this time
- there should be no talking or movement around the class during the session
- this is a time to enjoy reading and not a preparation for future work although, after the session, some children might recommend a book, which they have particularly enjoyed reading, to the class.

Many teachers have found that periods of silent reading work best if they occur after a natural break in the school day such as play time or lunch time. Before the break the children select their books so that they are ready for the session when they return to class. Although ideally this should be a silent time, with very young children, who often read aloud to themselves, the time may be quiet rather than silent. As long as the rules of silent reading are explained to the children and it becomes a regular feature of the school day, children as young as 4 will happily read or look at a book for five minutes or more. By the time children are 7 the silent-reading period may be as long as 20 minutes. Normally the whole range of books in class will be available for children to choose from but, every so often, the pattern of silent-reading sessions may be varied by having a theme for the session such as information books or books by named authors.

Paired reading: With paired reading children choose or are allocated a regular reading partner. The two children take turns in reading aloud to each other from a book of their choice. During the reading the partner can give the reader help by supplying words or trying to work out unfamiliar words. The teacher and other adults can also be partners. If children have not yet reached the stage of reading alone they can 'tell' the story to their partner by reading the illustrations in the text. Paired reading can take place regularly as a whole-class activity or may appear on the daily plan for group activities with a different group engaging in paired reading each day throughout the week.

As part of the weekly literacy plan for the class, these ways of organizing for reading enable children to gain a great deal of reading practice at school. If they are explained carefully and occur regularly they enable teachers to make good use of their time and provide opportunities for children to enjoy meaningful time with books rather than a hurried few minutes with an adult.

Resources for reading

After the encouragement provided by knowledgeable and supportive adults, the major resource for learning to reading is books. Because books play such an important role in learning to read it is important that they are selected with care and thought. They are used and reused, they must embody all that the teacher thinks is important for children who are learning to read, they are expensive and they play an important part in influencing children's short and long-term attitudes towards reading, since 'What the beginning reader reads makes all the difference to his view of reading' (Meek, 1982). Because books are central to learning to read and perhaps because of their power to affect and effect emotions in those who read them, the selection of books for young readers has been and continues to be an area which is surrounded by debate.

Until the 1970s it was accepted that children in school learned to read using books specially written to provide practice in phonic and word-recognition skills. This often resulted in texts containing unnatural language and lifeless stories, which attracted criticism as long ago as 1908 when Huey (p. 279) wrote: 'No trouble has been taken to write what the child would naturally say about the subject in hand, nor indeed to say anything connectedly or continuously, as even an adult would talk about the subject.'

During the 1970s some accounts of practice appeared which suggested that children could and should learn to read using picture books selected from the increasing array of books that were being written for young children (Spencer, 1976; Bennett, 1979; ILEA, 1979) This move was officially supported by the Bullock Report (DES, 1975) where reading schemes were described as 'an ancillary part of a school's reading programme, and nothing more'. During the 1980s increasing numbers of schools began to use picture books rather than scheme books for developing children's reading, a move that was supported and explained by the publication of Waterland's (1988) account of learning to read with picture and story books. Appearing at a time when a great deal of political and public attention was focused on education, this book reached a large audience of teachers, educators, journalists, parents and politicians and seemed to become the catalyst in a public debate about resources and approaches to reading in schools.

In popular jargon the label 'real books' has become associated with holistic and interactive approaches to reading and the use of reading schemes with the development of reading skills, particularly phonics. The move towards 'real books' has been labelled as a 'non-teaching' movement (Phillips, 1990) and criticized for bringing about an alleged fall in reading standards (Turner, 1990). Neither of these criticisms has any substance. The practices outlined earlier in this section indicate the importance of the teacher's role as a facilitator, model, adviser and observer with developing readers. According to the 1989–90 HMI survey of reading standards in school there was no evidence that standards in reading had fallen since 1978. In the same survey they wrote, 'Poor work is not strongly associated with any particular method of teaching reading'

(HMI, 1991). To associate the use of schemes with phonics teaching and high standards is a very simplistic representation of practice. Teachers who use picture books with young readers rather than schemes may also introduce children to phonics as one of a number of strategies that will help them to read more efficiently. Schools which use scheme books may also use supported practices, such as those described in this chapter, and may not have a structured phonics teaching programme. The careful choice of picture books for beginning readers does not equal failure to teach or failure to learn. On the contrary it classifies reading as an activity that is about a search for meaning and emphasizes children's integrity as learners.

As a result of continued criticism, the increased attention given to the role of stories in learning to read and the recognition of the importance of children's own attitudes to reading, every scheme that has been published since the 1960s has claimed to contain 'real' stories, natural language and to be motivating to children. Many publishers and authors of reading schemes now make strenuous efforts to ensure that the texts in their books are written in natural language, contain stories that have some relevance to children's interests and lives and include colourful and lively illustrations. However, schemes still attract criticism for a number of reasons. They are criticized for their uniform appearance, the way in which they encourage competition, the distinction that their use creates between learning to read and reading, the way that they delay children's access into the world of books and their bland content. It is this last point that is most frequently mentioned by those who write about reading. Although 'reading schemese' (Wray, 1994) is not as common as it once was it seems to have been replaced with an almost arbitrary choice of simple words which are used to describe everyday events that are familiar to most children. This type of story and use of language does not compare well with books written by authors who have a commitment to a story and a sensitivity to language. Meek (1988) writes about the disconnection, emptiness and arbitrariness of reading-scheme books in contrast to the coherence, fulfilment and pattern of individual books written for children. Her remarks are not dissimilar to those made by Stebbing and Raban (1982, p. 159) who described one reading scheme as containing 'narrative without structure. There is no plot requiring resolution . . . There is no introductory 'Once upon a time . . .' or anything suggestive of development . . . The characters are insubstantial and little occurs in the train of events to make the reader wonder what will happen next'.

While some individual books within reading schemes are enjoyable, even the best stories can be emotionally barren. By concentrating on the instant appeal of 'fun', they seldom, if ever, contain new material or stories which evoke an emotional response from the reader. How many reading-scheme books are set in the Caribbean or a tropical rain forest? How many explore issues such as the environment, ambition, friendship or loss? How many have stunning illustrations as diverse as those by Reg and Ann

Cartwright or Anthony Browne? Scheme books are rarely 'an instrument for entering possible worlds of human experience' (Bruner, 1984).

It is very difficult for all the books in any series to be of a high standard, particularly when they have been written to meet a number of constraining requirements, such as • introductory books containing very few words • a simple, limited vocabulary • some phonic regularity • word repetition • appeal to a mass audience • attending to all the prevailing 'isms' of the day • a uniform appearance (cover, illustrations, layout, size) for ease of identification • a grading system for ease of administration • commissioned rather than written with the emotional investment of an author who has a story to tell • often written by a committee.

Some of these criteria may now be inappropriate given our awareness of the oral language expertise and expectations children bring to print, and the knowledge about story and story structure they can draw upon when beginning to read.

It now seems time for teachers and educators to move away from criticizing and defending reading schemes and to ask themselves instead, do we really need them? As Southgate, Arnold and Johnson (1981, p. 122) concluded: 'Are the basic reading schemes being used the ideal reading materials either to grip the children's interest or to increase their reading ability or fluency? Are these schemes such as to convince children that reading is a desirable pursuit?' Who benefits from using schemes, with their implicit messages of learning to read as a competitive activity, the distinction they create between learning to read and real reading and the way in which they keep children away from the rich store of books that are now available for them? Real books can teach everything that scheme books can teach and more. They can teach children about enjoyment and satisfaction, book selection, the purposes of reading, a love of books, a delight in language, as well as offering humour, excitement, a recreation of the familiar and an extension of experience. They can even teach children about phonics and provide them with a sight vocabulary of function words.

Reading schemes only work as well as the teachers who manage them and it could be seen as a misuse of expertise for teachers to operate a system rather than to respond to children's individual interests and needs. Teachers with a thorough understanding of the reading process, who are organized, who know how children learn, who are aware of the abilities and needs of pupils in their classes and who are familiar with children's books will experience little difficulty in selecting suitable books and using these rather than scheme books for reading.

As a halfway measure between schemes and other texts written for children some schools have adopted a system for putting all their books (including schemes) into broad bands of difficulty. This system is often based on the suggestions in *Individualized Reading* (Moon, 1994). The children choose their own book from the level that is appropriate to their developing expertise, progressing from one band to the next when sufficient books at one level have been read. This system gives children an indication of the books they should be able to read independently but may also limit choice. Sometimes children can gain pleasure and satisfaction from a book that might be considered too difficult or too easy for them. It may also foster competition between children; learning to read can become a race to reach the next level and those children who progress slowly can suffer damage to their self-esteem. Colour coding books is a very time-consuming exercise and may not repay the effort it involves.

As an alternative to reading schemes, individualized reading or complete freedom for each teacher and child to select the books that are read, some schools work with a core of books. Core books are a carefully selected but small number of books (about 30 titles) which provide a framework of reading materials for each class. Unlike reading schemes, which are often written by a group of fairly anonymous authors and illustrators who share a house style, core books include the best literature and information texts that are available for young children. Multiple copies of each core book are kept in each class and used for group reading, quiet reading, reading with story tapes, retelling with story props and thematic work in class. The children can make models, collages, their own story props, tapes and games based around the books. They can be used as starting points for drama and promoted through posters and reviews produced by the children. Enlarged texts of some of the core books may also be available or made in class by the children or the teacher. Through frequent encounters with a limited number of core texts children's understanding of books, narrative structure, book language and the relationship between spoken and written language is developed; they establish a sight vocabulary and, as their confidence and success with reading increase, see reading and books as meaningful and enjoyable. Although core books are important, particularly in the initial stages of learning to read, they are not the only books that the class read and share, but they are often the ones that are used most frequently since they have been carefully selected by the staff to embody the school's approach to reading.

Organization for reading

As the teacher plans the weekly activities for the class she needs to consider when and where reading will appear in order to ensure that every child will read. Table 2.1 gives two sample literacy plans for an infant class indicating the reading that is possible each day and each week. These schedules are not exhaustive and will change from day to day and week to week. They are intended to indicate how literacy activities may be integrated within the teaching day and week.

The groups have not been allocated for the final activities as these might follow on from previous activities, might not occur each week and might vary as the teacher checks the progress made by each group in completing earlier activities. However it is possible to see from this timetable that every

Table 2.1   Two sample literacy plans

Daily plan for literacy

What	Who	When
Shared reading	Whole class	After break
Silent reading	Whole class	After lunch
Paired reading	Blue group	During the day
Reading to the teacher	Red group	During the day
Group reading with classroom assistant	Green group	Afternoon
Listening area	Two children from Orange group	During the day
Computer	Two children from Orange group	During the day
Phonic activities	Whole class	After shared reading
Shared writing	Purple group	Before break
Children in the writing area	Two children from Orange group	During the day
Writing and illustrating books (follow-up to yesterday's shared writing)	Yellow group	Begin after lunch
Story time	Whole class	End of the day
Oral word games	Whole class	Five minutes before lunch

Weekly plan for literacy

Practice/activity	Monday	Tuesday	Wednesday	Thursday	Friday
Shared reading	All	All		All	All
Silent reading	All		All		All
Paired reading	Blue	Red	Green	Orange	Purple
Reading to the teacher	Red	Green	Orange	Purple	Yellow
Group reading with classroom assistant	Green	Orange	Purple	Yellow	Blue
Listening area	Orange	Purple	Yellow	Red	Green
Computer	Orange	Purple	Yellow	Red	Green
Phonic activities	All	Yellow	Green		All
Shared writing	Purple		Blue		Red
Children in the writing area	Orange	Purple	Yellow	Red	Green
Writing and illustrating books	Yellow	Purple	Blue		Red
Story time	All	All	All	All	All
Word games	All		All		All
Sequencing activities	Green	Orange	Purple	Yellow	Blue
Matching games	Red	Green	Orange	Purple	Yellow
Extending stories into art/craft/music/drama/technology/science					
Making story props					
Children telling stories on tape					
Children writing individually/in pairs					
Making a word collection					
Making a wall display of a story					

child can experience frequent and varied literacy activities over the course of a week as long as the teacher includes these in her weekly planning.

All that has been written in this section on planning and implementing a reading curriculum is in line with the Programmes of Study for reading at Key Stages 1 and 2 (DfE, 1995a), which requires that children read an extensive range of children's literature and other texts alone, with others and to the teacher; that they understand the nature and purpose of reading and read with understanding, fluency, accuracy and enjoyment, drawing from a range of strategies. The practical suggestions outlined here should help teachers to realize all their aims for the reading development of all young children.

Conclusion

Since learning to read is a complex undertaking teachers need to be informed and reflective about reading in order to teach it successfully. By understanding the process and respecting the integrity and ability of young children it may be possible not just to produce readers but to foster in them an enduring love and need for reading. This chapter has attempted to set a programme for reading, containing practical activities and organizational strategies, in an up-to-date theoretical framework. This should help practioners to formulate their own reasoned approach to reading with the aim of helping all children to become successful readers.

Suggestions for further reading

Barrs, M. and Thomas, A. (eds) (1991) *The Reading Book*, CLPE, London.
Wade, B. (ed.) (1990) *Reading for Real*, Open University Press, Milton Keynes.

Publishers of big books

Collins Children's Books tel.: 0171–493 7070; Book Bus Big Books.
Heinemann Educational tel.: 01933 58521; Sunshine Books, All-Together Books.
Mary Glasgow Publications tel.: 01926 640606; Readalong Rhythms Big Books.
Oliver & Boyd tel.: 01279 26721; Storytime Giants – *Each Peach Pear Plum, The Lighthouse Keeper's Lunch, Two Monsters*, etc.
Tadpole Books, Kingscourt Publishing Ltd tel.: 0171–741 8011; Giant Books – *The Three Billy Goats Gruff, The Gingerbread Man, The Life of a Duck, Tadpole Diary*, etc.
Thomas Nelson tel.: 01932 246133; Story Chest, Big Big Books.

Chapter 3

Writing

Introduction

The past decade has been characterized by enormous changes in the way that writing is now taught in many early-years classes. The main impetus for the change arose from the publication of the first National Curriculum documents in 1989 and the work of the National Writing Project (1985–89). The first version of the National Curriculum for English (DES, 1989a) separated writing, the 'growing ability to construct and convey meaning in written language', from the skills of spelling and handwriting. This separation acknowledged and validated the distinction between the composition and the transcription of writing. The 1990 Programme of Study also drew attention to the significance for teachers of children's early, spontaneous writing, stating 'Initial efforts – marks on a page – will be followed by writing which is characterized by invented spelling and letter formation and partial understanding of many of the conventions of standard English' (DES, 1990). The revised National Curriculum (DfE, 1995a) continues to distinguish between the composition and the presentation of writing and urges teachers to acknowledge children's 'early experiments and independent attempts at communicating in writing, using letters and known words'. Both these aspects, the distinction between composition and transcription and the importance of recognizing and developing children's early unaided or emergent writing, were thoroughly explored during the course of the National Writing Project.

Prior to 1989 some practitioners were already working developmentally and in a way which took account of the distinction between transcription and composition. They were following a writing curriculum based on the research and ideas expressed by Temple *et al.* (1988) (developmental writing), Bissex (1980) (preschool knowledge about writing), Graves (1983) (drafting and conferencing) and Smith (1982) (the need to teach the different elements of writing individually), but such practice was not widespread. It was the appearance of the English National Curriculum which prompted many schools to examine and alter their approach.

Although there have been substantial shifts in the way in which writing is taught, the picture is not uniform. Currently there appear to be two approaches. Some teachers continue to work in a traditional way which ignores much of what is now known about the process of writing, about children's early understanding of writing and about how writing might be taught using this knowledge; while others follow a developmental writing approach incorporating many aspects of practice described in the literature mentioned above.

This chapter begins with an account of traditional approaches to teaching writing. This is followed by a summary of what is now known about the process of writing. There is a description of what young children know about writing when they start school and how their use and understanding of writing develops. These sections provide a rationale for a purposeful and developmental writing curriculum which is described in the final part of the chapter. The focus in this chapter is on generating and composing writing; the transcriptional aspects of writing, spelling, handwriting and punctuation are treated separately in Chapter 4.

Traditional approaches to teaching and learning writing

Traditional approaches to teaching writing in school usually begin from the premiss that young children have little or no knowledge about writing and need formal instruction from a teacher in order to learn. People who work in this way often have difficulty separating the teaching of composition from the teaching of transcription. They feel that children need to use correct spellings and correctly formed handwriting from the start. A typical traditional programme might involve the children in copying and tracing handwriting patterns, writing and tracing over the teacher's writing, copying underneath the teacher's writing and copying from the board. When children are considered ready to begin writing independently they are expected to use word books to obtain spellings of words which are unknown to them. They present their word books to the adult, who writes down the correct version of the word for the child to copy into his written work.

Traditional approaches tend to pay limited attention to audience, purpose and outcome for the early writing which children do in school. The main purpose for much of the writing appears to be to gain practice at writing and the audience for the writing that is produced is usually the teacher. When the writing is finished it is corrected by the teacher and generally remains in the child's writing book. Writing done in this way is rarely drafted and is often expected to be completed in one session, although if it is to be displayed it may be copied out by the child once it has been corrected by the teacher.

The writing in Figure 3.1 was produced by a 6-year-old working in a class with a traditional approach to writing. The activity was intended to encourage the children to consider the subject of recycling everyday

the adventures of a
plastic cup   25/1/94

yo can im a kelam odd' and
yoran yseit a again
and again and again
and yocan useitto
a Mould and put
plasticne in it.

Figure 3.1   Recycling

objects. The writing was done straight into the children's writing books and the only person to read the writing was the teacher. The spelling is good, since it was supplied by the teacher, and the handwriting is clear, although the letters are not formed correctly. However what is worrying about this writing is the tired content and lack of enthusiasm for writing that this child seems to have. In order to finish the task the child has merely repeated the same phrase until presumably, he judged that he had written enough to satisfy the teacher.

Traditional approaches to teaching writing have a number of limitations and disadvantages. Copying and asking for words encourage children to become reliant on the teacher. A great deal of time can be wasted by children as they wait for help, as they follow the teacher around the classroom with their word books open, or as they sit at their tables with their hands up waiting for the teacher to write their sentence for them to copy in their 'news books'. When the teacher gives the required assistance she is generally helping children with getting the writing to look right rather than responding to what the children have written and encouraging them to develop this. Whilst urging children to produce exciting, interesting, detailed and well constructed pieces of writing it is possible to spend most of the time in writing sessions not helping with any of these aspects of writing. A study of 'good' teachers of 6-year-old pupils revealed that 'The predominant aim expressed in more than 70% of tasks intended to promote writing was to "practice" writing . . . [and] Requests for spellings constitute the predominant teacher/pupil exchanges in language lessons' (Bennett *et al.*, 1984, pp. 101, 124).

Teaching writing in this way does not acknowledge the degree of linguistic learning children already have and makes it difficult for the teacher to see what children can do alone. It encourages dependence, inhibits children's willingness to write for themselves, wastes time, causes organizational headaches, puts the emphasis on transcription rather than composition, and generally fails to give children a sense of the communicative or personal uses of writing.

In spite of the disadvantages with traditional approaches to writing some schools continue to teach writing by getting children to copy from an adult model written in children's writing books or word books. There may be a number of reasons for this. Some teachers feel that young children's inability to produce letters, words and sentences which can be read and understood easily is a problem when children start school. So before teaching children about the uses and composition of writing they focus on the transcriptional elements of the writing system including letter formation, neatness, spelling and presentation. Teachers' assumptions about parental and other adult's expectations of what children's writing should look like may also affect how they approach writing with their classes. There seems to be a belief that writing should either look perfect or should show evidence of having been corrected, otherwise children will not learn, will internalize incorrect models and the teacher will be failing to do her job properly. However no one can be fooled by examples of perfect writing by young children. Even adults have difficulty in producing well presented and well thought-out writing at a first attempt. What is often seen in children's writing books are copies of the teacher's writing and evidence of the teacher's industry rather than examples of children's learning. Even if young children can copy writing well this is unlikely to be a true reflection of what children know and what they can do alone.

It is no longer sufficient to begin the teaching of writing by asking children to draw a picture, dictate a sentence about the picture to the teacher who writes this down and then for children to copy beneath the teacher's writing. This method of teaching takes little account of the broad communicative nature of writing or its distinctive power. Copy writing denies the child the opportunity to demonstrate what he might already know about writing and prevents the teacher from seeing what the child can do and what needs to be taught next. If this type of task is repeated daily the teacher is ignoring the many purposes for which written language can be used and placing the emphasis on what the product looks like rather than on the process and use of writing. Overall traditional approaches limit learning, teaching and the development of understanding about writing.

Findings from the literature about writing confirm that teaching writing in a traditional way is no longer appropriate, as educators are now aware of

- the importance of purposes, audiences and forms when writing
- many children's negative attitudes to writing
- children's early understanding of the functions of literacy
- young children's understanding and use of the forms of writing.

The writing process

Purposes for writing

Writing is a significant feature of life in the twentieth century. It surrounds and affects everyone and can be used in both the public and private aspects of people's lives. Publicly, it can be used to persuade, to suggest and indicate appropriate behaviour and responses, to establish contact with others, to communicate information, to entertain, to express one's individuality and to question. Part of the power of writing, as a means of communication, is that it offers the writer the time and opportunity to reflect on what information the message will contain and how it will be transmitted. It can also give the recipient time to consider what has been written: 'we write to share thoughts and feelings with others through communications ranging from hastily written notes to formal, carefully argued essays on complex issues' (Willig, 1990).

Privately people may write to explore and clarify ideas, to organize thoughts, to reflect, to exercise the imagination, to evaluate and to provide a record of events or ideas. 'Writing can be an extension and reflection of all our efforts to develop and express ourselves in the world around us, to make sense of the world and to impose order upon it' (Smith, 1982); it 'is a key element in the search for meaning because it allows us to reflect on and to order our encounters with the world and the impact they make upon us' (Willig, 1990).

Audience and form

Writing is an act of communication and as such has both an author and an audience. Before beginning any writing, writers identify not only why they are writing but also whom they are writing for. During the course of a week an adult might write to the person who delivers the milk, to a friend, to the bank manager, to a colleague, to readers of a newspaper, to oneself. Each piece of writing will have a clear purpose, an intended audience and be written in a particular way. A note asking for an extra pint of milk may be written quickly, on a piece of scrap paper with any writing implement that is to hand. It will probably be brief. A letter to a friend may be quite lengthy, describe events and feelings in some detail, may contain advice or comment and may vary in style from the humorous to the grave. It may be loosely structured, may refer to shared knowledge and experiences and convey the personality of the writer. A letter to the bank manager might be quite formal. The writer may take a great deal of care in organizing the content, presenting the information clearly, ensuring that the handwriting is legible and checking spelling and grammar. It might be written out a number of times and the writer may use a typewriter or word processor. A shopping list written for oneself may contain abbreviations, words which are crossed out and it may be added to over a few days. In all these pieces of writing the interplay among the purpose for writing, the audience and the content will affect the form and style of the writing, the care with which it is undertaken and the length of time spent on it.

Writing is affected by ● the writer's purpose ● the audience; *these affect* ● form ● style ● vocabulary ● transcription (handwriting, spelling, punctuation, drafting, choice of tools, care and time).

Children and writing

Children's attitudes to writing

Children's poor attitudes towards writing at school have been evident for many years. The 1988 APU survey of language performance revealed that 'not less than two out of ten pupils have developed negative views about writing by the time they are eleven' (Gorman *et al.*, 1989, p. 57). The same report also stated: 'such attitudes are established long before pupils reach the age of eleven. It can be assumed that they are established primarily when children are first being taught to read and write' (*ibid.*, p. 57). Although poor attitudes may arise for many reasons, children's feelings about writing and their view of themselves as writers are likely to be influenced by the way that writing is taught and the messages that the teacher transmits about writing. Children may become discouraged with writing because they think that they have nothing to say that needs to be communicated through writing, that the demands that are placed on them to produce neat, correctly spelt writing at the first attempt are difficult to meet, that their writing is not very good, even when the content is fine because they are poor spellers and their handwriting looks untidy. They may decide that writing takes too long if they have to wait for every spelling from the teacher or for the teacher to write their sentence down before they copy it. Writing sessions may not occur regularly enough for children to spend sufficient time on producing something that is worth reading by others. Alternatively, writing may happen too often, when everything that happens in the class is followed up with a piece of writing. Writing in the class may be organized so that children do not see the purpose for it, particularly if the only audience for what is written is the teacher. Finally, even if children have something to write about and someone to write for, if the teacher attends to the transcription rather than the content, children may assume that the message is unimportant. In the long term asking children to write with the emphasis on transcription and without any clear sense of purpose and audience conceals the communicative function of writing and prevents children from seeing the relevance of writing.

Children's early understanding of the functions of literacy

Children are active and avid learners almost from the moment of their birth. This is clearly demonstrated through their achievements as oral language users. However two conditions need to be present for their learning to take place. They need to see a purpose for their learning and that purpose has to be relevant to their present needs. In Whitehead's words, children seem to ask themselves two questions when engaging in a task: first, 'What is it for?' and, second, 'What's in it for me?' (Whitehead, 1990). Most young children are aware of writing in their homes, their communities and from books and stories which have been shared with them. They will have seen adults responding to written messages and using writing. Children may have been encouraged to join in with the writing that adults do, when writing greeting cards or letters to relations and friends. They may well have begun to formulate some ideas about the use of writing in the world. What seems to be more difficult is for children to understand the relevance of writing to their own lives. During the course of the National Writing Project (1990) children were asked why they wrote. They gave replies such as because 'teacher says so' and 'so we don't get told off'. These children saw writing as a school activity whose primary purpose is to show adults what has been learned. They were unclear about the reasons for doing the writing they were asked to do in school and could not relate writing to their own lives or their present needs. If children learn most effectively when they can see reasons for what they are learning, then it is important to present children with writing activities that have a purpose and to make these purposes explicit and relevant to their present lives.

Writers write because they have something to communicate and someone to communicate with or because they have something to remember or clarify. They do not write if the message can be transmitted more easily and just as successfully through speech. Children can very often tell elaborate stories or pieces of news at school but when it comes to putting this down on paper they produce one sentence. This was the case with Stuart, whose writing was reproduced in Figure 3.1, and who spoke at some length about how everyday objects could be reused before he began his writing. This difference might arise because children can see no advantage in communicating this information again through writing. They have already communicated with a wide audience, probably wider than the audience who will read what they write. Writing down what they have said will involve them in the chore of wrestling with transcription and seems to offer no reward to them. They may well wonder what advantage is to be gained from writing at school.

Just as oral language is learned in purposeful situations and in order to satisfy immediate goals set by the child, so the writing curriculum that is presented in school must, as far as possible, engage children in relevant, purposeful writing activities. It would be inappropriate to expect children to become interested and adept users of written language if they are not offered reasons for becoming so. Adults need to explain, demonstrate and indicate the communicative functions of writing and the many reasons for writing, through the writing activities that they present to children.

Children's understanding and use of the forms of writing

Writing is a system containing regular features and forms including letter shapes, print direction, consistent spelling and punctuation marks (Clay, 1975; Temple *et al.*, 1988). Studies of young children's early writing reveal that before starting school many children know a great deal about the forms of writing. They often know that, in English, print goes from left to right across the page and from top to bottom down the page. They may know about letter shapes and symbols and how these represent meaning. They discover that not all symbols are writing and not all letter combinations are words. Children gain more experience of writing through seeing it around them, imitating what they see, exploring its features for themselves and discovering what is and what is not acceptable as part of the system (Ferreiro and Teberosky, 1983; Browne, 1993). By the time they start school they have abstracted a great deal of knowledge about the writing system from the examples they have seen around them, they may have hypothesized about what it is for and how it works, and the majority of children will be able to construct or represent what they have learned so far (Bissex, 1984). Children who intentionally produce a series of marks on a page which they call writing and who realize that writing communicates meaning have already learned some important lessons about writing.

The example in Figure 3.2 was spontaneously written by a 3-year-old, Abbie, as she was playing in the nursery home corner. The letter was intended for Ann. Abbie has positioned the recipient's name perfectly, showing a commendable awareness of the layout of writing on envelopes. She has seen both Ann's name and her own name many times, recognized that they begin with the same letter and drawn on her memory of both names in order to write a recognizable and very close approximation to the recipient's name. Abbie, who was just a normal, playful young child, already has a great deal of knowledge about writing.

Figure 3.2   Abbie 'Ain' envelope

Developmental approaches

Teachers who work developmentally, work with the knowledge and ability that children bring to school. From the start children are expected to try to write for themselves. They are given the opportunity to 'have a go' at writing without copying or waiting for the teacher to help them with spellings before they write. Initially children are encouraged to write without worrying about spelling and handwriting. This is totally in harmony with good early-years practice since it offers opportunities for learning through active exploration. The children are given a purposeful task that focuses on one of the many uses of writing and, wherever possible, an audience other than the teacher is provided for the writing that they do. The teacher provides encouragement and support as the children write. She encourages children to discuss their writing, to think about the content of their writing and to think about how things should be written. Children are asked actively to engage with the process of writing by being expected to think about what writing looks like and how they can best represent meaning and ideas in print. The teacher works with what is constructed and with what children know in order to help them to revise and extend their understanding of writing. It is after the writing has been produced that the teacher gives the children feedback and help with the transcriptional elements of what has been written. In this way teachers place the emphasis on purpose, composition, structure, clarity and meaning. What children can do is extended through adult observation and sensitive intervention, which is intended to help them to write more fluently and more easily.

Children do not learn to write quickly. It takes time for them to learn about writing and to move from marks on a page to fluent writing. Expressing what is meant through the written word can be both time consuming and hard work and success and involvement with writing can vary from task to task and from day to day. However it is important that

Figure 3.3 Emmanuel

children are given the time to experiment with each stage of the writing process and to feel that their written efforts are valuable if they are to continue to learn and to develop positive attitudes to writing. To this end the teacher does not correct every error that the child makes when writing; instead she provides correct models for the child to see and works with the child on one or two mistakes or difficulties at a time. The examples which follow show how children's writing can develop when teachers respond positively and sensitively to what children can do.

The first example was produced by 3-year-old Emmanuel. The children in the nursery were drawing pictures of their favourite playthings for a class book. Before beginning his picture Emmanuel had seen some of the completed pages in the book when the teacher had read the text and discussed the pictures with the class. After Emmanuel finished his picture he told the teacher that he was going to write his name at the top just like it would be in the book. Unaided he wrote three very clear letter shapes. To reinforce and extend what Emmanuel knew, the teacher wrote his name and the caption for the picture with Emmanuel, talking about the letters and words as she did so. Later, when the book was shared with the class, Emmanuel was asked to read his page aloud with the teacher (Figure 3.3).

Sally, aged 4, wrote the words in Figure 3.4 about herself. The teacher responded positively to what Sally had written and then modelled the correct version. Next she wrote out a question for Sally to answer in her writing. Sally's response shows how attentive she has been to the adult's intervention. She has thought carefully about the spelling of *Funnybones* and included several letters from this word in her own response. When the teacher read Sally's answer she was able to draw her attention to the letters which Sally wrote and those present in the title of the book.

Michelle, aged 6, a speaker of Ibo as well as English, was writing in her duck diary shortly after some eggs, which had been kept in an incubator in the class, had hatched. Michelle wrote very quickly and could be quite

Figure 3.4   Sally 'I am reading a book'

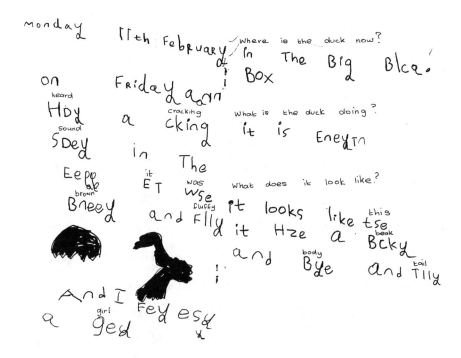

Figure 3.5 Michelle Duck Diary

careless. As Michelle read her entry aloud, the teacher wrote some of the correct spellings above Michelle's words. She did not particularly draw Michelle's attention to the correct versions as she had written these to remind herself what had been written rather than for the child's benefit. She did think that Michelle could write more about the ducklings, so she wrote out a series of question which were intended to show Michelle how to include detail in her writing. Michelle's responses show how she has incorporated some of the teacher's models into her own writing, for example, 'it' rather than 'ET' and 'is' rather than 'esy'. She may also have used the teacher's spelling of 'look like' in order to write 'looks like'. After writing her answers to the questions, the teacher commented positively on the correct spellings that Michelle had produced. She then discussed with Michelle how the answers could have been made into complete sentences in order to produce an extended and structured text of her own (Figure 3.5).

Although the two previous examples have shown the teacher responding to pupils' writing by asking questions, this does not always need to be the case. The teacher's oral and written comments should always express genuine interest in what the child has written and this could be in the form of a statement or a question.

Darla

here are the dogs

Ouce a pon a time we bote a
litle kitten and you no how
they are win there little
They are little rascules.
But this one loved to climb
tree and scach pepple He was
a mean rascule.

Figure 3.6   Darla

The final example (Figure 3.6) shows a very lively story written by
6-year-old Darla. She had taken a great deal of care with it and any
comments about presentation could have damaged Darla's appreciation
of the power of writing to entertain the reader. The teacher responded
only to the content and showed her enjoyment of Darla's choice of words.
Darla read this story to the rest of the class. The teacher had noted Darla's
confusion with 'Once upon a time' and her misspelling of common words
and later that week, during a shared-reading session, drew the attention
of the whole class to the way in which some of these words were written.

Developmental writing is principally about understanding how writing
develops and understanding how children learn to write in the context of
how children learn. This understanding is central for the teacher since it
enables her to make decisions about when and how to intervene in order
to develop each child's writing ability, as these examples have shown.

A developmental approach to writing offers learners and teachers
many advantages since it encourages children to

- believe in themselves as writers from the outset, since the teacher accepts
  and teaches from the knowledge and understanding that children have;

- participate actively in their own writing development;
- take a chance and to risk being wrong;
- be independent by using their own resources and knowledge, a factor which leads to smoother classroom organization by removing dependence on the teacher for all that is written;
- develop positive attitudes towards writing by not being overly concerned with correct letter formation, correct spelling and neatness;
- employ strategies that enable them to complete a whole piece of writing;
- understand that writing is primarily about communication of content;
- discover the ways in which writing is used; and
- think about spelling, handwriting and punctuation by considering how words look and how their audience needs to be able to read what has been written.

A purposeful writing curriculum

It is important when designing a writing curriculum for children that, first, they are given tasks that involve real reasons to communicate meaning to a range of readers through writing. Secondly, that children are given time to work on a piece of writing and time to return to it later either alone or with the teacher's help. Thirdly, that children have opportunities to write in different styles and with different degrees of concentration depending on the task.

Writing has a range of uses, audiences and forms. It is important to demonstrate this to children wherever possible. The writing curriculum at school can cover all the purposes for which writing is used as children write stories, personal journals, poems, letters, responses, questions, invitations, explanations, labels, notices, adverts, posters, reviews, scripts, jokes, accounts and talks. Providing real audiences for children's writing can be more difficult but these might include other children in the class, younger children, carers, children at other schools, authors, and the general public. Each piece of writing that is done should be set in its context so that content, style and presentation are also varied and suited to the purpose and the audience. As children gain experience as writers, writing for different purposes and audiences, adults will be able to show them how to make choices about content, organization and vocabulary. They will be able to introduce children to the idea that control over words, the ability to manipulate meaning and to select words from a vast repertoire makes writing a powerful method of communication.

The role of the teacher

The teacher is responsible for managing children's learning in the classroom. As she teaches writing she has a fourfold role, acting as a facilitator, a model, an adviser and an observer in order to plan, teach and refine the writing curriculum and to extend the writing abilities of the pupils.

As a facilitator the teacher provides the resources that children need when they write. She makes sure that there is a varied and plentiful stock of writing materials and other resources such as alphabet friezes, collections of words and dictionaries to support the children's independent writing. The teacher designs a reading-writing classroom with a writing corner, displays of writing, a well stocked library and literate role-play areas. As a facilitator the teacher is responsible for planning writing tasks that are necessary, purposeful, varied and interesting and for ensuring that the writing that is produced is valued and displayed. As well as organizing resources and activities the teacher may organize other adults in the classroom to work alongside children as scribes, to operate the computer keyboard or in other ways that help children to learn about writing.

The teacher demonstrates what writers do through her attitude to writing, her own writing in the classroom and in shared-writing sessions with the children. She may want to demonstrate her own use of a dictionary to the children and she may draw their attention to textual features of writing when reading stories and sharing big books with the class. When the opportunity arises the teacher will explain the function of the writing that she does in the classroom to the children. Situations such as taking the register, writing for displays and writing letters and notes provide these opportunities. She will also engage in written dialogues with the children. Through the examples of writing she provides she demonstrates what writing is for.

When working as an adviser the teacher works with the pupils on their writing. At all times she will be responding positively to what the children do while looking for ways to enhance their achievement. In the early stages of writing she may be encouraging children to have a go at writing, to focus on what words look like or what letter words begin with. She may write the correctly transcribed version of what the child has written beneath the child's writing and discuss this with him. As the child progresses in confidence and competence she may teach specific skills such as letter formation or strategies for spelling correctly, such as 'look, cover, remember, write, check' or how to use word banks and dictionaries. Later she may demonstrate strategies such as drafting and revising. The teacher may advise on various ways of representing written responses such as using lists and diagrams as alternatives to prose. She will also be making suggestions about how to improve the content, organization and vocabulary of writing.

Finally the teacher acts as an observer of children as they write. As she monitors the children and their work she considers how successful she has been as a facilitator. Would the children benefit more from different tasks? Do they need more or different resources? She considers her role as a model. Is this sufficient for the children's development, or do they perhaps need more shared-writing sessions? She also thinks about when she should intervene and how to intervene to support each child's writing development. In the light of her observations she can then change aspects of her teaching.

Classroom organization

It is easier to help children with their writing if only one group of children is writing at a time. It is difficult for the teacher to provide effective teaching if she is dealing with 30 writers at once. Daily organization needs to take account of this. A classroom where groups of children are engaged on a mix of activities that demand different degrees of adult attention will put less pressure on the teacher as she responds to the children's learning needs. A typical classroom scene might reveal one group of children making a circuit with bulbs, wires and batteries, another group making a large model house which will be lit by the circuits, another group may be illustrating a book that they have written about their homes, a fourth group might be writing a first draft of an information text about homes and the final group of children might be engaged on a mathematics task involving measuring their model homes and recording the results. The science and the technology activities currently underway in the classroom may be the starting point for the next writing activity for these groups of children when they write about what they did, what they needed and what they found out as they completed their tasks. The writing and the illustrating activities may be part of the preparation for the model building; they may be helping the children to plan how they will go about practical tasks. The children who are measuring and recording are also writing. Not all these activities will demand the same degree of attention from the teacher. Planning a range of activities that demand different degrees of teacher attention can give the teacher more time to spend on productive intervention with the children who are writing.

Children who are writing do not always need to write alone. The teacher may ask children to work in pairs to compose and write using each other as sources of ideas and help. This again helps the teacher to use her time more effectively as she can work with two children at once when she checks on their progress or, if the children are providing effective help for one another, she can let them get on alone and spend time with other children in the class.

If the writing that is done in school is to mirror the way writers write in the world outside school, the children will plan, draft, revise and publish many of the pieces of writing that they produce. All this takes time and not all children will finish each stage at the same time. Within a group of writers there may be children who are planning and some who are making a final copy of their writing. The teacher can expect children who are involved with what they are doing to carry on with a piece of writing over the course of a few days. Again this helps to take pressure off the teacher since at the final draft stage she will not be needed by the children and will be able to concentrate on working with those pupils who are planning or revising their work.

Organization for writing varies according to the activity, but when children are used to working independently and to thinking about their work there is less demand on the teacher for fragmented help with individual spellings and more time for the teacher to give help on all aspects of writing including content, structure and style as well as transcription.

Above all the teacher is responsible for the general learning ethos in her classroom and amongst the children she teaches. It is important that the classroom climate is one that encourages risk taking and where mistakes are regarded as opportunities for learning. Learning at school should be seen as a collaborative enterprise between the teacher and her pupils and between the pupils themselves, not as competitive or individual. All classroom activities should encourage the pupils to share what they know with others and to listen to the ideas that others offer to them. When schools and classes work in this way they are truly a community of learners.

The classroom as a writing environment

A well planned and resourced classroom offers children many models of writing, the opportunity to practise writing in a variety of ways and promotes a positive image of writing to the children. Children are more likely to respond positively to writing if it is given a high profile in the classroom and if it is clear that the teacher values writing.

The writing area

Most classrooms contain resources that promote children's writing development. Such resources include books, alphabet friezes, wooden, plastic, velvet and magnetic letters, paper and writing implements. It is often helpful if these are generally available and stored in one part of the classroom that is known as the writing area. This area often becomes a focal point for writing. An attractive and well resourced writing area transmits the message that writing is important and worth while and signifies its status to the class. Practicalities such as the size of the classroom influence the amount of space that can be given to the area, determine whether the area is used for writing and how many children can work there at one time. Children can choose either to work in this area or they can collect the resources and materials they need for writing from it.

Resources in the writing area might include ● a variety of different sizes, shapes, colours and quality of paper ● card ● coupons and forms ● envelopes ● postcards and greeting cards representing a variety of festivals and featuring a range of languages ● note and message pads ● ready-made booklets of different sizes ● a typewriter ● in and out trays ● felt-tips, biros, pencils, pens, crayons, a stapler, a

Figure 3.7   Patrick 'Thank you for the Smarties'

hole punch, rubber stamps, glue, labels, pencil sharpener, Sellotape, string, paper clips, ring binders, scissors, rulers ● old diaries and calendars ● line guides and borders ● a paper trimmer ● Letraset, stencils, ● a waste bin ● reference materials such as alphabet books, dictionaries, thesauruses and word banks and lists ● a post box ● a word processor.

It helps to keep the children's interest if the resources are changed regularly. If they are to work independently and use the area purposefully the children need to know how to use resources such as the paper trimmer and the stapler and how to mount their work and make their own books. The children can also be involved in organizing the writing area. They can make labels for the equipment and write notices for the area. The use of the writing area should be discussed with the class and some of the writing that is produced there can be shared, displayed and responded to by others.

The writing area should invite children to use it. It should be a quiet place where writing is seen as an enjoyable and purposeful activity. There might be notices such as 'Come and Make a Book' or 'Make a List of Your Favourite Books', encouraging children to use it both at set writing times and when they can make choices about their activities. Written suggestions about what children might write when they choose to use the area, such as an invitation to rewrite a story that has recently been shared with the class or to write to a child who is away from school, can maintain the children's involvement in using the writing area. If it is available for use at any time by the children it can give them the chance to experiment with writing for their own purposes and at their own pace, without pressure for particular results and usually without needing much adult intervention. Used in this way the writing area can help to foster independence and be a place where children are in control of the writing process, giving children the space to initiate and carry out ideas of their own. Using the resources provided, Patrick, aged 5, wrote the letter in Figure 3.7 to his granny as he experimented alone in the writing area. It reads, 'Thank you for the Smarties'.

The writing area can also be used to display writing including writing in a variety of scripts and languages, writing from home, a range of handwriting styles, writing that has been received by the class and writing that has been done at school. Writing that is displayed may reflect current events in the classroom or in the locality. The writing area can demonstrate writing used for a variety of purposes and in a variety of styles.

The relationship between reading and writing

An important part of the classroom writing environment is provided by books. This includes books that are in the library or book corner, books that are taken home by the children, books that are read to children, books that are made by children, books that are made by the teacher and big books that are shared with the class. Familiarity with books provides children with important lessons about how writing works, what it can do and how they can use it.

Learning to read supports learning to write in many ways. From books children learn that print carries a message and as they begin to write they will want their writing to convey meaning. When reading they learn that symbols used in writing are not arbitrary – writers use a set of symbols with a particular form. They can see that writing is arranged in a particular way. In the English language it moves from left to right and top to bottom on a page. Spaces separate words and punctuation is used to separate ideas. As children read they are engaging in a visual examination of words and as they read aloud they are using the grapho-phonic aspects of written language. Both of these are important in helping to increase children's awareness of letter shapes and in developing their knowledge about spelling. Written language is used in particular ways that have to be experienced and understood before they can be produced. Experience with reading introduces children to the pattern, style and the explicit nature of written language. Children may also learn about structuring their own writing by thinking about how different sorts of texts are organized. When stories are shared with children teachers are familiarizing children with the notion of authorship. As children realize that books are written by people they can be introduced to the idea that they too can be authors and produce texts for others to read. Books and other forms of text provide ideas for writing – as Smith (1982) wrote: 'composition is stimulated by reading.' For reading to benefit writing development as much as possible, it is essential that children have access to a wide a range of good-quality books which present a range of ideas, styles and organizational structures.

Writing and role play

The classroom environment cannot always provide the opportunities for the full range of writing that children encounter in the world outside school. Role play is one way of extending the range of purposes, audiences and variety of writing available to children in the classroom. It is also a means of demonstrating the variety and purpose of writing. Role-play areas often arise from the theme that is being undertaken by the class. For example a clinic, a hospital or a garden centre might be set up if the children are working on the theme of 'Growth' or a visit to a fire station could lead to a fire station control-room being set up in the classroom.

Whatever type of role-play area is established, it is important that children have some knowledge and experience of the context to support them as they engage in the writing activities that may arise. When setting up the area it might be appropriate to ask the children to write the signs, notices, menus and price lists that will become part of the play area. The children may also benefit from the teacher joining in and modelling the types of writing that are appropriate, for example writing a shopping list or taking a phone message. By doing this the children will understand the purpose, style and audience of the writing that accompanies their play.

The sort of writing that might emerge from setting up a post office in the classroom could include ● letters, postcards, cards, notes, invitations ● filling in forms ● keeping records of money deposited and distributed ● notices, signs, posters, advertisements ● stamp design ● making passports ● writing addresses.

If the play area is used as a home corner this too can be a valuable source of literacy activities. Children can write books to read to the dolls, invitations for a dolls' party, greeting cards, telephone messages, shopping lists, notes for the milk deliverer, items in a diary, labels for jars and containers and fill in forms such as football coupons. It is useful to use the home corner to illustrate the different sorts of writing that may be found in the home. To this end it might contain magazines, newspapers, letters, greeting cards, postcards, recipe books, a calender, a telephone directory as well as packets and containers with writing on them. It should also have resources for writing such as pens, paper, postcards and notepads which are present in most homes.

By using writing in role-play activities children may come to recognize the uses of writing and the many types of writing that exist. They are given the opportunity to experiment with writing in a relaxed environment. The writing they produce need not be assessed, improved or re-drafted, but by observing children writing in play situations the teacher can gain insights into their understanding of the writing process and may seek to extend this in the more formal writing sessions that take place in the classroom.

Writing across the curriculum

Writing is both part of a distinct curriculum area, English, and a part of every other area of the curriculum. It is easy to identify writing as a part of the English curriculum when children are writing stories, poems or letters. However the starting point for writing may well be science, technology, geography or history. The children may write up a recipe as part of a science investigation into change. They may describe and evaluate how they made a musical instrument as part of a technology session so that others can copy their idea. The focus may be on geography if children are planning a route from the school to a local park in preparation for a class picnic. Writing can arise from history if the children are compiling a set of questions to ask a visitor about his childhood in the 1950s. Because writing can arise from every part of the curriculum the teacher can provide a range of writing activities requiring a variety of formats.

There should also be opportunities for personal writing at school and children can be provided with their own private journals where they are free to write anything they like without it being read by others. When children write in journals they may be organizing their thoughts, recording feelings or experimenting with different forms of writing. The opportunities for writing and the possible types of writing that can emerge in school are plentiful and varied. Writing does not need to be a distinct part of the curriculum only taking place with status during 'creative-writing lessons'.

Writing activities

As far as possible, the writing activities that form the writing curriculum for the class or the school should have an audience and a purpose that extends beyond the teacher and her requirement that the children should write. They should be meaningful and motivating for all the children. Activities that fulfil these criteria include

- labels, captions and commentaries for paintings, models and displays
- information and story books written by the children for others to read
- collections of poems written by the children
- cards and letters that receive a response from others or written to thank visitors to the school
- invitations to parents and carers to attend events at school
- records of books read or projects that have been undertaken
- instructions to users of games or equipment
- reviews of books and posters to display in the book corner
- charts or graphs recording surveys and discoveries
- newspapers for the class or school
- information leaflets about the school for new entrants to the class or school.

Not all writing at school will have an outside audience. Some writing will take the form of drafts, notes, plans and personal writing. Writing in this form may be used to organize thinking and ideas and be determined by the needs of the child. It may vary in length and appearance and may be left incomplete.

When setting writing tasks it may be useful to ask oneself the following questions: Who is to read the writing? What is this writing for? What will happen to the writing when it is finished? How might this affect the way children set about it? Is it appropriate to draft, redraft, put it on tape, use the word processor, work with others, publish or display it? How might it be presented, as connected prose, a list, a diagram or a commentary?

Considering these questions may affect the guidance that is given to children. A well planned writing curriculum where time is given for children to produce purposeful and careful pieces of writing motivates children as writers and extends their repertoire of writing skills and styles.

Shared writing

Shared writing refers to the times when a group of children compose a text together, with the teacher acting as the scribe for the group. When children are familiar with the format they may take over some of the scribing but initially it is more helpful if the teacher does this. It is generally best organized by having the children sitting as a group on the carpet and the teacher writing on large sheets of paper on a flip chart or an easel. It is essential that all the children can see the writing.

The activity usually begins with the teacher and children discussing the topic for the writing. If the activity is new to the class it may be best to use shared writing to retell a familiar story, write a letter, produce an account of a visit, make a sign to go with a display in the classroom or to compose a poem, as these have a clear structure that can be followed by the children. It is important to be clear about the aims and purposes of the writing with the children as this will affect the style and content. After the initial discussion the teacher takes the pupils through all the processes of writing as she scribes for the pupils. The first stage is to brainstorm ideas to be included in the writing. As the children contribute their ideas the teacher records these as a list or diagram. After collecting the ideas on content the group considers which ideas should come at the beginning, middle and end of the writing. The teacher then numbers the ideas in the order that they will occur in the text to form a plan. Working from the plan, the children and the teacher begin to compose the writing. The initial ideas are reworked, words are changed and sentences are composed as the group focuses on the writing. At the end of this stage the first draft of the writing, probably containing false starts and crossing out, is complete. The first draft is read through and may be revised or edited before the final draft is produced by the teacher or the pupils.

A piece of shared writing may take a number of sessions to complete. This provides a useful message about the permanence of text and how it helps people to remember ideas. It also signals that writing that is worth doing need not be completed in one session. Reading and reviewing what has been written at the beginning of each session may lead to further revisions and may help pupils to see the benefits of rereading a piece of writing. Writing often benefits from taking place over a longer period than one session since the writer has had time to think about what has been written and may bring new ideas to the writing.

The completed writing may be copied out by the children to form individual letters or books that they can illustrate. With a long piece individual children may copy out one section of the text to form the writing for one page of a class book. They can then illustrate their page. Alternatively the teacher may make the final draft of the writing and the children may provide the illustrations. The text and the pictures can be placed in a large book that can be used for shared reading. Sometimes the teacher may stop scribing before the final draft of the writing and the children can use the plan and the draft to compose their own individual ending to the story, poem, letter or account. Whatever the final outcome of shared-writing sessions it is important that the teacher has thought beforehand about how the activity will end.

Shared writing encourages children to reflect on all aspects of the writing process. The children see all the stages of reflecting, planning, drafting, editing, evaluating and redrafting taking place and from this model they can learn valuable lessons about how they might work on their own writing in class. As the children see the teacher writing, their attention may be drawn to spelling patterns, punctuation, word boundaries, layout of text as well as the patterns and conventions associated with different genres of written language. The children benefit from seeing how the transcription of writing takes place and this will help them in their own writing.

Writing in this way enables children to work collaboratively and to draw on each other's strengths and knowledge. As the transcriptional aspects of writing are taken over by the teacher the children can focus on the composition and as a result can often produce longer, more complex texts than they could do alone. In particular, less confident or less able writers benefit from shared writing since they can see that writing does not have to be perfect at the first attempt and that writing is as much about composition as transcription. Such children may also experience a great sense of satisfaction from seeing their ideas in print.

The skills and practices that are modelled during shared-writing sessions provide a structure for the children to use when they write and the teacher can expect these routines to be adopted by older first-school children in their individual or paired writing. Depending on age, experience and level of confidence groups of children may be able to work on shared writing alone or with very little teacher help.

Scribing

More experienced writers, such as older children, parents, carers or other adult volunteers, can be invited into the classroom to write with and for the children. They can transcribe for individuals or small groups of children leaving the children free to concentrate on the composition of text.

While they write they can discuss the choice of words, spelling, the use of punctuation and layout with the children. They can also act as prompts if the composition dries up and they can encourage the children to get ideas by reading and reflecting on what has been written so far. The scribes may do all the writing involved in planning and writing first drafts. They can write by hand or on the computer. They may tape record a child's story and then work with the child as he writes his story using the tape recording as a first draft. Before volunteers start to work with the pupils it is essential that they know exactly what is required of them. The teacher needs to spend some time explaining the way that she would like them to work with the children and the purpose of the activity. Experienced writers, writing alongside children, can encourage children to compose at greater length than they could manage alone and enable children to see how writing should be tackled. The satisfaction children gain from seeing their words in print is enormous and often motivates children into wanting to write alone (Smith, 1994).

Shared writing and scribing fulfil the requirements of the 1995 Programme of Study for English at Key Stage 1, which states:

> Pupils should have opportunities to plan and review their writing . . . Teachers should, on occasions, help pupils to compose at greater length by writing for them, demonstrating the ways that ideas may be recorded in print. To encourage confidence and independence, pupils should be given opportunities to collaborate, to read their work aloud and to discuss the quality of what is written. Pupils should be helped to make choices about vocabulary and to organize imaginative and factual writing in different ways.
>
> (DfE, 1995a, p. 9)

Writing conferences

A conference is a time for a child to discuss his writing with the teacher. It can last from two minutes to as long as the child needs and classroom organization permits. The main aim is for the teacher to provide the child with feedback about his writing and to discover and provide help for the difficulties that the child identifies. The conference may begin with the child reading or summarizing his writing so far. The teacher then asks the child questions about the writing. These questions might include: How is your writing going? What do you think that you will do next? Could you add anything else to interest the reader? Do you need to give the reader more information? What do you do when you aren't sure about how to spell a word? How do you work out where to put full stops in your writing? What will you do with your writing when it is finished? Are you pleased with your writing?

The questions are intended to focus the child's attention on his writing and to find out about the writing strategies he uses. Depending on the child the teacher might provide help with the composition or the transcription of a piece of writing. The conference should occur as the child is engaged on his first and subsequent drafts so that he can revise and improve his writing as a result of the conference.

Holding a writing conference is like listening to a child read. In it the teacher is trying to listen to the child write and to respond to the strengths and weaknesses that the child reveals as he talks about the process of writing for him. The teacher responds to what the child can do as well as what the child finds difficult. Graves (1983) describes how conferencing can lead to 'dramatic changes in children's writing', since it is an opportunity for the teacher to provide the help that the child identifies as important and that meets his current needs. During the conference the teacher should be aware of the context, purpose and audience for the writing. She needs to be aware of the child's attitude to writing and to temper her comments to fit the child's effort and feelings about himself as a writer. When she receives the writing she needs to understand the message, analyse the composition, analyse the transcription and in consultation with the child decide on what the child should do next.

Response partners

The idea of pairing children to act as consultants for each other's writing developed during the course of the National Writing Project (1989) where it was found that children as young as 5 were able to work successfully in this way. In their pairs children listen to or read their partner's writing and comment on how the writing might be improved or extended. They can comment on clarity of meaning and order as well as helping with spelling and punctuation. Children need to be instructed about how they can best help to improve the work of others and they will probably benefit from their own experiences of working in this way during conferences and shared-writing sessions with the teacher.

They can be given simple instructions about how to act as a supportive partner, such as ● say two good things about the writing ● ask questions if anything was not clear ● suggest two ways of making the writing better.

Drafting and redrafting

Few writers have the skill of producing perfect writing at the first attempt. Most writers need to draft important pieces of writing before producing a final copy. Children too need to be introduced to this method of working. The Programme of Study for writing at Key Stage 1 states that 'Pupils should have opportunities to plan and review their writing' (DfE, 1995a). The document gives further guidance on this aspect of writing for children at Key Stage 2, declaring that

To develop their writing, pupils should be taught to:

● **plan** – note and develop initial ideas;

- **draft** – develop ideas from the plan into structured written text;
- **revise** – alter and improve the draft;
- **proofread** – check the draft for spelling and punctuation errors, omissions or repetitions;
- **present** – prepare a neat, correct and clear final copy.

(Ibid., p. 15)

The process of drafting encourages children to shape and reshape their ideas on paper, on the computer or on tape before producing the final version of their writing. It encourages children to reflect on their writing and to evaluate and self-correct as they read through what they have written. If children are to spend time drafting and redrafting their writing it is essential that the writing task is important enough to demand this degree of attention from the child. It is also important that, before the child writes, he knows the purpose and the audience for his writing as this will affect the content, style and organization of the writing. For example a letter to a friend reads very differently, is set out in a different way and includes different sorts of information than a letter written to a stranger. Not all writing needs to be drafted; it depends on its purpose and audience, but all writing can benefit from applying the drafting process. Children can be encouraged to draft in their heads or to plan through drawing a picture or a sequence of illustrations and they can be given thinking time before they commit their thoughts to paper.

During shared-writing sessions the teacher models the ways in which writers draft and redraft their writing. She may need to give children further explanations and examples of how to draft and redraft and why it is helpful to work in this way before children are confident with the procedure. Before writing the first draft the first stage for the writer is to focus on what he is about to write. He may spend time recollecting and remembering information, incidents or feelings. He then needs to make a note of the ideas that he had thought of, perhaps in the form of a spider diagram or a list. This brainstorm may contain key words and expressions as well as ideas. For younger or less experienced writers, recollection and planning can be done by drawing either one picture or a sequence of pictures that help the writer to organize his thoughts and reflect on what he is going to write. Next the ideas need to be organized into a coherent plan, perhaps by making a list or numbering the ideas in sequence.

After the first stage of thinking about the ideas and making a preliminary outline the writer is ready to write. The first draft of the writing is about getting it down fast, without worrying about the transcription elements such as spelling, punctuation or handwriting. As long as the child can read his own writing there is no need to interrupt the creative flow of the writing. At this stage the child may make false starts and rethink as he writes and this may result in what looks like a messy piece of work containing misspellings and crossing out. This does not represent careless or poor work; many adult writer's first drafts look like this. A first draft represents the writer's struggle with the process of translating thoughts and ideas into the written form. There is no need for the child to use an eraser to conceal mistakes at this stage; an adult writer would be unlikely to use a rubber on a first draft, crossing out is far quicker and interrupts one's thoughts far less. It is also unnecessary for the child to check his spellings by asking the teacher or consulting a dictionary. As long as the words can be read back they can be checked after the first draft has been written. The mistakes that a child makes at this stage provide a useful insight for the teacher into the difficulties that a child may have in writing and how the child tackles these. They may also provide starting points for discussion during a writing conference.

When the first draft is complete it is time for the child to read through his writing. He can look for clarity of meaning and change words, phrases and sentences to make a more satisfactory piece of writing. He can also proofread for spelling and punctuation errors. It is at this stage that the child might use a dictionary to check or find spellings. Problems that the child cannot resolve himself, such as parts of the writing that do not make sense or spellings that he thinks may be wrong, can be indicated by the child using a highlighter pen. After rereading his work carefully the child may be ready for a writing conference with the teacher. The child and the teacher can discuss the work so far to see if further revision or more ideas are necessary. It is also at this stage that the teacher might teach the child some spellings and demonstrate correct letter formation. If the child has a response partner, the partner may read what has been written and offer suggestions.

The writing may go through another draft to incorporate any ideas and changes which have been discussed and which the child feels would improve the piece. Alternatively after the first draft the child may move straight on to the final draft. At this stage the child should be clear about how he is going to present the work. Is it going to be in the form of a book, a letter or for display? This may determine layout and the choice of writing materials. The focus at this stage is on presentation. The child needs to write carefully with clear handwriting and attention to spelling if the work is to be read by others. The teacher can expect the child's work to reflect the help that he has received. At this stage the child will begin to incorporate illustrations into his writing and will at the end of the final draft have a piece of writing that is satisfying to him and interesting for others to read.

The time spent on drafting and redrafting will vary depending on the child's age and experience as a writer, as will the exact drafting procedures that are used. Very young children may plan through drawing, or through talking to the teacher or to other children about what they are going to write before producing a sentence of their own. The teacher may then discuss the writing with the child and either write the correct version under the child's writing or correct one or two errors and ask the child to rewrite the sentences incorporating the corrections in the final draft.

Older, more experienced writers who can write at greater length can be expected to go through all the stages of planning, editing and producing a final draft. It is very difficult to assign ages to these procedures but very young children may be nursery, reception and Year 1 pupils and older children may include Year 1, Year 2 and Year 3 pupils.

In order for drafting to work, the class has to be organized so that a piece of writing can be worked on over a period of days. One day's writing may only cover the planning and first draft stage. Children need to be able to store their first drafts in their own writing folder or in their first draft book. They can then return to their writing the next day.

Drafting takes pupils through the real stages of writing. It enables pupils to take risks since it does not matter if they make mistakes in a draft; these can be rectified later. It helps pupils to focus on composition and content rather than transcription and can result in a very satisfying piece of writing of which the writer can be proud.

Making books

Making books and writing stories that are read by the author and others is highly motivating for children. It enables them to feel that their writing is valued and it provides a purpose and an incentive for writing. Through making books children's writing reaches a wider audience than the class teacher. Books can be read to others and by others, in class, in assemblies or in the school library.

Children are able to incorporate the features of published books into their own books, features such as an index, a list of contents, chapters, notes about the author, summaries, dedications and reviews by others. In addition when writing the book the children will have to plan, draft, revise and produce a best copy either on the word processor or by hand so they will be going through all the stages of writing. Before beginning to write children will have needed to identify the audience for the book and to have considered how this might affect the length, style, content and organization of their book. After composing the text they may need to share the writing with their peers or with the teacher to gain a reader's perspective. The redrafting stage may then involve them in making decisions about the organization of the text, reshaping the writing and choosing the format and layout for their final draft.

The sorts of books children can write or contribute to include • poetry • imaginative stories • personal stories • information books • biographies • recipes • jokes • cartoons • stories based around superheroes • rewrites of well-known stories • dual-language stories • stories in home languages • books containing records of work undertaken during a theme • books written for younger children • books made by parents and children • cumulative books such as a reviews of favourite books • flap or pop-up books • zig-zag or concertina books • big books • little books • diaries

● magazines ● photographic sequenced books ● books with audio tapes ● instruction manuals ● instant books.

Publishing

Publishing means making writing public mainly through books but also in other forms, such as posters, notices or letters. Not every piece of writing done by a child needs to be published. Personal writing, diaries, notes, diagrams or plans may never have been intended for an audience beyond the writer or the teacher. The child and the teacher should discuss whether a piece of writing should be published. The original purpose of the writing as well as the quality of the finished product may influence the decision. Publishing should be viewed as the end of a long process where the teacher works through the drafts with the child and both have agreed that the writing is good enough to be published. Quality must take account of each child's experience and the degree of effort that has been invested in the writing. This will differ from child to child even in the same class or age group.

The subject matter and the presentation may determine what form the publication takes. Accounts of learning and discovery may become part of a display. Captions, labels and explanations may be placed next to models or drawings. Stories or information may be published in books that are placed in the class library to be read by the writer and other children in the class.

Conclusion

Writing at school should represent our understanding of how children learn to write and include activities and resources that reflect this understanding. The curriculum should take account of what children know, of writing as a communicative act, of audience and purpose, of variety and of activities that enable children to write in a meaningful way. The classroom should provide a context within which children's writing can develop and within which the teacher and the children work together to enhance achievement. This chapter has presented practitioners with a number of suggestions about the ways in which they can organize the physical resources of the classroom and the variety of activities that may form part of their writing curriculum.

Suggestion for further reading

Browne, A. (1993) *Helping Children to Write*, Paul Chapman Publishing, London.

Chapter 4

Spelling, handwriting and punctuation

Introduction

This chapter covers the teaching and learning of spelling, handwriting and punctuation, which are often referred to as the conventions of writing or as presentational, surface, secretarial, mechanical or transcriptional skills. They frequently preoccupy adults when they examine and discuss children's writing, particularly those who are unclear about the distinction between the purposes for writing and the tools which facilitate that communication, or those who do not understand how children learn language and judge young children's logical but incorrect explorations of the writing system as indicative of falling standards in literacy.

Spelling, handwriting and punctuation do have a place in writing development. They enable clearer and more effective communication to take place between the writer and the recipient of the message and their efficient use gives the writer greater freedom to concentrate on content. But in spite of their value, they should not become the prime concern of the teacher or the child; they should not take on a significance that is out of proportion for the beginning writer who needs to explore the purposes of writing and to learn about content, structure, coherence, clarity, choice of language, style and audience, not just the conventions.

Surveys of children's understanding of writing have revealed that they may also have learned to place too much importance on transcription. During the National Writing Project (1985–88) teachers found that 'Children often judge the success of their writing by its neatness, spelling and punctuation rather than the message it conveys.' (National Writing Project, 1990, p. 19).

Two further surveys, one conducted by Shook, Marrion and Ollila in 1989 and another reported by Wray (1994), found that the majority of young children thought that good writing was synonymous with correct spelling, good punctuation and handwriting, neatness and length. Wray suggests that these results reveal as much about the priorities of the children's teachers as they do about the pupils.

Teachers who are trying to develop children's abilities in all aspects of writing will know that writing is, first and most importantly, about the creation and transmission of meaning rather than the accuracy of presentation and that it is important not to overemphasize transcriptional skills to children. They will realize that these form only one part of the Programmes of Study for writing at Key Stages 1 and 2 and that too much attention to the conventions will undermine children's confidence and limit their experiments with the other important features of writing. Adults should not have unrealistic expectations that conventional spelling, neat handwriting and accurate punctuation will develop quickly. They will develop as children gain greater familiarity with written language both as readers and as writers, as they appreciate the need to take account of the reader's ability to understand what has been written and as a result of sensitive, well timed intervention by the teacher.

Within this chapter spelling, handwriting and punctuation are examined separately. The consideration of each will include sections on the development of that skill, what children in the early years need to know about each of them and practical suggestions for teaching in a way that is relevant and appropriate to the needs and experience of young children.

Spelling

Learning how to spell is an important part of learning to write. Correct spelling makes writing more readable and enables the writer to communicate more easily with his audience. However it is not the main purpose of writing. It is easy to focus on spelling errors first and the content of what was written second when reading children's writing, perhaps because spelling is more immediately obvious than style, structure or choice of vocabulary. This is perhaps even more the case in the very early stages of writing when children's writing can be very simple and brief. Unfortunately if teachers concentrate on spelling, particularly with children who are just beginning to write, they risk inhibiting children's desire to write. Too much emphasis on correct spelling may produce writers who are frightened to 'have a go' alone and who play safe with the words they include in their writing, limiting their choice of words to those which they think they can spell correctly rather than using words which add colour and atmosphere to writing. If the role of spelling in writing is overemphasized, teachers may be teaching children that learning to write is just about learning to spell correctly and that children who cannot spell cannot write. It is possible to transmit this message in many ways, not just by overly correcting children's spelling errors but also by only displaying perfectly spelt work, by training children in the indiscriminate use of word books and by encouraging children to use erasers to correct every mistake they make as they are putting their thoughts on to paper. It is important to maintain a realistic awareness of what children may be expected to achieve in unaided spelling as they begin to discover how the spelling system of the English language works and to let this sense of proportion guide the response, assessment, correction and teaching of spelling to young children.

The problem with spelling

Unfortunately adults can present the knowledge children need when learning to spell in an oversimplified and incorrect way. They may give children simple rules such as 'i' before 'e' except after 'c'. But what about 'their', 'eight', 'weigh' and 'height', words that are frequently seen and used in the early-years classroom? Adults can also transmit the message that English is a phonically regular language in which solutions to spelling difficulties can be found by 'sounding out' a word. When children ask for help with spelling a word an adult's first response is often to ask the child to say the word and to listen for the sounds that it contains, or the adult may pronounce each letter sound slowly. Not only is it difficult for a child to take in auditory information and translate it into a visual image but also spellings such as 'like', 'play' and 'house' cannot be given in this way. Moseley (1990) suggested that only one-third of the words used by beginning readers contain a one-to-one correspondence between letter and sound. Another strategy provided by adults is slowly to articulate each syllable in a word. This is not helpful either. When each syllable is articulated separately the emphasis and intonation alter our hearing of the word and may result in incorrect spelling, for example 'stable' could become *stay . . . bull.*

The problem is that the English writing system has 26 symbols or letters with which to represent the 44 sounds or phonemes of the language. Each symbol or grapheme does not always directly relate to the same phoneme. The sound of letters is affected by the position of the letter in a word and the letters that surround it. For example *a* sounds quite differently in '*bat, cake, play, tail, ball, was, what*' and '*road*'. The way in which the same grapheme can occur in different phonemes can cause terrific problems for the speller who relies totally on phonics. A further example is provided by the word 'through'. To try to spell this word by sounding it out could be very difficult. In the first place 'through' could be and is represented by the letters 'threw' depending on the context. Moreover the phoneme represented by the letters *ough* may also be represented by *ou* as in 'you', *u* as in 'prudent', *oo* as in 'boo', *oe* as in 'shoe' and *ue* as in 'clue'. In addition *ough* can also stand for the *off* sound in 'cough' or the *ow* sound in 'bough' and the *up* sound in 'hiccough'! If writers could rely on rules and the regularity of sounds then spelling correctly would be a lot easier than it is. Regrettably, presenting rules and systems to children not only confuses but also often distracts the adult from teaching and the child from learning about how to spell correctly.

Although adults may give a great deal of attention to spelling by writing in children's word books and correcting spelling in children's writing, traditionally there has been little attention paid to helping children to learn how to spell (Barnes, 1994). For, in spite of the difficulties English may present to the inexperienced writer, children can be taught to spell. By being aware of how children learn about spelling without a great deal of adult intervention and by examining the strategies that competent spellers use, it is possible to identify some effective ways of helping children to learn how to spell.

The development of children's spelling

Research suggests that accuracy in spelling develops as children explore the writing system for themselves and as they gain more familiarity with written language (Read, 1986; Temple *et al.*, 1988). Each of the stages they pass through shows children developing new insights into writing and attempting to understand and use a system for conventional spelling.

During the first stage, known as the prephonemic or preliterate stage of spelling development, children are imitating the writing that they see in the world around them and in doing so are making their first discoveries about writing. The writing that is produced at this stage may take the form of scribbles or pretend writing and may incorporate numerals or the letters that are found in the child's name. The child may be able to explain what he intended to write but the text will generally be unreadable, as in the example in Figure 4.1.

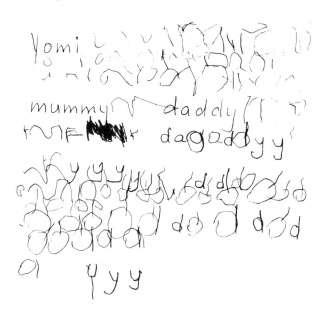

Figure 4.1   Yomi

Figure 4.2   Tile layer

The next stage, known as the early or semi-phonemic stage, shows children developing an awareness of the alphabetic and phonic principles of the English language and exploiting their understanding of this complex relationship. Letter names are used to represent words, for example *R* for 'are' and *NIT* for 'night'. Elements of this stage may persist for some time and are helpful to the speller and the reader in communicating and understanding the message. In the example in Figure 4.2, John, who is at this stage, has written 'TIYL LAYA' for tile layer.

In the third stage, known as the phonetic, the child recognizes that all the sounds in words can be represented by letters. More letters are

Figure 4.3   Marcus 'when I was young'

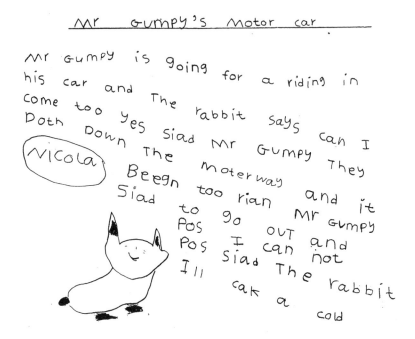

Mr Gumpy's Motor car

Mr Gumpy is going for a riding in his car and The rabbit says can I come too yes siad Mr Gumpy They Doth Down The moterway and it NICOLA Beegn too rian Mr Gumpy Siad to go OUT and Pos I can not Pos Siad The rabbit I ll cak a cold

Figure 4.4   Nicola

included in the words and the words become more complete. Examples of spellings at this stage include *baf* for 'bath', *cist* for 'kissed' and *cercul* for 'circle', and in the example in Figure 4.3, the words *cwyuet* for 'quiet' and *care* for 'carry'.

As children move closer to conventional spelling they move away from being almost wholly dependent on phonic strategies and into what is known as the transitional stage. Their increased experience of words gained from seeing adult models and through their reading helps children to become aware of the visual features of words. They begin to combine their understanding of how words sound with their knowledge of how words look. Increasingly they begin to write words that look right, showing an understanding of letter combinations that are frequently found in the English language. This can result in spellings such as *howld* for 'hold' and *coloer* for 'colour'. In the example in Figure 4.4, *too* and *moterway* and the experiments with letter strings in *rian* and *siad* show Nicola's growing awareness of how words look and sound.

The final stage is when correct spellings are produced almost all the time. At this stage writers use a combination of strategies including letter sounds, letter names, letter strings, visual strategies and memory to produce close approximations or correct spellings of short and multi-syllabic words. The writing reproduced in Figure 4.5 is an example of this stage.

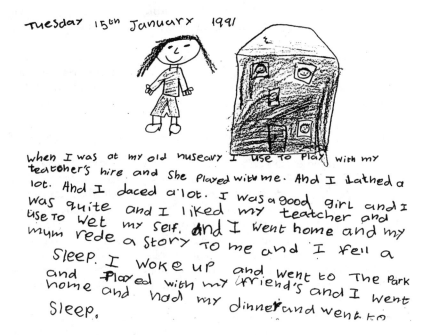

Tuesday 15th January 1991

when I was at my old nuseavy I use to Play with my teatcher's hire and She Played with me. Ahd I ~~Lathed~~ a lot. Ahd I daced a lot. I was a good girl and I was quite and I liked my teatcher and use to wet my self. And I went home and my mum rede a story To me and I fell a Sleep. I woke up and went to The Park and Played with my friend's and I went home and had my dinner and went to Sleep.

Figure 4.5   Tandi correct spelling

Adults frequently call upon a variety of strategies to help them spell correctly. They may use aids such as dictionaries and spell checks, exaggeratedly pronounce each syllable of a word or write down several versions of an unknown word. Sometimes writers use a known spelling to provide clues about the spelling of a more difficult word, for example using 'finite' to spell 'definite' or 'lie' to spell 'believe'. On occasion adults draw on their awareness of how the English language is constructed, using their understanding of roots, prefixes and suffixes or their knowledge about the sequence of letters in words. When spelling difficult or unfamiliar words adults often use a combination of these strategies.

The developmental model indicates that the mistakes that children make are usually systematic and transitory. They are a necessary part of their learning about spelling, providing them with the opportunity to experiment with and internalize the system and enabling them to make intelligent and informed attempts at spelling words correctly. Another lesson to be learned from this model is that inexperienced spellers almost always draw upon phonic strategies without having to be formally taught to do this. Children who spell in this way are making good progress but they need to proceed beyond this stage. To teach and overemphasize the role of auditory or phonic strategies when helping children to spell may prevent them from developing beyond the phonetic stage of spelling development. Children need to be given access to the variety and combination of strategies that adults use, including the visual appearance of words, knowledge about language, memory, external resources as well as awareness of sounds and syllables.

Appreciating how children learn to spell and examining adult spelling strategies helps teachers to respond positively to what children can do, appreciate progress, identify good errors and establish a framework for teaching spelling.

Practical ways of supporting children's development in spelling

There is considerable evidence to suggest that accurate spellers draw on visual rather than phonic strategies when spelling (Peters, 1985). Good spellers can often 'see' correct spellings inside their heads, they 'know' by 'looking' at words whether they are spelt correctly. To help children 'see' and 'know' they need opportunities to look at and visualize words that are relevant and frequently used. Asking children to copy out corrections, to learn lists of words, to copy from word books or to sound out words does not help children to become good spellers and does not provide them with reliable strategies for spelling unfamiliar words independently (Peters, 1985; Moseley, 1990; Redfern, 1993).

Devising a programme for spelling begins with assessing what children can already do. It has been suggested that until children have reached the transitional stage of spelling they are unlikely to benefit from direct teaching (Whitehead, 1990; Palmer, 1991). Children need to have some understanding of the principles of English orthography and the opportunity to produce their own invented spelling before they can understand and absorb instruction about correct spelling. Indeed, an emphasis on correctness at too early a stage can make children anxious about writing and inhibit the experiments which give them valuable insights into the principles of spelling. The strategies that follow are intended to develop and activate children's visual awareness and memory for words. They should be used regularly as part of a systematic approach to developing spelling.

Becoming aware of words

Regardless of the stage that they have reached all children benefit from examining and discussing print. When teachers draw children's attention to classroom displays, labels and notices they are providing them with opportunities to visualize and remember words. Children also benefit from activities involving making letter shapes and letter strings in a variety of media. They need to share and read books and to write. Seeing adults writing either as scribes or during shared-writing sessions provides children with visual models of words and letter combinations. The teacher can use story and reading periods to draw attention to print. For example after reading the 'big book' *Mrs Wishy Washy* (Melser and

Cowley, 1980b) with the class, the teacher could ask the children to think of words that they know that contain the letters *sh*. These could be recorded by the teacher on a flip chart while she spells out the letters. After a list has been compiled the teacher could ask individual pupils to find particular words on the chart. This activity involves the careful visual examination of words. During the later stages of spelling, that is the phonemic and the transitional stages, correction of individual words in writing, 'try' books, look, cover, remember, write, check, compiling family groups, looking at spelling patterns, suffixes, prefixes and using dictionaries should be introduced.

Collections

The teacher and children can make other collections of words, for example issuing a written invitation to the children with the heading 'How many words do we know that begin with *B* or *b*?' written on the flip chart. The children can be encouraged to find words themselves and add them to the collection. This activity can continue for several days. The collection can be examined daily and the words discussed by the class.

Language games

The game of word snap using the names of children in the class and later using common words that are familiar to and used by the children can be productive in encouraging the visual examination of words. To make this even more relevant and useful to the children, they can be asked to make the game. Making the cards and writing the words carefully will help to develop their memory for conventional spellings and provide them with a real reason for spelling correctly.

Reciting and singing rhymes and sharing poems and jokes provides a rich opportunity to interest children in language and to discuss words with them. Even very young children understand the humour of a 'Knock, Knock' joke, such as:

'Knock, knock, who's there?'
'Mary.'
'Mary, who?'
'Merry Christmas.'

This depends for its effect on the ambiguous sounds of the words.

Recognizing letter patterns

Teachers can talk about letter patterns in words to children in order to help them 'see' words more clearly. For example, one could list the words contained in the word 'heart' – *hear, ear, he* and *art*. After a discussion about all the words and the letters they contain, the children are more likely to remember how to spell the original word and may have added more words to their spelling vocabulary. Children may also remember some of the spelling patterns found in the English language, in this instance *ear*. This may help them when spelling other words such as 'tear, wear' or 'dear'. Games such as 'What's the Word?', formerly known as 'Hangman', can help increase children's awareness of letter combinations in words. For example the letter *B* can only be followed by one of the five vowels or by *L, R* or *Y* and this and other letter sequences become clearer as children play. An associated activity is to find a long word that is of interest to children or drawn from the current theme in the classroom, for example a word such as 'gardening', and ask the children to make as many words as possible using the letters that are contained in the word. Other words to discuss include families of words, for example, 'play, playing' and 'played' and words that have prefixes and suffixes.

Look, cover, remember, write, check

The most helpful way of giving spellings is to write the word down for the child using the 'look, cover, remember, write, check' routine originally devised by Peters and Cripps (1980) and recommended in the nonstatutory guidance for spelling (NCC, 1990). First the teacher writes the word for the child and then asks the child to look at the word and to memorize it. The correct version is then removed or covered and the child is asked to write the word from memory without help. The child's spelling is then checked against the correct version. If the spelling is correct the child can incorporate the word into his writing. If the word is incorrect the teacher and the child compare the two versions, identify where the problem lies and repeat the whole procedure.

This strategy helps children to ● memorize the correct spelling ● look at the whole word ● get the overall visual pattern of the word.

Positive correction

When correcting children's spelling it is best to work with the errors that arise in what the child is writing. These words are of use and interest to the child and for that reason the correct spelling is more likely to be remembered. Some teachers ask the children to identify the words that cause them problems or those that they think are incorrect. One way of doing this is to ask children to put a mark such as a dot next to words that they think are incorrectly spelt and which they would like help with. If the child has made a good attempt at the word the teacher might write the correct version of the word beneath the child's version and draw attention to the number of letters that are correct in the child's word. The teacher might illustrate this by putting a tick above each of the letters in the child's word that correspond with the letters in the standard spelling of the word. The teacher might then ask the child to look at the letters that

Figure 4.6 Positive correction

are incorrect and compare these with the correct letters. After doing this with one or two identified errors the teacher can then ask the child to follow the 'look, cover, remember, write, check' routine. One or two words from a piece of writing might be corrected in this way. The extract in Figure 4.6 shows a teacher working in this way.

Having a go

If children are totally stuck on a word and unwilling to have a go, the teacher can suggest that they write down any letters that they think are in the word and indicate by lines or dashes where the missing letters are. A word attempted in this way might look like 'be—s' for 'because'. When the teacher reads through the writing with the child she can talk about the word with the child and fill in the spaces. This strategy encourages less confident children to 'have a go' without risking an error and it helps the teacher to identify the words to tackle first when she is helping the child with his spelling.

Some children feel more confident about 'having a go' in a 'try book' or 'try pad' before writing their chosen version in their writing. This practice encourages children to have several attempts at a word and to compare the versions visually. It promotes the habit of visualizing and recalling the appearance of words.

Drafting and redrafting

If children are in the habit of producing first and second drafts of their writing, help with spelling can be given when the first draft has been completed. Before the teacher reads the writing the children can be encouraged to proofread their own writing, identifying words that they think are incorrectly spelt and either trying to correct these by having another go at the word or searching for the word in a dictionary, or they can indicate the words that they are unsure of by means of a mark. In addition to rereading their own writing pupils can ask another child in the class to read it and identify mistakes in the text before it is shown to the teacher. The response partner need not just focus on spelling but may also make suggestions about content, clarity and structure. This routine introduces an audience other than the teacher for the children's writing and helps to make writing a collaborative rather than an individual activity.

Computers and spelling

It has been proposed that children's spelling may improve when they use word processors for writing (Potter and Sands, 1988). They suggest that incorrect spellings are more easily identified when they appear on the screen or on a print-out than when they are handwritten. Spellings that are identified as incorrect can be deleted and replaced more easily with the computer than in a piece of handwritten text. With the computer the whole text does not need to be rewritten in order to remove misspellings and insert the correct versions. Finally they suggest that children are more motivated to produce correct spellings in writing that is produced on the word processor since the print-out, with its similarities to commercially published texts, emphasizes the public nature of writing and the understanding that others will read what has been written. With the possibility of an audience the need for correct spelling has more significance.

Using the word-processing facilities of the computer to motivate children to check spellings and to correct spellings presupposes that children use the computer for first drafts and for redrafting their work after identifying things that they want to change. If the computer is only used to copy out perfectly spelt final versions of writing the ease of correction that it provides is lost along with the incentive it provides to make redrafting less time consuming.

Some teachers feel anxious about introducing drafting and redrafting to young children since they feel it may turn writing into a chore. The use of the computer to produce first and subsequent drafts of writing can lessen this chore since the child does not have to copy out each draft afresh. The computer can certainly reduce emphasis on the transcriptional elements of writing since it automatically produces clearly written text that is easily readable, can make the correction of spellings simple and takes the effort out of redrafting. All this means that the child can be freed to concentrate on the composition of writing and yet still produce a perfectly presented piece of writing.

Spell checks provide another source of help for children's spelling. They can enable children to check the spellings of words that they think may be wrong or the programme itself may identify words that are incorrectly spelt. In order to prevent children from becoming too engrossed with correct spelling at the cost of composition it is suggested that spell checks are not used until after the first draft of a piece of writing has been completed.

Dictionaries

Children can be introduced to the use of commercially produced dictionaries by making a large class dictionary to which new words are added when different themes are undertaken by the class. The new vocabulary can be entered by the children, giving them a purpose for spelling carefully and correctly. Making a dictionary gives children a sense of alphabetical order and introduces the idea of looking for spellings in other dictionaries and books that are available in the class.

For younger children or as an alternative way of introducing knowledge and understanding of alphabetical order, the children can produce an alphabet frieze or poster. A good starting point for the words on class-made alphabet friezes are the names of the children in the class and the school or topics such as food and animals. To reinforce alphabetical order older children can be asked to write an ABC book for younger children in the school.

When introducing the more difficult alphabetical ordering skills using letters beyond the initial letter, children's names are again a good starting point. The children may begin by producing an alphabetical list of class names using initial letters and then asked how they could order Saloni and Sophie or Rosie and Rinku. The principle of using the second and subsequent letters of the alphabet when looking for words in a dictionary can then be explained. Class names can be extended to include the names of family members and friends if there is not sufficient variety within the class.

Practice at using alphabetical order may also be gained in play situations in the classroom – for example making patient record cards that are kept in name order in the doctor's room or hospital, or entering names in an address or telephone book in the home corner and referring to this when making phone calls.

Spelling and handwriting

There have been suggestions that introducing young children to cursive script can help with correct spelling. When a writer prints, each letter is isolated from the one before it and the one after it and the hand does not build up a memory for how it feels to produce certain patterns of letters. When letters in words are joined there is an increased possibility that the correct version of a word will be remembered since both the visual and the motor memory are being used. Peters (1985) suggests that this is particularly helpful for memorizing letter strings such as *ough* or *ight*. The multisensory approach to learning spelling has been advocated as a useful way to support learning for children needing intensive remedial help with spelling (Fernald, 1943), but there is no reason why the principles cannot be applied to all children.

Some children adapt their handwriting to help their spelling on their own initiative. For example, it is quite common to see children use a capital *B* in the middle of a text that is mostly written using lower-case letters. This is often a device for avoiding reversals and distinguishing between letters that are commonly confused. Handwriting corrections involving words that are incorrectly spelt because of letter reversals, as with 'bog' for 'dog', may improve some children's spelling.

Spelling conferences

Conference time between the teacher and the pupil might sometimes focus particularly on spelling. Not only might spelling errors in the piece of writing that has just been completed be discussed but the teacher might also ask what the child finds difficult in spelling, what strategies he uses when spelling unfamiliar words and which words he would like to be able to spell correctly and easily. As a result of a spelling conference the teacher might have a better understanding of the child's needs and be able to plan her daily interventions more appropriately.

Handwriting

The aims of teaching handwriting

One of the aims of every school's English policy should be to teach children to write legibly, fluently and with reasonable speed. Since the purpose of all writing is to communicate, the writer needs to do this easily and the recipient of the writing needs to understand the message easily. Clear, quickly formed handwriting aids this act of communication. Thus it is important that handwriting is legible. Fluency in writing means that the writer is at ease with the writing system and with writing implements, pencil or pen grip is firm but not tense and the letters are correctly formed. Speed and fluency go together; if the child knows how to form letters he will form them quickly. The main reason that 'infant script' is thought of as the 'correct' method of letter formation for young children is that it is economical and legible and for the most part leaves the pen in the appropriate place for a joining stroke when cursive script is introduced. Clear, well formed handwriting does not develop naturally, it needs to be taught carefully and sensitively so that all children are helped to form and join letters quickly, easily and legibly.

Handwriting style

Many models of handwriting exist for use in school and most are accompanied by manuals that give teachers information about letter formation and the development of good handwriting. Schools may have individual preferences about the style they choose. The important point is that one style is taught and modelled consistently throughout the school.

The debate about whether cursive script should be introduced to children as soon as they begin to write at school has been with us for many years. Joined-up writing has been viewed as a progression from preliterate patterns (Jarman, 1993), as an aid to spelling (Peters, 1985) and as a means of maintaining the flow when writing creatively (Graves, 1983). However it is only recently that the issue has been discussed seriously in many schools. The statement, 'Handwriting is joined', which occurs in the description of a Level 3 writer (DfE, 1995a), will no doubt ensure that the debate about handwriting styles will continue as some teachers may feel that they are disadvantaging pupils if cursive script is not introduced early.

A question that is often asked about handwriting styles and that is central to this debate is: 'Is joined-up writing compatible with a developmental approach to writing?' In some ways it may be seen as incompatible. When children first begin to write they often produce capital letters, then a mixture of capital and lower-case letters and finally lower case with the correct use of capitals. To expect children to move from the preliterate marks on paper to joined-up writing might exclude the other stages that children go through as they are learning about the writing system. The use of capitals plays a part in spelling development when children use letter names to help them write words. As the type face in children's books is usually print script it would seem to be at variance with the models children see and the materials teachers use to teach children lessons about writing if joined-up writing was introduced from the start.

Sassoon (1990) has suggested a compromise and a possible way forward for those concerned about the merits and demerits of the early introduction of cursive script. She proposes that from the start, children should be introduced to letters with exit strokes. Letters that are made in this way retain the print form similar to that found in books, give children the opportunity to absorb and use correct letter formation and provide a model for the flowing movement needed for cursive script. With this style children will only need to extend the exit strokes to form joins as their handwriting matures. The example in Figure 4.7 illustrates how this works. The teacher has written the correct spelling of 'home' using print with exit strokes.

For schools which prefer to teach a traditional form of infant script to younger children and cursive script to older children, the order of introduction might be as follows:

- Beginning writers – print script.
- Children using lower-case print confidently with only a few incorrectly formed letters – introduce joined letter strings when modelling or discussing children's spelling.
- Children using lower-case print well and forming letters correctly – begin to introduce them to joining letters when it is comfortable and quicker for them.

Figure 4.7   Home – handwriting

This sequence implies that joined writing would be introduced when individual children were ready. The majority of children should begin to reach this stage by their third year at school.

Writing for different purposes and different audiences may entail different degrees of care in the handwriting that is produced. A first draft may be written quickly and contain a number of crossings out and corrections. Normal everyday writing will need to be both legible and fast. Writing for special occasions such as public writing on invitations, letters home and displays will require care and attention. In time each writer will develop his own personal style of writing and this need not be a problem. There is nothing wrong with a personal style as long as it is legible, fluent and economic.

Practical ways of supporting children's development in handwriting

The teacher's role when teaching handwriting is to provide the appropriate resources which children need to practise the skill and to demonstrate to children how letters and words should be formed. Corrections and demonstration should arise from the child's own writing. The purpose of well presented and correctly formed writing should always be explained to children so that they understand the reasons for attending to the skills of writing. They should be told that good handwriting helps the reader to read what has been written and helps the writer to write more quickly. Children should never be given the impression that perfectly formed writing is more important than content.

Writing implements

Sassoon (1990) writes that thick pencils are not necessarily helpful for small infant fingers and suggests that a variety of writing implements should be made available to children. A range of writing implements can make writing more interesting and should include different sizes of pencils, fibre-tipped pens, felt-tips, wax crayons and pencil crayons. Biro can look messy so it is probably not a good tool for a final best draft but it can be used for rough work. Teachers may like to put a biro in the home corner for children to use there since many children will be familiar with biros at home. Pens can be introduced to children as soon as they start school. It is likely that most children will have had experience of using pens before they come to school. If children do not use rubbers when writing first drafts they can write in any medium, but it might be most appropriate for children to use pencils for first drafts of writing and roller-ball pens, fountain pens or felt-tips for final drafts where presentation is important. The type of paper used may influence the writing implement that is chosen.

Paper

Traditionally beginning writers have used unlined paper to write on. Young children may have problems keeping to lines. They are not always sure which part of a letter rests on the line and may place the tails of letters such as *p* and *g* on the lines if given lined paper too quickly. Unlined paper gives young children the freedom to experiment with letter formation and size as well as giving them the flexibility to incorporate drawings into or near to their writing. Drawing can be an important part of the writing process since it can be used as a planning and thinking aid. As children begin to use smaller writing and to form letters correctly they can be introduced to line guides to help them keep their writing straight. Line guides are made from strong white card on which bold black lines are drawn at the desired width. The guides are placed beneath the child's writing paper and can be kept in place with paper clips. The lines show through and provide a guide for writing. They have the advantage over lined paper of allowing children the freedom to choose where to place their illustrations. It is also a good idea to have different shapes, sizes and colours of paper available.

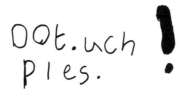

Figure 4.8 'Don't touch please'

Alphabets

Most classes contain commercial or pupil-made alphabet friezes that children can refer to when writing. Sassoon (1990) suggests that each child could also have an alphabet strip which could be placed on the table when writing. This might help children to remember the order of the alphabet and help them to sort out which way letters face. They also remind children of the writing style that the school favours.

Developing handwriting across the curriculum

Whitehead (1990) suggests that the skills needed for handwriting – hand and eye co-ordination, muscle control and visual sensitivity – develop through play activities, art activities and exposure to displays and writing seen in school. Handwriting can be practised in all areas of the curriculum, for example in art children can produce patterns using letters, print with letter shapes and produce patterns when finger painting. Close observation drawing can be particularly helpful in developing children's visual discrimination and attention to detail (Sassoon, 1990). In mathematics children can use plastic and wooden letters for matching and sorting. To extend play activities children can make labels for the home corner, shop, office, etc. They can also make labels for their models, giving the name of the model, their own name and a message, such as 'This model was made by Shippu and Maria-Elena'. The label in Figure 4.8, which reads 'Don't touch please!', was placed next to an unfinished model that the children wanted to complete later.

Intervention

Handwriting is best taught individually to pupils through the writing that they produce rather than through class writing lessons involving copying from the board or from cards. Even if one uses a particular style of handwriting formal exercises are not necessary. During class handwriting sessions it is not usually possible to observe whether children are forming their letters correctly and there seems to be very little transfer from handwriting sessions to handwriting used at other times. Instead it is good practice to match the teaching of handwriting to individual children's needs and to correct errors with the child as one observes them occurring in everyday writing. While observing writing look for the ease with which the child holds the pen, the mixed use of lower and upper-case letters, the arrangement of writing on the page and incorrect letter formation. The aim is for children to start in the right place and move in the right direction. This is more important than the final letters produced. Problems with handwriting can lead to tense and uncomfortable posture and grip, reluctance to write, slow writing and difficulties with cursive script. Suggestions for correction should only be made about one or at the most two mistakes in one piece of writing, and the teacher should focus on poorly formed letters or incorrect joining strokes. Having identified the errors that will be discussed with the child, the teacher may demonstrate the correct formation of these letters and ask the child to practise making them correctly. The child may be asked to produce a line of correctly formed letters and then to rewrite the word in which the mistake occurred. The best time to emphasize careful presentation of written work is probably just before the child is making a final draft when corrections that have been made should be included. It is at this time that children can see the point of making writing legible and attractive since others may read what has been written.

Models of writing and writers

When teachers write underneath children's writing in the early stages of developmental writing or when they work with children on spelling corrections or in shared-writing sessions, they should make sure that their writing provides a good model for children. They should ensure that children have the opportunity to see well formed, clear handwriting as it is produced. Good models provide examples that children can see and imitate.

It is important that whole-school decisions are taken about the style of handwriting adopted and how it is taught in order to ensure continuity and progression as children develop as writers and as they move through the school. All the staff need to be aware of the style of handwriting chosen by the school and should use this when writing for displays and providing models for children.

Left-handed writers

Left-handers may have particular difficulties with handwriting. It may help if teachers consider the following points:

- *Light* – ideally a left-hander needs the light to come over his right shoulder so that he is not writing in the shadow of his own hand.

- *Paper* – a left-hander needs to have paper on the left side of the centre of the body. The paper needs to be tilted to the right so that the writer can see what he is writing.
- *Pencil hold* – encourage a left-handed writer to hold the pencil or pen a little further from the point than a right-hander so that the writing is not obscured. It may be helpful to introduce children to a pencil grip to find the right place for their fingers.
- *Position* – make sure that a left-hander is not sitting too close to the right of a right-hander when writing. This will avoid their arms colliding.
- *Speed* – allow for slower writing until competence increases.
- *Teaching* – demonstrate to left-handers with your left hand whenever possible.

Computers and handwriting

Word-processing programs are an ideal way of varying the writing process. Children usually enjoy working at the computer and gain a great deal of satisfaction from seeing their stories printed out in a professional way. Typed script can be an excellent way of producing public documents such as class books. Computers can speed up the process of producing first and second drafts of written work and encourage children to correct and change their writing using the editing procedures. Very young children can be invited to play with the keyboard or to try to write their names as a way of helping them to recognize the connection between upper and lower-case letter forms.

Punctuation

The problem with punctuation

Punctuation marks such as full stops, question marks and commas help readers to interpret sentences and help writers to express their meaning more clearly. The correct use of punctuation helps to decrease the possibility of ambiguity for both the communicator and the recipient of the message and for this reason it is an important part of the writing system. However understanding the correct use and conventions of punctuation even at the simplest level may not be easy: 'although in one sense educated adults all know what a word like sentence means, there is no denying that linguists find it exceptionally difficult to produce a watertight definition of even such a common term' (Perera, 1987, p. 38).

In order to understand where full stops should be positioned it is necessary to know what constitutes a sentence – to understand what characterizes the group of words that occur between one full stop and another. Most adults and some primary-age children may have an intuitive grasp of what a sentence is, but this does not necessarily make it easy to explain to others. Smith (1982, p. 84) echoed the sorts of conversations that must be familiar to every teacher when he wrote:

> 'Begin every sentence with a capital letter.'
> 'What is a sentence?'
> 'Something that begins with a capital letter.'

He goes on to suggest that the 'rules' of punctuation and capitalization, although seemingly obvious, tend to be very difficult to explain simply. When adults try to explain what is meant by a sentence and therefore where to place a full stop, they may use phrases such as • 'a complete thought' • 'a group of words that make sense' • 'where you stop' • 'where your voice falls' • 'where you take a breath'.

Complete thoughts and groups of words could refer just as well to phrases as to sentences, and stopping places, particularly during the composing process, may occur virtually anywhere. In the Kingman Report (DES, 1988a) a sentence is described as 'what it is that is enclosed between a capital letter and a full stop', but this still leaves the problem of what should be enclosed. Some readers may be familiar with the 'rules', 'never begin a sentence with and' or 'you can't start a sentence with because', but this is not always true. For example, one could write, 'Because of the difficulty involved in explaining grammatical rules to children one wonders why we try to teach them to very young children and why we expect children to be able to use them competently in the early years of schooling'.

It is true that punctuation is a way of marking meaning. However until children can confidently create their own meanings through writing they cannot clarify what they want to express. They have to know what they intend to mean and be aware that it might be misunderstood before they can knowingly apply punctuation marks to indicate how what they have written should be understood. This entails having a sophisticated level of awareness about grammar, about one's own use of language and about the requirements of an audience. In spite of these difficulties, the National Curriculum Orders for English (DfE, 1995a) tell us that at Key Stage 1 children 'should be taught to punctuate their writing, be consistent in their use of capital letters, full stops and question marks, and begin to use commas'. At Key Stage 2 inverted commas, apostrophes and exclamation marks are added to the list of what should be taught and known.

The development of punctuation

In order to discover how young children use and learn about punctuation, Cazden, Cordeiro and Giacobbe (1985) analysed samples of writing from a class of 22 first-grade (6-year-old) children collected over a period of nine months. They found that children begin to incorporate full stops, question marks, commas and apostrophes into their own writing when they become aware of punctuation in the writing of others. At first children place punctuation marks in the wrong places in their writing, but as they experiment more and receive feedback on their attempts its use becomes increasingly correct. Cazden, Cordeiro and Giacobbe found that direct teaching about punctuation did not hasten its development. Their research showed that on the way to using punctuation appropriately children passed through six stages of experimenting with the positioning of full stops. Examples from these stages showing where the children placed full stops appear below:

Between each syllable in words
DN. USOS dinosaur
RAS.ING racing

Between each word
I. AM. WOKEING. MY. BIKE. AP. THE HEL.
I am walking my bike up the hill.

At the end of each line
WE PRT ON THE.
FORTH FOR.
We parked on the fourth floor.

At the end of a page

Between phrases
ON THE WA HOME. MI CAR IT SPLODID
On the way home my car it exploded

Both between phrases and correctly
WE ARE SILE [still] DRIVING TO NEW YOK.
WE TOK MY GRMS CAR. MY DAD MY MOM AND
MY BROTHER MY GRAMY AND MY GRAPY. WAT
TO NOW YORK WITH ME.

They comment that the last two examples are particularly significant since these show children using their intended meaning to guide their decisions about where to place the full stops. They show children on the way to understanding what a sentence might be and consequently where to position full stops correctly.

These examples show that young children's use of punctuation is rarely random. They indicate that children are trying to discover the appropriate unit of meaning which should be demarcated by a full stop. Their errors do not become permanent bad habits; instead they provide learning opportunities. Just as with the development of oral language or the development of spelling, children are using what they know so far of the system, to overgeneralize, play with the rules, experiment and discard guesses as they learn more about language.

It is probably when the teacher observes children experimenting with full stops at the level of intended meaning that her discussion with them about its correct use will be most productive. However children will still need to experiment with positioning the full stop at different points in their writing as their usage approximates closer and closer to the adult system, until they come to 'know' what a sentence is. As Smith (1982, p. 190) wrote,

> How then does a child ever learn to recognise a question, a clause, a sentence . . . ? The answer is in much the same way that children come to recognise dogs, cats, chairs, tables . . . Adults do not often try to define for children what constitutes a cat, dog, chair or table. They do not attempt to teach the rules of catness, dogness or whatever. They simply point out instances of each category and leave the children to work out the rules themselves, implicitly.

Practical ways of supporting children's development of punctuation

As with all language skills it is likely that young children's appreciation of punctuation will precede production. Even very young children may comment on the use of punctuation in picture books. Many books for young children contain punctuation marks that are prominent and integral to the meaning of the book. Teachers and children may naturally comment on these non-alphabetic marks on the page as they discuss the illustrations and stories. These early discussions, which may well begin in the nursery, will enlarge children's understanding of how and when punctuation marks are used in writing and may begin before there is any expectation that children will incorporate punctuation marks into their own writing. However young children often surprise adults with their understanding and observation of textual features and may begin to use

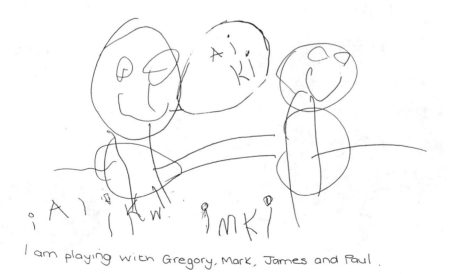

I am playing with Gregory, Mark, James and Paul.

Figure 4.9 Jay punctuation

full stops, question marks and speech bubbles earlier than expected, as the example in Figure 4.9 by Jay, aged 4, demonstrates.

However whatever stage the child has reached in the production of punctuation marks the teacher will be alert to signs that children are aware of these symbols as they enter Key Stage 1 of the National Curriculum. Before aiming to teach any aspect of punctuation the teacher will need to discover what children know and understand and to ensure that children are confident in their production of writing. Children for whom some form of teaching about punctuation is appropriate will probably be beginning to use punctuation at the level of making meaning. At this stage the teacher may introduce punctuation by continuing to discuss punctuation in books and by acknowledging what children can do.

Using books

The teacher will want to give explanations about punctuation in the context of experiences that are meaningful and familiar to children. She may introduce the topic as children comment on and discuss a story after a big book or picture book has been shared with the class. Or she may comment on the use of full stops and capital letters after a shared-reading session with an individual child. It will be important to ensure that the books that are available to the class contain written language that is realistically rather than artificially divided into sentences. Books containing sentences that stop at the end of every line are poor models for children, as are books containing repeated or short, simple sentences of the type found in many scheme books since they are unlikely to resemble the writing that the children produce and need to punctuate (Kress, 1994).

Figure 4.10 'What's the time, Mr Wolf?'

Figure 4.10 gives two sample pages from a well-known children's book. The following commentary indicates how picture books may be used to teach children about punctuation.

Figure 4.10 is taken from *What's the Time, Mr Wolf?* (Hawkins, 1983). On each double spread of pages the narrative follows the same pattern, a question asked by the reader, 'What's the time, Mr Wolf?', with the answers provided by the Wolf contained in speech bubbles. It is very likely that after an initial sharing of this book at story time the teacher would invite the children to join in with the questioning and one child at a time might read his answers in response. No doubt the teacher would make comments, such as 'We can all ask the questions together'. This would provide a model of written dialogue for the children that shows how questions are indicated by question marks and how responses can be demarcated by speech bubbles. As questions and punctuation marks are a large feature of this text it is likely that the teacher or the children would talk about the non-alphabetic marks. Each answer ends with a full stop so the text provides a good example of how two different types of punctuation can be used to mark boundaries in different types of sentences. If the teacher wished to she might also mention the use of the apostrophe to indicate missing letters in 'What's' and 'o'clock'.

Using children's writing

The child's own writing may act as a starting point for a discussion about punctuation, particularly if the child has incorporated but mis-used punctuation marks in his writing. Before the teacher makes any comments about punctuation in a child's writing, she might ask herself: 'Do I want to work on punctuation or are there other features of the writing such as content, structure or length that are more important at this stage?' Then if she decides to discuss punctuation she might con-sider ● How has the child used punctuation? ● What has the child done well? ● At this stage in the child's development as a writer, what could he do better? Initially it is important to discover what the child knows about the use of punctuation and ask why the child decided to use punctuation marks as he has. Then by referring to what the child

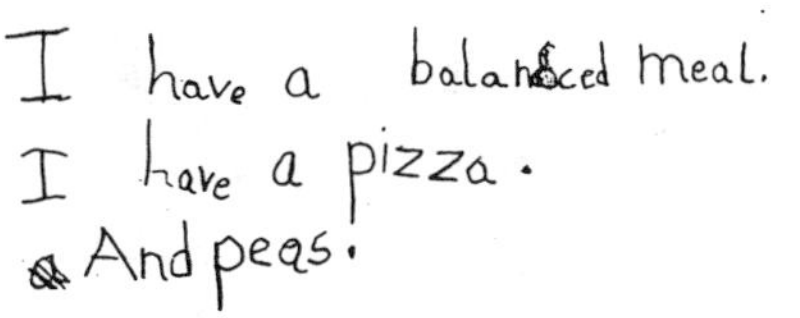

Figure 4.11   Nelson healthy meal

has written and remembering that the role of punctuation is to clarify meaning the teacher might comment on what the child has done. The teacher might next explain about the correct use of punctuation marks. Figure 4.11 is given as an example.

This was a second draft of a description of a healthy meal by Nelson aged 6. It was written to accompany his meal picture and displayed in a class book about food. The content and spellings had been commented on after the first draft had been written, and as the child had, on his own initiative, included full stops in his final draft, this provided a good opportunity to discuss punctuation. The teacher might begin by finding out what Nelson knows, asking questions such as: 'You've put some full stops and capital letters into your writing. Where did you get that idea from? Why did you decide to put the full stops here?' After listening to the child's responses the teacher might suggest that full stops do not need to occur at the end of each line of writing. She might explain that full stops are used by the writer to help the reader make sense of what has been written and ask Nelson where he wanted the reader to pause as the description was read. Does the inclusion of a full stop after pizza help the reader to make sense of what he has written? Nelson could be asked to follow up this discussion by looking at print in a picture book to reinforce the point that full stops are not always placed at the ends of lines.

Figure 4.12   Mrs Armitage on wheels

Figure 4.13   Tom, Tom

Providing models

Another form of teaching is provided by an adult's written responses to children's writing which contains punctuation marks and provides the child with models of punctuation in use, as the example in Figure 4.12 illustrates. The teacher may begin to draw attention to her own use of punctuation during shared-writing sessions or when she scribes for pupils. Modelling provides an opportunity for teachers to make explicit the specific thought processes involved in deciding where to place punctuation marks in writing. This may enable children to understand and see the use and reasons for punctuation.

The picture and piece of writing in Figure 4.13 were included in a class book about sounds and were prompted by the teacher's question, 'What do you hear?' after the class had listened to a piece of music. Tom, a reception child aged 5, wrote his name twice as requested by the teacher and then the teacher wrote the question and 'I hear a . . .', as Tom watched. After Tom had written 'lion' the teacher wrote the correct version of this word and completed the sentence with a full stop. By doing this, even at this early stage of Tom's writing development, she was providing the child with a model and drawing his attention to how punctuation is used in writing.

Writing activities

With older children the teacher might follow such modelling episodes by asking the pupils to engage in a writing activity that encourages them to

Monday 10th December 1990
Where's Jacquie?

Where's Jacquie.? Is she under the christmas tree? The bath room No. No. Is she in She gone to the. Park. Then where is she.

Figure 4.14   Tandi – Christmas tree

use an aspect of punctuation. The children could be asked to compile a list of questions about a mysterious object that the teacher has brought in. These might then be displayed around a collection of unusual objects that the class are examining. Or, again, using an object as a starting point, the children could be asked to write statements about it to form part of a display. The first writing activity is intended to encourage the use of question marks, the second the use of full stops.

Writing a class or individual book based on *Where's Spot?* (Hill, 1980) could again encourage the children to use question marks and full stops, as in the example in Figure 4.14.

Making and publishing books is likely to encourage children to pay attention to all aspects of transcription as there is a real purpose for care and effort. After writing the children's sentences could be discussed in a group and the children asked to explain their use of punctuation to others providing an opportunity for children to learn from each other. Other writing for public audiences, such as making posters for the book or imaginative play areas, might encourage children to think about punctuation.

As well as set activities that encourage children to incorporate punctuation into writing the children should also be free to experiment with punctuation in all the writing that they do. Correct use of punctuation will not develop quickly or in a strictly linear fashion. The teacher will need to be patient, to continue to demonstrate, discuss and respond to children's attempts as their understanding and use of punctuation develops. It is worth waiting for as once children have established sentence boundaries in their writing and understood what a sentence might be, the most fundamental aspect of their knowledge about written grammar has developed and further learning about other aspects of punctuation will follow (Kress, 1994).

Correcting transcriptional errors in children's writing

When the teacher receives a piece of writing from a child the first step is always to respond to what has been written, the content, language, structure and style and then to respond to the transcriptional elements of spelling, handwriting and punctuation. Before giving feedback on corrections to be undertaken she needs to consider how the child has presented the writing and whether this represents an appropriate response to the task for this particular child. If she decides that the child and the writing would benefit from comment about and changes to the transcriptional aspects of the piece she should limit her suggestions and advice to what the child is likely to remember, probably no more than two or three comments overall. Correction of errors in spelling, handwriting and punctuation is gradual and systematic and should be undertaken with the

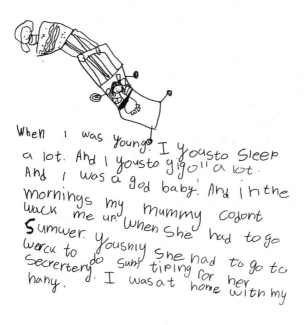

Figure 4.15 Lana

intention of teaching the child something that he will remember for next time. The example in Figure 4.15 illustrates how to respond to transcriptional errors in children's work. There are no hard and fast rules. Teachers will make their own judgements about what to correct based on their knowledge of their own pupils. The focus on transcription that follows has been deliberately constructed to illustrate some of the points made in this chapter.

Lana, aged 6

Context

The children had discussed some of their early memories in preparation for a piece of writing for their individual personal history books. The opening phrase had been written on the flip chart. Before beginning her writing, Lana had jotted down some of her ideas about what she was going to include, using individual words. She wrote in pen and after finishing her writing, mounted it herself and stuck it in her book.

Teacher response

Many words in this piece of writing are spelt correctly. Lana has not been deterred from being adventurous in her choice of words by being over-concerned with correctness, although it is clear that she has thought carefully about her spelling. *Codont* shows Lana drawing on her knowledge about English and her understanding of how words are constructed in quite a sophisticated way. The majority of spelling errors arise from Lana's use of phonic strategies and indicate that she needs continued help with strengthening her visual strategies. Lana could be asked to read her writing through, looking for any misspellings. If she recognized that she had omitted an *o* from 'good', she could correct this herself. After her rereading the teacher and Lana might work on two mistakes that Lana had identified. If Lana had not recognized any errors the teacher could work on the words 'some' and 'somewhere', using the look, cover, remember, write, check system.

Lana's handwriting is clear and all her letters appear to be formed correctly. She writes fluently and quickly. The long tails on many of the *y*s show that Lana is beginning to develop her own individual style of writing and indicate that she is ready to begin cursive writing. The tendency for Lana's writing to slope down the page could be helped by reminding her to use line guides.

Lana has incorporated full stops and capital letters into her writing. Their use shows that Lana is well on the way to understanding that punctuation is used to separate ideas. The teacher and Lana might discuss whether the full stop between 'young' and 'I' in the first line of her writing is necessary.

Lana's transcriptional skills are developing well and she will continue to make progress if she is encouraged to think about what words look like and to proofread her writing.

Standard English and language study

Opportunities to develop children's understanding and use of standard English and to study language are a necessary part of the English curriculum. The requirements for these run through each aspect of English and are present at each Key Stage. All children know a great deal about language by the time they start school and this implicit knowledge is drawn upon whenever children speak, listen, read and write. Helping children to learn about the conventions of writing is one way in which teachers can help to fulfil the requirements of this section of the National Curriculum for English (DfE, 1995a).

As she talks to children about spelling, handwriting and punctuation the teacher will be using the vocabulary and terminology associated with language and needed for language study, as well as introducing children to the 'characteristic language' associated with writing. Words and phrases such as letter, word, capital, small, lower case, upper case, direction, full stop, question mark, penhold, position, sentence and space will be presented naturally and in context. Discussions about the surface features of writing will involve references to the differences between spoken and written language, the rules and conventions of grammar, spelling and punctuation and the characteristics and features of different kinds of texts. Many of the activities that develop children's writing skills will involve them in reflecting on and discussing language and may stimulate children's interest in language. Thinking about spelling, handwriting and punctuation can extend children's understanding of how language works, which is one of the aims of the standard English and language study sections in the National Curriculum.

If they wished teachers could develop this incidental learning through a project on written language. This might begin with an examination of the particular features of different forms of writing, such as diaries, letters, postcards, records, lists, newspapers, advertisements, etc. Different ways of spelling children's names could be considered, for example Ann and Anne or Jon and John. Why certain spellings are chosen might lead to finding out about the origins of words, their meanings, language change and famous people in history. Within the project teachers might like to look at scripts and handwriting in different cultures and the way in which the presentation of writing has changed over time. *Scripts of the World* (Bukiet, 1989) is a useful introduction to the five main scripts used around the world and includes an account of the development of handwriting. An investigation along these lines might interest children in language and its conventions and stimulate them to take more care with their presentation of written language.

Conclusion

Spelling, handwriting and punctuation are skills that need to be taught sensitively and their place within writing needs to be explained carefully to children if we are not to emphasize transcription at the cost of content. Not every piece of writing that children produce needs to look perfect but some of the writing that children do should be used to demonstrate correct models of spelling, handwriting and punctuation. The transcription skills of spelling, handwriting and punctuation do not always transfer if they are isolated from real writing situations but they will improve as children gain more practice and experience as writers, if they are made aware of the communicative function of writing and if transcription is discussed and learned within activities that have a clear communicative purpose. Children learn best if they are given real reasons for making their writing clear and receive sensitive guidance and intervention. The key strategies for teaching transcription skills in the early years should not involve exercises and practice for their own sakes or correction of mistakes without reasoned discussion. Instead they should be to ● provide examples in books and other resources ● model the process ● teach in the context of meaningful experiences ● discuss ● let children experiment ● respond positively to children's efforts.

Suggestions for further reading

Peters, M.L. (1985) *Spelling: Caught or Taught? A New Look*, Routledge, London.
Sassoon, R. (1990) *Handwriting: The Way to Teach it*, Stanley Thornes, Cheltenham.

Chapter 5

Children's books

Introduction

This chapter considers fiction and non-fiction for young readers. It begins by examining the role of books in children's learning and includes sections on ways of selecting and promoting children's books.

Learning to read is generally regarded as the most important aspect of education in the early years. Carers often consider that learning to read is as significant for children as learning to speak or learning to walk and teachers and schools are proud of their success in teaching children to read. Being able to read is not sufficient, it is the active use of reading that is important, since it is this which enables children to function in school and in a literate society, and offers them the opportunity to engage in a life-long pleasurable activity. Books are the mainstay of the early-years reading curriculum and so are a major force for exciting children into reading. Books also transmit messages to children about the enjoyment of reading and the power and uses of literacy. Because books are such an important resource, teachers need to pay as much attention to them as they do to ensuring that children can read. Teachers who want children not only to learn to read but also to appreciate that reading is a source of learning, experience and entertainment will make careful selections of the books that they offer to children.

The importance of books

What books offer to readers

There are many sorts of books, but for ease this chapter will refer to two main types, fiction and non-fiction. Both are important in school and outside school, both require special selection criteria and both demand particular styles of reading.

The uses to which information and references texts can be put are obvious. If we need to know how to . . . or we want to know about . . . we can consult the relevant text and discover the answer that we need. Children need to be able to read and use non-fiction to further their learning at school and to access information out of school. The majority of adult readers who do read usually read for functional reasons rather than for sheer enjoyment (Wray, Bloom and Hall, 1989). As a preparation for the learning demands of school and the literacy needs of adulthood, learning to read and use information texts should be an important part of the reading curriculum at school and should probably receive more attention in the early years than is often the case.

Fiction is less obviously useful. It is seen as 'recreational' (Meek, 1991) and is often seen as a leisure or holiday activity, rather than as important for learning or for work. Since much of the reading curriculum in the early years is structured around stories, whether these are the mischievous escapades of Billy Blue Hat (McCullagh, 1969) or the multiple versions of Shirley's adventures at the seaside (Burningham, 1977), early-years practitioners need to be able to justify their use of story as the major resource for introducing children to reading.

The ability to tell stories based on their own experiences and developed through their encounters with stories in books, on television and on tape is a skill that all children bring to school (Barrs and Thomas, 1991). Introducing children to reading by providing them with story books to read is one way of building on what children can already do and know. Although this is important it is not the only justification for a literature-based reading curriculum. Stories have a value in their own right. Well written stories invite readers to re-create and examine familiar and unfamiliar worlds and experiences and offer readers the opportunity to know themselves, others and the world more fully. In the words of D.H. Lawrence, a story 'can teach us to live as nothing else can' (quoted in Wade, 1984).

To illustrate this, perhaps readers of this book would like to think about a story that they have read recently and consider what they gained from that reading experience. Recently I finished reading *The Bone People* (1985) by Keri Hulme, a book that provoked a strong response in many people. For me reading *The Bone People* was a significant, rewarding and disturbing experience. It enriched and challenged me in a number of ways, personally, socially, intellectually and linguistically as well as stimulating me to look for more of Keri Hulme's books.

At a personal level, reading *The Bone People* was an overwhelming emotional experience. As I began reading I admired the strength and sympathized with the dilemmas of the central character but, as the events of the book unfolded, I experienced a whole range of emotions including anger, fear and disgust at her actions and those of other characters in the book. Socially, the book gave me access to a society of which I have no direct experience. I was introduced to Maori traditions and values. I was confronted with the complexity of human actions and interactions and the recognition that these were linked to individual histories, relationships, communities and one's position in society. I was stimulated intellectually by examining the moral issues that confronted the characters. As I read, the unorthodox style of the book and the inclusion of Maori words and phrases encouraged me to pay close attention to the way in which the author used written language. And finally, because this was a book that had engaged my attention throughout, I wanted to read more by this author and to know more about her. I had experienced the power of story.

Whilst this was an adult text, written for readers with abilities, understanding and experiences far greater than those possessed by young children, well written children's books should offer readers similar opportunities to those outlined above. Good stories should offer children the possibility of personal, social, intellectual and linguistic enrichment and leave children with the desire to read more. The list which follows identifies what stories have to offer young children as individuals and as learners.

To offer opportunities for personal development, books should ● give enjoyment ● extend imagination ● develop empathy ● widen experience ● develop imagination ● reflect experiences ● present other perspectives.

To offer opportunities for social development, books should ● reflect the nature of society ● give access to secondary worlds ● explore human relationships ● express a variety of cultural traditions and values ● demonstrate different ways of viewing the world.

To offer opportunities for intellectual development, books should ● make abstract ideas accessible or intelligible ● reveal deeper levels of meaning about familiar situations ● invite consideration of moral issues ● encourage reflection ● modify or influence attitudes, values and understanding ● give access to new ideas and knowledge ● add to the understanding of new concepts.

To offer opportunities for language development, books should ● use writing conventions and story structure ● permit readers to encounter models of vocabulary, spelling, dialogue, punctuation and grammar ● contain a range of writing styles ● be a source of ideas about subject matter and writing techniques ● demonstrate the power of language.

To offer opportunities for developing positive attitudes to reading, books should ● leave the reader with the wish to read more.

Since books have the potential to enrich children's lives in so many ways, it is essential that books for school are selected carefully so that every child will be given opportunities for worthwhile reading experiences.

Selecting books for the early years

Every school needs a large, varied and balanced collection of books to cater for the children's current and changing needs and interests. Some books should be kept centrally in the school library and the remainder distributed between each class. It has been suggested that every classroom should contain approximately one hundred books and that part of this selection should be changed once or twice each term (Somerfield, Torbe and Ward, 1983). A collection that is changed will stimulate and maintain the children's interest in books and encourage them to discover the range of books and authors that are available.

Types of books for young children

There are so many different types and formats of good books available for children that it is worth making sure that any collection covers the full range. Each collection should contain books that will entice children, sustain their interest in reading and extend all the skills associated with textual and visual literacy. Outlined below are the main categories of books available for young readers. Each class and library collection should include books from each category in order to provide a balanced and varied selection catering for all the readers in the school from the youngest to the most sophisticated and experienced.

Books without words

These are usually considered to be most appropriate for very young readers as they do not demand that the reader is able to read text, yet they can teach children about books, directionality and story telling. However, their appeal is not limited to inexperienced readers, the quality of illustrations and the detail they contain often makes them attractive to mature readers. In order to enter into the story and construct the narrative the reader needs to read the pictures by closely observing the detail in the visual text. Each picture acts as a time frame containing a single stage of the action. The size of these frames often indicates the pace of the story, with fast action being signalled by a number of small frames and slow action by one picture to a page. The size of the frames may also suggest the significance of the incident that is portrayed. Making sense of wordless books requires a number of reading skills similar to those employed when reading comics and cartoons, material that is often considered too sophisticated for the very young.

Caption and concept books

These are very often alphabet, counting or naming books and contain limited text. Some books in this category consist of photographs each of which describes an independent event. They are usually considered suitable for very young children.

Picture books

These comprise the majority of story books available for young children and form the largest part of every collection. There are a number of subcategories in this section including traditional, dual-narrative, cartoon-style, art and novelty books.

Traditional picture books are books, written for young readers, which contain a combination of pictures and text. In the best books the pictures and the text combine to produce a satisfying and harmonious visual and textual experience. The illustrations support and clarify the text, helping the reader to understand and read the story. The illustrations may elaborate on the text by providing details of the setting or indicating the mood and the tone of the book. The pictures invite the reader to linger over the page and encourage children to reflect on and understand what is read. The length of the text on each page can vary from brief, repetitive sentences to long, complete paragraphs. Although they should be conceptually accessible to young children they need not be trite and can cover a range of themes ranging from the familiar to those of universal and enduring significance. Some picture books are created by artists such as Mitsumasa Anno and Kit Wright, who are famous in their own right. In these books the illustrations may dominate and the text may consist of a loosely connected narrative. The visual delight of these books can make them very appealing to children.

Although in dual narratives the pictures and text are connected and may at first glance seem simple, the visual images often contain layers of meaning, which show different perspectives and feelings. The illustrations extend the story far beyond the text and sometimes create a separate story. These books need to be read actively to fully appreciate the complex interweaving between the text and the several meanings expressed in the pictures. Reading books in this category can really develop children's understanding of the subtlety and meanings of books.

In cartoon-style books the narrative is usually found in the captions; dialogue, thoughts and dreams are contained in bubbles. The reader is asked to shift between at least two different styles of writing arranged within and around the pictures. Again these books encourage the reader to use all the clues on the page, in the text and in the pictures, to make sense of the story.

Novelty books include books with pop-ups, flaps, cut-outs and hidden pictures. At the simplest level they can be used to entertain and maintain children's interest in books. But they also ask the reader to predict what is hidden beneath the flap or concealed on the next page and to scrutinize the illustrations.

Longer text

These closely resemble paperbacks for adult readers. They vary in length, difficulty and in the number of illustrations they contain but generally provide a more sustained read than picture books. They may contain chapters or a number of short stories. Adults sometimes see these as the bridge between picture books and 'proper' books.

Picture books for experienced readers

Picture books are not just for beginning readers. Many of them can be read at different levels and evoke different responses depending on the age, experience and situation of the reader. Some picture books demand to be read by older children and adults because of the sophistication of the message, the length of the text and the intricacy of the illustrations. Even simple picture books should be read by older children since they can provide all readers with a visual treat and a satisfying read. Teachers need not be reluctant to recommend picture books to fluent readers, even the most ardent adult reader will select short, familiar and less demanding material at times.

Books for sensitive situations

Feeling that it is 'their story' rather than 'my story' can give young readers and listeners a sense of safety when they encounter a subject that may be difficult. Death, loss, fear, bullying, abuse, illness, disability and inequality are all topics that have been written about by authors sensitive to young children's feelings. Including books on these subjects in the class collection acknowledges the existence of complex issues, presents them as normal and may prepare or bring comfort to children who are faced with situations that they find difficult.

Information books for young children

Mallet (1992) has identified three broad categories of non-fiction texts that have been written for young readers. These are narrative, non-narrative (reference) and non-narrative (exposition) texts.

Narrative texts

These can be written chronologically as information stories, biographies, autobiographies or diaries or they can describe procedures such as a set of instructions. Information stories have a narrower focus that true stories, since their function is to enable the reader to explore familiar and un-familiar experiences, such as going to hospital or to find out about topics linked to particular curriculum areas, for example facts about places and people. Children's first encounters with procedural texts may occur through reading displays of instructions written by the teacher, recipes and instructions for using computer programs. Books containing instructions about making models or conducting experiments are procedural texts.

Non-narrative texts

This category includes dictionaries, thesauruses, encyclopaedias and at-lases. It also includes alphabet books, counting books and simple word books as well as those which provide facts through a combination of pictures and personal accounts. Expositionary texts which describe, explain and present arguments within their text are another, more complex, form of non-narrative information book. They may contain a considerable amount of text and make substantial demands on young readers. However they are likely to be of most use in providing new information and extending the children's understanding of a topic.

Criteria for selecting books for the school, the class and the individual across the 3–8 age range

Good books for young children are written by authors and illustrators who care about what children read, have something worth while to say, are committed to writing well and are concerned about the quality of young children's encounters with print. In good books, the illustrations and the language unite to capture the reader's attention and support the child in his attempts to read. They can be read and reread by adults and children, revealing something new at each reading (Meek, 1982).

Not every book that is offered to children needs to be a modern classic, but as more than 5,000 books for children are published each year and added to the backlist of 35,000 children's books in print, teachers can be selective about the books they buy and recommend to children. They are in a good position to apply as many of the following criteria as they wish to the selection of books for school.

Criteria for selecting and examining individual books

Is the external appearance of the book attractive? Will it encourage the potential reader to look beyond the cover? Is the book well written? Does it contain a story that is worth reading? Is it inspiring, entertaining or thought provoking? Is the story coherent and convincing? Is the language vivid yet accessible to young readers? Can today's readers identify and sympathize with the characters? Are the moral and social assumptions in the text positive and constructive? Are the illustrations of good quality? Do the illustrations enhance and support the text? Is it a book that children will like? Do I like it? Will the book contribute to the breadth, balance, range and variety of the present book collection?

More specifically: What positive attitudes does this book present to children about the lives of girls and women, boys and men? Are girls shown as active, assertive, autonomous, clever, competent and successful at home, at play, in school? Are women shown at work outside the home? Are boys and men shown as enjoying caring, working and responsible roles or quiet pursuits in the home? Are girls and women shown as equal in importance to boys and men? Are male and female figures shown to be co-operating, working and playing together? Are there positive images of people from a diversity of cultures? Do children and adults with disabilities take active roles in the book? How far does it offer a fair representation of the world in the 1990s? How far does it represent the experiences of the children in this school?

Specific criteria for selecting information books

Many of the criteria referred to in the previous section also apply here but there are some additional considerations about the choice of non-fiction books for very young children. They should ● look inviting ● be clearly laid out ● contain a factually reliable summary of information about the subject appropriate to the age and knowledge of the pupils ● introduce key words and technical language in context ● contain the key features of information texts such as a list of contents, index, glossary and headings ● have illustrations, diagrams, photographs or drawings which complement, extend and explain the written text ● be free of bias, stereotyping and misrepresentation ● make reference to disturbing as well as cosy aspects of subjects, for example, controversial practices related to farming ● help young learners to organize their existing knowledge and provide unfamiliar information to extend what is already known.

Considerations about the overall collection of books in school

When selecting individual books, teachers are often conscious of the omissions and strengths of the overall collection of books in school. They will want to maintain a balanced, varied and attractive stock which is suited to the needs and interests of all the children. In order to create a balanced collection it may be necessary to discard some books and purchase others. Books which are worn or damaged should be thrown away, as should those that are now irrelevant or inaccurate. Increasingly we have come to recognize that books containing racist or sexist narratives or images, or which suggest that one cultural group is superior to another, have nothing to offer children in the classroom. Indeed, they can damage young children's belief in themselves as individuals and as learners, and limit their aspirations. Most professionals involved in education now believe that they should play a part in countering the racial and sexual stereotypes that abound in the world outside schools and that one way of doing this is by actively promoting carefully chosen books containing positive images of all children. The list that follows takes account of the need for schools to provide children with non-stereotypical material and a balanced selection of books. When appraising one's existing stock it might be helpful to use the following list to discover any gaps and to highlight one's priorities for future purchases.

Main characters ● female/male ● black/white ● working class/ middle class ● young/old ● disabled/able bodied ● active/quiet; *content*: ● fiction/non-fiction ● fantasy/real life ● traditional/new

- conflict free/conflict • sad or unresolved/happy endings
- serious/light hearted • timeless/current; *setting*: • urban/
suburban/rural • Africa/Asia/Australasia/America/Europe • nuc-
lear family/single-parent family/extended family/other family groups
- domestic/outdoors; *illustrations*: • photos/drawings/paintings/
cartoons • detailed/impressionistic/bold/sensitive; *language*: • re-
petitive/non-repetitive • wordless/simple text/longer text • dual
language/single language • rhyming/non-rhyming; *values*: • positive,
co-operation, compassion, success, sensitivity, bravery, fear, anxiety,
love, care, independence; *style*: • simple, sincere, authentic, relevant,
humorous.

All teachers will need to be aware of the sorts of books that can be
offered to children, as an important part of their role is to help children to
make choices about reading material. At times the teacher will need to
extend the range of books that the child is reading, suggest more books
that appear to match the child's current interest and increase or reduce
the difficulty level of the books for the child. Teachers do this by sharing,
guiding, suggesting and promoting good books. In order to be able to
recommend a wide and rich reading journey for all children teachers
need to be familiar with all the books in the classroom. They need to be
aware of the demands they make on readers, their subject matter and
other books by the same author. Keeping up to date with books that are
available is an important, time-consuming but often delightful part of
every teacher's role. As well as reading children's books, teachers can
keep up to date through reading book reviews, sharing information with
colleagues, attending book exhibitions and visiting bookshops and children's libraries.

Promoting books

Using the book stock

Having a range of carefully selected books is important but teachers have
actively to promote the books if they are to be used to their full potential
in the classroom. As Klein (1986) wrote, 'resources . . . cannot in themselves teach the pupils'. The teacher's own enthusiasm and knowledge
about books plays a great part in influencing children's attitudes and
interests but there are also a great many practical ways of encouraging
children to read and use the book stock in the class and in the school
library. What follows is a list of suggestions for developing children's
interest in books and for promoting books in school:

- Have a variety of books in the classroom. Don't forget joke books,
recipe books and poetry.
- Make sure that the books are interestingly, attractively and accessibly
displayed; that they are in good condition and clearly organized.

- Regularly change the books that are displayed.
- Have a comfortable, welcoming, inviting reading area in the classroom.
- Read regularly to the class.
- Have commercial and home-made taped stories available with the appropriate books. Keep a stock of blank tapes available for children who wish to record favourite stories.
- Have books available that span a range of difficulty levels.
- Include books written and published by the children in the book displays and library area.
- Use adults, parents, helpers, visitors and other children to share books.
- Have specific times such as silent or quiet reading periods set aside for reading.
- Make time for children to share opinions with others about books they have read at home and at school.
- Have classwork that links with books and culminates in the production of a class book which can be placed in the library.
- Discover individual children's reading interests and recommend titles that will appeal.
- Make sure children take books home.
- Organize a book week every year.
- Organize a book club.
- Have a book sale of second-hand books once a year. Make sure it is well publicized and start collecting early.
- Use the school library for story times and for class projects.
- Organize visits to the public library.
- Introduce new books at assembly time or class-sharing times.
- Make a display of new books.
- Half read a book, ask the children to predict the ending then offer the book to the children for reading in their own time.
- Offer inspection copies of books to children to evaluate.
- Make displays of each chapter of the class book as it is read.
- Organize story-telling or story-reading sessions for groups of children. The teller or reader can be an adult or an older or more confident reader.
- Be alert to children's book programmes on the TV or radio and sometimes match the book that is read to children in class with these.
- Have a 'Book of the Week' display. After reading this the children could write or draw a response to go on to the display.
- Play games based on books. For example, 'I'm thinking of a book in which the young girl is ill and has to stay at home with her dad . . . I wonder who can guess which book I'm thinking of . . . ?'
- Use extracts from books on computer programs such as TRAY.
- Use computer programs that are based on books.
- Begin and add to a large chart listing good books as and when children mention them.
- Have a puppet box to provide opportunities for children to act out stories and repeat the language of books.

- Before buying books for the class ask the children, 'What is the best book you have read?', to give you an indication of what to buy.
- Put some of the children's book reviews inside the back covers of books for others to read.
- Have a class discussion, such as 'If you could only take one book to a desert island, which would it be?'
- Have a permanent display board for children to pin up their spontaneous book reviews and for others to display their responses.
- Use author-bank videos.
- Invite more confident readers to read to the class.

Story times

These are often the most valuable times for promoting children's interest in books. Traditionally story time occurs at the end of the day or at the end of each session in the nursery, but there are sound reasons for introducing story times at the beginning of sessions so that children can follow up a story with activities that relate to it. Alternatively, a story read in its entirety the previous afternoon can be discussed at the beginning of the next day and used as the starting point for a series of story-based activities. In the course of a week a teacher will probably select a range of stories that offer children opportunities for personal, social, intellectual and language development, that are varied in content, style and length and that appeal to the children she teaches. It is at story time that the teacher's enthusiasm for books is transmitted regularly to children. Her choices of books and the way in which she reads or tells the story will do much to affect children's attitudes to books, authors and reading.

Telling and reading stories to children is a real art. One only has to listen to and watch professional story tellers to realize how inadequate one's own performance is and what a spellbinding experience it can be. Listening to and watching actors telling or reading stories on TV, radio and story tapes can provide teachers with ideas about how to share stories well. Sharing stories with children is a communicative activity, bringing together the teller and the listener and enabling the teller to respond to the feedback he receives from the audience. It depends not only on the use of the voice, including clarity, projection, level, varieties, intonation, pace and the use of pauses, but also on the use of a whole range of facial expressions and gesture. This means that story times can be particularly valuable for children with special needs and those whose home language is not English. There are a few guidelines that may help to convince children that stories are extraordinary and that make story time a truly magical time for children and adults.

Selecting the story: • choose a story that you like or enjoy • make sure that you are familiar with the story • make sure that what you have prepared is appropriate for the audience • consider where you will be able to use sound effects, emphasis and repetition • prepare and use props such as puppets or examples of items that are mentioned in the story.

Before the reading or telling: • ask the children to look at the cover, title and author of the book • ask for the children's ideas about the content and the characters • make links with stories they have previously encountered • explain any words that may not be understood • ensure that you have the children's full attention before beginning the story.

During the reading or telling: • do not be afraid to take a risk; children enjoy something different • allow the children time to respond and use their contributions by incorporating them into the story • encourage the children to examine the illustrations to enrich their understanding of the story • leave plenty of time for story sessions • do not rush to finish the story; pauses and silences can be very effective for creating tension and drama • involve the children by keeping them guessing, asking them what they think might happen next and by encouraging them to help with props and sound effects • if you are sharing a story in episodes, summarize with the children what has happened so far before beginning the next session • enjoy yourself and so will the children.

After the story has been shared: • give the children the opportunity to express their opinions and reactions • take the children through the illustrations again • provide opportunities for the children to re-create or retell the story orally • place the book in a prominent place in the classroom so that the children can read or browse through it at their leisure • if a tape of the story is available place this and the book in the listening area • ask a group of children to create story visuals for the book so that the story can be retold and enjoyed in a different way.

Reading stories is important and enjoyable but telling stories allows even more contact between the adult and the audience, so using some of these suggestions teachers might sometimes consider telling rather than reading stories.

Activities to foster responses to books

Activities that are based on books that are shared with and known to children can • promote children's interest in books • extend their enjoyment of stories • enable children to express and develop their responses to text • encourage children to approach books critically • foster reflection.

They can be used by teachers when they are planning to meet the requirements of the Programme of Study for reading which specifies that children at Key Stages 1 and 2 should be able to 'understand and respond to stories and poems' and 'evaluate the texts they read' (DfE, 1995a).

The following activities can be used with a range of books. The majority are suitable for use across the 3–8 age range but their success may vary according to the children's experience of stories and the books that are selected. The activities will become increasingly successful as the children become more familiar with them.

Discussion and questions

All stories can be followed by a discussion and questions. This may take the form of comparing the events in the story with the children's own experience, for example how does the action described in *Mum's Strike* (Ritter, 1988) compare with events in their own homes? Or, after reading *Phoebe and the Hot Water Bottles* (Furchgott and Dawson, 1977), one might ask whether the children have ever received a present they did not want and what has been their favourite present. When asking questions adults need to be careful that discussion times do not become quizzes about how well children have been listening, but that they are genuine starting points for exploring the story.

To vary the format of these sessions the children can sometimes be asked to discuss their answers to questions that the teacher has asked about the story in pairs or groups. The questions can be written on a flip chart and the children given 10 minutes discussion time before they report back to the class.

Collections

It can be useful to use a collection of objects related to the story when sharing a story with children. This is especially useful if the story contains unfamiliar vocabulary or experiences that are distant from the children's lives. Real objects may help to increase children's understanding of the story and extend their vocabulary. The collection might also contain items related to the subject or the issue that is being raised. After using the items during the story session, the collection could be used to make a display and the objects labelled in English and other languages known to the children in the class.

Retelling the story

Children can retell a story in a number of different ways. It can be done orally as children take turns to recall an episode from the story. It can be done using role play, puppets, cut-out figures on a magnet board, or by using models of the characters. The objects that form part of a story collection can also be used. Sometimes children can be asked to retell the story by identifying four significant elements in the story. These can be recorded in the same order that they occurred in the book using pictures or words and pictures. All these activities can be done individually or in pairs. They help children to consider story structure, language, characterization and content. Retelling a dual-narrative story where the words and the illustrations tell different stories can be an exacting and revealing activity. Retelling a wordless story can be a stimulating talk activity for a group of children. The teacher might want the children to use books without words as a stimulus for writing. One way of organizing this is to ask groups of children to rehearse orally the dialogue that could accompany the pictures in the book. They could then draw some of the pictures, adding speech bubbles containing the dialogue that they had composed. Written retellings could be incorporated into a large book of class stories or made into individual books. When asking children to retell the story it is important that the book is presented carefully, time is given for the children to discuss the events and issues contained in the story and for them to rehearse orally their retelling so that they will be able to remember the events and their sequence in the story.

Role play

The role-play area can be transformed into the setting for a favourite or important story. This can provide children with the opportunity to explore the characters and repeat and adapt the action. By asking the children to make a large window for the home corner, this could easily become the setting for *Through My Window* (Bradman, 1986). During their play the children could experiment with the roles of Jo and people she sees during her day at home. With the addition of a wicker basket or a cardboard box painted by the children to resemble a large toy box, the home corner could become the setting for *Bet You Can't!* (Dale, 1987). Involving the children in the production of props can give them further opportunities to reflect on the story.

Visits and visitors

These are another way of bringing stories to life for young children. They can extend the story, give children a deeper understanding of the book and create real opportunities for using the language contained in the book. After listening to *Mrs Lather's Laundry* (Ahlberg, 1981a) groups of children could visit a local launderette to observe it in use. They might have prepared questions to ask of the person in charge of the launderette. Afterwards they might compare what they had found out during their visit with the events in the book. They could also write to the launderette manager to say thank you for his or her help. As a follow-up to *The Baby's Catalogue* (Ahlberg and Ahlberg, 1982), a carer who has recently had a baby might be asked to come in to talk and answer questions about the preparations for the birth and the items she uses for the care of the baby. Some of these items could have been introduced to the children when the book was read with them, and after the visit they could be placed in the home corner to stimulate role play.

Writing a sequel

Some stories are part of a published series, for example *Through My Window* (Bradman, 1986) was followed by *Wait And See* (1988) and *In A Minute* (1990). Reading all three could give rise to a discussion about further events that could form part of Jo's life and the children could produce their own book about the further adventures of Jo. The children could write replies to the letters that are delivered in *The Jolly Postman* (Ahlberg and Ahlberg, 1986) or they could write about what happened after the original letters were received. Sequels to individual class favourites can also be written, perhaps during a shared-writing session.

Book reviews

These are sometimes considered difficult for young children to write, but if the activity is clearly defined most children can successfully review some of the books they read. Children can review books orally after a period of quiet reading. They can paint or draw a picture representing one of the scenes from their favourite book and write the title, author's name and a caption on their poster, such as 'THIS IS A GREAT READ! READ IT TODAY'. This could be displayed in the book area.

During a close-observation drawing session children can carefully copy the cover of their current book and at the bottom of the picture draw the

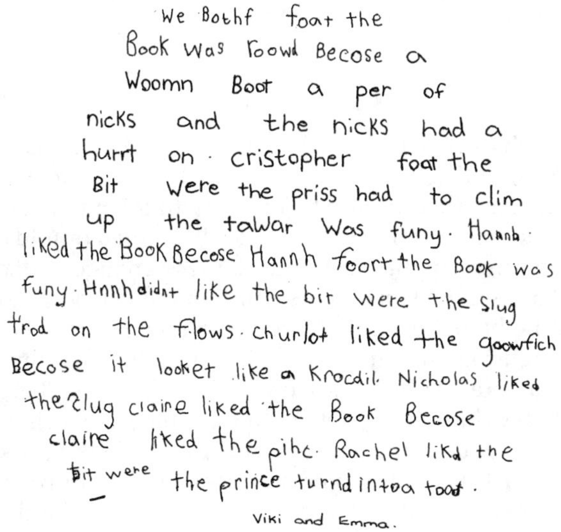

We Bothf foat the Book Was roowd Becose a Woomn Boot a per of nicks and the nicks had a hurrt on cristopher foat the Bit Were the priss had to clim up the talwar Was funy. Hannh liked the Book Becose Hannh foort the Book was funy. Hnnh didnt like the bit were the slug trod on the flows. churlot liked the goowfich Becose it looket like a Krocdil. Nicholas liked the slug claire liked the Book Becose claire liked the pihc. Rachel likd the bit were the prince turnd intoa toad.

Viki and Emma.

Figure 5.1 Book review

number of stars that they thought it merited. More experienced writers could be asked to review one of the books they had read recently giving three reasons why others should read it or, if appropriate, three reasons why others should not read it. Pictorial or written book reviews could be published in a book of reviews, displayed on a chart for others to read or hung up as a mobile in the library area at child-eye level. Over a period of time the children could compile a data base on the computer containing details of books that had been read by the class. From time to time this could be printed out and children could see the most and least popular books and authors in the class.

Author study

The books of an author, such as Anthony Browne or Pat Hutchins, who has written a number of books for young readers, could be used as the basis for a class exploration of books. The teacher might collect and display all the books by this author. Each book could be read with the children and some of the activities described in this section used to examine the books in detail. The children might be asked to find out as much as they could about the writer and this could involve searching through book catalogues as well as writing letters to publishers and to the author. If the author could visit the class as part of the project this would be ideal. The project might be drawn to a close by asking groups of children to compile a list of questions about the author and the author's books for their peers to answer; it could then end with a class quiz.

Exploring language

Using books such as *A Dark, Dark Tale* (Brown, 1981) and *Don't Forget the Bacon* (Hutchins, 1976), the children could be asked to remember the repeated sequences of words and to join in with them when they occur in the story. On another occasion the story could be read or told omitting the refrain. The children might discuss how these changes affect the story. After reading a rhyming story to the children the teacher could write out the words of the book omitting every other line of text. The class could read this through together and then think up their own lines that fitted into the text. Before reading *Each Peach Pear Plum* (Ahlberg, 1978) the teacher could play the game 'I Spy' with the children. During the reading the class could play the game with the illustrations in the book. The large-format version of this book would be ideal for this purpose. Using an alphabet book such as *A, B, C, I Can Be* (Wilkins, 1993), the children could look at initial letters of words and make up a similar alphabet frieze based on the names of the children in the class and their friends. This helps in the learning of letter sounds and names and in becoming familiar with alphabetical ordering.

Exploring messages in books

Some books contain messages about important issues within their stories. Gender stereotyping is explored in books, such as *William's Doll* (Zolotow, 1972), *Princess Smartypants* (Cole, 1986), *Henry's Baby* (Hoffman, 1993) and *Piggybook* (Browne, 1986). Reading one of these books to the class and following this with a discussion can be a valuable way of exploring ideas and issues with young children. After reading *Piggybook* the children could be asked questions such as: What is a piggyback? Look at the front cover of the book. Who is giving a piggyback to whom? What does this make us think the book is about? What does 'pigs might fly' mean on the inside cover?

These initial questions might be followed by going through the book and making a list of the images of pigs that occur in the book. In groups the children could be asked to think of words that are used to describe girls, boys, women and men.

Finally the children could be asked, 'What do you think *Piggybook* is about?' 'What do you think about this?' As part of the process of understanding the message contained in the book the children might be asked to write to a character in the book expressing empathy, giving advice or stating an opinion about his or her actions. Other representations in books of girls, boys, women and men could be examined and the children could be asked to retell or rewrite a familiar story changing the sex or actions of some of the characters.

Rewriting a story

Children can rewrite or retell a story using a different starting point from that used by the author. For example *Rosie's Walk* (Hutchins, 1970) could be rewritten from the fox's perspective, beginning 'One day I saw a hen in the farmyard . . .' Using *On The Way Home* (Murphy, 1982) each child could write an account of the grazed knee in the role of one of the characters in the book. They might begin and continue their account with phrases such as 'My friend told me that . . . , but I think . . . , because . . .' Activities such as these can help to develop empathy and understanding of different perspectives.

Organizing a book week

A special week, devoted to books, can help children to become more informed about books and stimulate them into reading more widely. A school book week can help to reinforce the idea that reading can be exciting, stimulating and informative. Organizing a successful book week needs a great deal of prior planning as authors, illustrators, story tellers, book sales and displays provided by local bookshops need to be booked and organized well ahead. The *Children's Bookweek Handbook* available from Young Book Trust provides up-to-date and detailed information on all aspects of organizing a book week for a school. Any of the activities outlined in this section could be usefully incorporated into a week devoted to books.

Games based on books

Who am I?

One child thinks of a character from a book and gives the class a brief description, the children then have to try to guess who it is and what book the character comes from. For example a child might say, 'I am a girl who wants to be a star in the school concert. Who am I?' (*Amazing Grace*; Hoffman, 1991). Alternatively, after the first child has selected the character the rest of the class take turns to ask him questions, such as 'Are you a girl?', 'Are you an animal?', 'Do you go to school?', in order to identify the character. They may only be given yes or no answers to their questions.

Snap

Each child needs to make two identical playing cards. On one side they should draw a character from a book they know well and on the other side write the title of the book in which the character appears. The cards are used to play a conventional game of 'Snap', using a match between the words, the pictures or either. A set of similar cards but blank on one side can be used to play matching games such as 'Pelmanism' or 'Memory'.

Lotto

In order to make this game the children need to divide a piece of A4 card into four sections. In each section they should draw a character or a scene from a book. On smaller pieces of card that will each cover one section of the playing board the children should write the title of the book or the name a character they have drawn. Four boards are needed to play the game. One player reads the title or name of the character from the small cards and the other players look for the match on their lotto boards. A variant that is particularly useful for very young children is to ask the children to draw four items or characters from a book that they know well, as described above. Before they colour these in the A4 boards are photocopied. The children should then colour their boards and the photocopies taking care to use identical colours. The photocopies are cut into four pieces and used to cover the cards when the lotto game is played.

I read a book . . .

In turn the children think of a book, author or character beginning with each letter of the alphabet. For example, 'I read a book called *Anancy and*

Mr Dry-Bone' (French, 1991). 'I read a book written by Anthony Browne.' This activity could arise from or lead on to making an alphabet frieze based on books in class.

There are a great many activities and games that can arise from stories. Books containing more ideas are listed in the further reading at the end of this chapter.

Using non-fiction

Reading non-fiction can be enjoyable, entertaining and satisfying, particularly if one is reading a text that matches a current interest and some information texts are both informative and visually sumptuous. Consequently, many of the suggestions made in the previous section can be applied to non-fiction as well as story books. However there is also a need to consider information books separately. The texts that are read most often by the teacher and the children in early-years classes are stories and, although non-fiction is available, it is usually given a lower profile in the classroom. Reading in order to obtain information and reading to learn are important uses of reading. Reading in this way is also vital for functioning effectively in a literate society and within a learning environment such as school. Using books for learning gives children an important message about print; they will be able to see that print is permanent and can be returned to and reread until one understands the information it contains.

Key features of information texts

The appearance and presentation of text in information books differs substantially from that of story books as do the reader's purposes for reading them. Stories tend to follow an accepted structure, often contain characteristic phrases and tend to use familiar vocabulary. Information books have a different set of features to guide the reader and to help him understand facts. The number and use of organizing features of information texts vary, often according to the length and nature of the book, but all information books contain some of these features. Among the typical key features of information books for young readers are

- an introductory summary of what the book contains
- a description of the characteristics of the object, event or process
- text arranged around the key processes, stages or events
- a comparison of the information in the book with what might be known already
- a final summary
- an afterword containing extra information
- the use of retrieval devices such as a list of contents, index, glossary and headings.

(Adapted from Pappas, 1986; Mallet, 1992.)

These features are important because they guide readers through the text and are intended to help them to understand and use the book easily. However in order for readers to make use of these aids to understanding, they need to be aware of why they are there and how they are helpful. If these devices are to be used to help with reading their use needs to be explained and taught to children.

The difficulties with information texts

Because of the emphasis on story books in the early-years classroom, children are usually less familiar with this genre of text than they are with narrative. They are not always aware of the purposes of the structural devices they contain or with reading only parts rather than all of a book. Consequently many children do experience difficulties with reading and using information texts efficiently. If children are to use non-fiction texts to gain new information they need to be shown the purpose of these types of texts, they need to be introduced to the features and organization of information books and to understand how these guide the reader through the text. They also need to become more familiar with reading an impersonal style of writing and the use of sometimes unfamiliar and technical language that these books contain. Finally children need to be taught how to use the information that they discover.

Helping children to read and use information books

Using information books effectively has to begin with an understanding of their function. Children need to understand that they are a resource for learning, that if they wish to pursue an interest, explore an idea or discover the answer to a question an information book may be able to help them. The best way of illustrating this is for the teacher to model ways of reading and understanding information texts. Sharing non-fiction with children gives the teacher the opportunity to show children how many information books present an overview of a subject. This may include information that is already familiar to them but may also include new facts or ideas. Reading the list of contents, looking quickly through the book and reading the headings gives the reader a good idea about the range of information that the book contains. Then one can make a choice either to read the sections which look useful or interesting or to read the whole book. One can also reject a book because it does not fit one's purpose. If a book does not contain anything new or useful then it is not necessary to continue to read it. Using books in this way necessitates learning a new set of reading skills. Children who are used to reading fiction will not be familiar with reading selectively and often think that it is wrong to read in this way, but this is the key to making best use of non-fiction.

Neate (1992) suggests that the best time to teach the skills needed to read information texts is in the infant school. Teachers need to show children how to find the book that they need for a particular purpose, to appraise books quickly by using the cover, title, list of contents, index, headings and subheadings, to scan the book to locate the section that they want, to skim through the pages that they think will be useful and carefully to read the parts which contain relevant information. Finally children may need to be shown that new information extends what is already known and is a way of learning.

Teaching children to read non-fiction involves modelling and explaining the skills that are needed and giving children regular opportunities to practise these skills. Used during thematic work, the following suggestions, adapted from Mallet (1992), should help children to become familiar with and to use information books:

- Begin by discussing the topic with the children, find out what is already known and what the children want to know, identify possible areas for investigation.
- Providing the children with a tangible starting point for the investigation such as a visit, a display, a video or a talk from a visitor can stimulate some children into identifying a focus.

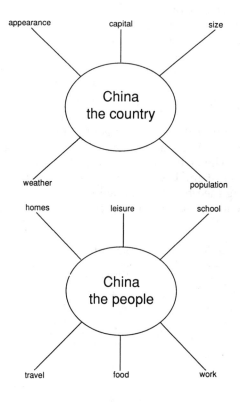

Figure 5.2 China

- Give the children a direction and purpose for their investigation by working with them to compile a list of questions about what they want to know.
- Teach and demonstrate ways of reading and understanding information texts.
- Introduce the children to ways of accessing and recording the information contained in non-fiction texts through using charts and diagrams.
- Provide opportunities for the children to share their findings with others in discussion.
- Show children how to make use of their findings through recording them for use or sharing them with others in oral presentations, writing, books, models or displays.

The following examples of introductory work with information books are taken from work in a class of Year 1 and Year 2 pupils. The first example (Figure 5.2) shows the initial activity which followed on from reading an information book about life in China (Flint, 1993) to the class The teacher began by recording what the information book had told the class about China.

After compiling these two charts from the book the children went on to consider which aspects of life in China are similar to life in Britain and which are different. They began with a chart like the one that appears in Table 5.1 and used their own experience and other information books to extend and complete the chart.

The question at the end of the chart was the starting point for reading other books about China, food and Britain. The results of the investigations could have been displayed in the form of a Venn diagram showing all the similarities and differences that the children had managed to discover. Some children did use the people in China diagram to identify what they wanted to know about life in China. One child began to investigate where and when Chinese people took their holidays. He had identified his own interest and had a real purpose for reading other information texts. By starting the project with a whole-class session, reading an information book with the children and constructing two simple diagrams

Table 5.1 Food and drink in China and Britain

Food and drink	China	Britain
noodles	yes	yes
rice	yes	yes
chicken	yes	yes
fish	yes	yes
pork	yes	yes
tea	yes	yes
rice wine	yes	no
beer	yes	yes

What other food and drink are found in China and Britain?

Table 5.2 'Play'

Game	What you need	Number of players	Where to play it
marbles	marbles	2+	inside/outside
bombadiers	marbles	2+	outside
brown girl in the ring	people/song	lots	outside
hopscotch	chalk, stone	2+	outside
slide	slide	1	outside
higher and higher	skipping rope	3+	outside
jacks	jacks	2+	
people puzzle	people	4+	
grandmother's footsteps	people	3+	
giant's footsteps		1+	outside
follow my leader	people	3+	

with the class, the teacher had introduced children to one way of using non-fiction texts, had demonstrated how to organize the information this text contained and had provided a structure and a starting point for the further use of information texts.

The next example (Table 5.2), arising from work in the same class, is of a chart constructed after the teacher had read an information text about games with the children (Deshpande, 1988). This was used during a theme on 'Play'. The intention was to play the games so those that were not fully explained in the book were investigated further using books and interviews with other people.

The final example (Figure 5.3 and 5.4) is of a class dictionary made by Year 1 children. It was inspired by *The Baby's Catalogue* (Ahlberg and Ahlberg, 1982). When making this book the children considered the use and format of published dictionaries and realized that they provide definitions of words as well as correct spellings. They also used some of the features of information books, such as an index, to make their dictionary easy to use.

These examples and the suggestions outlined in this section indicate how teachers can extend children's repertoire and application of reading. They are in keeping with the requirements of English in the National Curriculum (DfE, 1995a, p. 6) which states that at Key Stage 1 children 'should be encouraged to make use of a range of sources of information, including dictionaries, . . . encyclopaedias and information presented in fictional form', they should 'be taught to use reference materials for different purposes' and 'about the structural devices for organising information, *eg contents, headings, captions*' (*ibid.*, p. 8). At Key Stage 2 children are expected to be able to skim and scan and should be taught to

- pose pertinent questions about a topic they are investigating;
- identify the precise information they wish to know;
- distinguish between fact and fiction;
- consider an argument critically;
- make succinct notes;

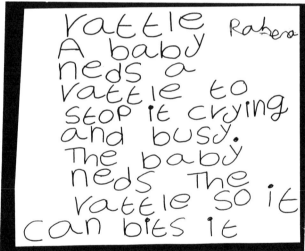

Figure 5.3   Baby Catalogue R

- use dictionaries, glossaries and thesauruses to explain unfamiliar vocabulary;
- note the meaning and use of newly encountered words;
- re-present information in different forms.

(*Ibid.*, p. 14)

Teaching children about non-fiction texts and developing their reading skills is best undertaken in the context of a theme. This can give children a

Author Index

Anh - May	11,18,25
Asvi	2
Claude	2,20
Craig	32
David	3,10,33
Grant	17
Joe	16,23
Jason	23
Loui	2,29
Michelle	14,22
Marcus	15,16
Marwa	18,26
Nicola	5,7,20
Rymell	12
Rahena	24
Sezgin	1,6
Shereen	27
Samantha	30
Tahdi	7,24
Toks	19
Yasmin	4

Figure 5.4   Baby Catalogue Index

real purpose for using the books and provide opportunities for using the information they discover. Most, if not all, themes will lend themselves to the use of different types of information books and, with careful planning, the development and application of reading.

Using books as a starting point for a theme

Using one book or a number of books as the starting point for a theme can be a very productive way to promote books and reading and to extend children's knowledge about and use of books, as well as offering opportunities for learning across the curriculum. What follows is an example of the initial planning undertaken in preparation for a theme based on a collection of carefully chosen books. The actual choice of books could make the theme appropriate for any age group in the early years.

The aims for the theme: To ● promote reading   ● extend the children's awareness of different types of books   ● give children practice at reading different types of writing   ● explore familiar and unfamiliar experiences, events, ideas and issues through reading   ● extend children's learning in all areas of the curriculum; *The criteria for the selection of books to be used during this theme are*:   ● variety of type   ● variety of authors ● variety of illustrative styles   ● books containing positive images of reading   ● books that will lead to work in all curriculum areas.

ENGLISH	MUSIC	SCIENCE
story structure characterisation writing reviews writing letters retelling stories making story tapes presenting work orally exploring book language library skills alphabetical order response to books	writing and making music to accompany stories and drama arising from books	investigations using books as a starting point cooking testing writing implements testing paper making paper

GEOGRAPHY
exploring the location of stories routes

BOOKS

TECHNOLOGY		MATHEMATICS
finding out about how books are made making pop-up, flap and zig zag books making games based on books models developed from books		measuring books charts & graphs of favourite books, authors, illustrators & subjects classifying & sorting books making board games keeping a tally of books read

ART
making book covers using different techniques·- printing, marbling, examining illustrations
illustrating books

HISTORY		I.T.
as represented in books and stories the development of books and printing personal history books reading diaries sequencing arising from books		constructing databases of favourite books word processing programmes based on books and stories

P.E.
gym and dance based on stories

Figure 5.5   Theme – 'Books'

Books to be used: • *How a Book is Made* (Aliki, 1986) • *I Like Books* (Browne, 1988) • *My Book* (Maris, 1983) • *Piggybook* (Browne, 1986) • *The True Story of the Three Little Pigs* (Scieszka, 1989) • *Tell Me A Story, Mama* (Johnson, 1989) • *K Is For Kiss Good Night* (Sardegna, 1994) • *The Jolly Postman* (Ahlberg and Ahlberg, 1986) • *Prince Cinders* (dual-language version) (Cole, 1987) • *Marcellus' Birthday Cake* (Simeon, 1992) • *Sunshine* (Ormerod, 1981) • *Miss Fanshawe and the Great Dragon Adventure* (Scullard, 1986) • plus a selection of story tapes, story videos and author videos (see Figure 5.5).

The theme could begin with a display of the books which had been selected. As different aspects of the theme were explored each book from the display could be shared and used with the class. After exploring some or all of the books in the initial collection the children could add their favourites and follow some of their own interests, perhaps by looking at a number of books by one author or examining a collection of poetry books. During the theme many of the activities outlined in this chapter could be used. The theme might also include a visit to the local library, a visit by a mobile library, a story session provided by a librarian and the book area in the classroom could become a library with an issue desk for the duration of the theme.

Conclusion

Literacy is prized in a literate society for two reasons: it is necessary for functioning in daily life, to perform tasks that range from selecting a greeting card to reading the situations vacant column in the newspaper. Secondly, it is a rewarding and enjoyable activity in its own right. If teachers are to meet the present and future needs and interests of all the children they work with they need to be as familiar with as many books for young children as possible and actively to promote books in school. If they do this they will be helping to foster a life-long use and enjoyment of reading with the young children they teach.

Suggestions for further reading

Ellis, G. and Brewster, J. (1991) *The Storytelling Handbook for Primary Teachers*, Penguin Books, Harmondsworth.
Hester, H. (1983) *Stories in the Multilingual Classroom*, Harcourt Brace Jovanovich, London.
Meek, M. (1988) *How Texts Teach What Children Learn*, The Thimble Press, Stroud.
Sylvester, R. (1991) *Start with a Story*, Development Education Centre, Birmingham.

Chapter 6

Bilingual learners

Introduction

The kind of good practice described elsewhere in this book forms the basis for working on the development of language with all young children. However children who start school with more competence in a language other than English may need additional support in order to become confident users of English. This chapter describes activities that are appropriate to fostering the development of oral language, reading and writing with young bilingual learners. As Britain is now a multilingual and multicultural society this chapter also explores some of the issues that are pertinent to all schools that wish to provide a curriculum that is relevant to the needs of their pupils as citizens of the twentieth and twenty-first centuries.

The background

Terminology

The children who are referred to in this chapter may be bilingual, trilingual or multilingual. The term bilingual is used to mean a speaker who is developing competence in more than one language. The exact definition is likely to vary as each bilingual pupil's proficiency in and use of two or more languages is likely to vary depending on context, audience and experience.

Throughout this chapter the terms first language, home language, preferred language, community language and heritage language are used to describe ● the first language a child speaks ● the language used at home ● the language in which the user is most competent ● the language of the community.

The words first, home, preferred, community and heritage are used in their broadest senses to describe the language the child has most competence in when starting school. In some instances the term that is used may not always accurately reflect the complex language repertoire of any one child and it may cover more than one of these categories. For example, at home one or more first languages, including English, may be understood and spoken if members of the household use different languages. These terms are not intended to stereotype children's experience, to attribute undue status to the developing language or to imply any limitation in language competence.

The context

Many British citizens are bilingual or multilingual and are able to speak English and at least one other language including a dialect form of a home language. Languages such as Arabic, Bengali, Cantonese, Greek, Gujarati, Hindi, Italian, Panjabi, Spanish, Turkish, Twi, Urdu, Welsh and Yoruba are familiar to and used by a significant number of young children in Britain today. Some schools may have substantial numbers of bilingual pupils; others may have small groups or individual bilingual pupils.

Developing bilinguals who enter school in Britain may be • British-born children who speak varying amounts of English at home • children who are joining their families in Britain • children whose parents have come to study or work in Britain for a few years • children arriving as refugees.

The suggestions for teaching contained in this chapter apply to all these groups and are intended to provide ideas for those who work with large or small numbers of children who are developing bilingual competence in English.

Bilingualism and the National Curriculum

The National Curriculum for England clearly identifies English as the dominant language. The label 'English' rather than 'language' in the National Curriculum documents symbolizes this dominance and the attitude of policy makers to bilingualism over the past few years. This is of some significance to teachers who work with children who enter school with a language other than English. If children begin school as developing bilinguals then one part of the teacher's responsibility will be to begin the process of introducing children to successive bilingualism by widening their language repertoire to include English. Teachers know that this is important, since the National Curriculum specifically refers to success in English and standard English usage for all children apart from those unable to communicate orally. Pupils who are fluent users of other languages 'should be encouraged to make use of their understanding and skills in other languages when learning English' (DfE, 1995a).

For Welsh children attending school in Wales the requirements are somewhat different. They have the right to a bilingual education and are exempt from the Key Stage 1 Programme of Study for English. The National Curriculum Orders (*ibid.*, p. 2) state that Welsh-speaking children will have developed similar skills in and knowledge about language as monolingual English-speaking pupils, and inform teachers that 'In Wales, the linguistic and cultural knowledge of Welsh-speaking pupils should be recognized and used when developing their competence in English'.

There are some important differences between the statement referring to Welsh bilingual pupils and that which refers to other bilingual pupils. The statement for Welsh children makes provision for continuity in their language learning and acknowledges the importance of Welsh as a language in its own right. Speaking and learning through two languages is officially recognized as a positive advantage and as beneficial to the overall development of both languages. The words that are used imply that teachers of Welsh-speaking pupils have a responsibility to build on their children's existing competence in language. For other bilingual learners their home language appears to be regarded as a stepping stone to English. The link between cultural identity and language is strongly signalled for Welsh speakers, but for speakers of other languages the link between home, community, cultural and religious languages and identity is not acknowledged.

Language development in two or more languages

Some teachers express anxiety about teaching pupils who have a first language other than English. They may feel that in order for children to learn English they need to leave their first language behind and begin to learn how to speak again. To treat young children in this way is to deny three, four or five years of valuable learning of a specific language and of learning about the purposes of language in general, both of which provide a strong foundation for the development of a further language.

Children who have learned one language are already skilled listeners and competent users of language. They are aware of the uses of oracy and they know that its use and form change in relation to audience, context and purpose. They are able to apply their understanding of how meaning is conveyed in the sounds, structure and intonation of language to their learning of English. From their learning of a first language children are intuitively aware that a language is made up of separate words and has a special word order and grammar. When they were learning their first language this took some time to discover, but as learners of a second language they are already aware of the way in which oral language works and are able to apply this knowledge when learning a new language.

Young children who begin to develop a second language at playgroup, nursery or first school have a second advantage as learners of language: they are old enough and physically mature enough to engage with others in meaningful activities that require the use of a common language. The activities and the contexts within which they take place support the development of the new language. Crystal (1987) suggests that 'If the language environment is natural, consistent and stimulating, children will pick up whatever languages are around'.

Not only is the learning of a second language more straightforward than some people believe but it can also be advantageous to the learner. It has been suggested that speakers who are proficient in more than one language have a greater linguistic awareness than monolingual speakers. Through gaining control over two language systems learners may gain an analytical awareness of language which contributes to a more conscious understanding of linguistic patterns, since a first language is acquired unconsciously but a second language is acquired with 'conscious realization and control' (Vygotsky, 1962). One of the findings of the LINC (Language in the National Curriculum) Project was that children's linguistic awareness makes an important contribution to their development as readers and writers.

It is now accepted that acquisition of a second language is not affected if the first language is maintained and supported. Supporting children's home languages helps them to feel valued and gives them the confidence that they will need in order to take the risks and make the mistakes which are necessary when learning and using another language. Indeed there is evidence to suggest that children who feel that their home language is rejected will make less satisfactory progress in English (ILEA, 1990b) and when the first language is suppressed or seen as an obstacle, the linguistic and cognitive gains, outlined earlier in this section, do not occur (Cummins, 1979). Children use language to clarify their understanding and express ideas and this is another reason for encouraging or at least permitting children to use their home language in school. In the early stages of learning English, the children's understanding and use of English may not be sophisticated enough to enable them to think and learn across the curriculum. Bilingual adults or other children may be able to help to explain unfamiliar concepts using children's home languages:

> Where several children speak the same language they should be encouraged to use their preferred language for talking through ideas. It does not confuse the children, on the contrary they are able to move in and out of their home language with an obvious understanding of the needs of their audience.
>
> (Norman, 1990, p. 25)

Developing bilingual children's language competence in English and supporting the development of their first language need not be as problematic as people sometimes fear. This is particularly true if the advantages and the suggestions about the use of a first language to positively develop a second language (that are ascribed to Welsh speakers in the National Curriculum) are extended to other language groups. This statutory advice may help teachers to appreciate the benefits of supporting all first languages at school and to accept that teaching bilingual children does not need to be viewed as disadvantageous for the child or a problem for the teacher.

Providing for bilingual learners

Britain is a multilingual society and provision for all learners, whether bilingual or monolingual, should reflect the diversity of languages and cultures found in Britain today. Schools who receive bilingual pupils will make more provision for them and their needs as learners of English. Such provision should exist, first, at the level of the school as an institution and, secondly, within the classroom. The way in which the school caters for bilingual pupils will be reflected in • the attitude of all the staff to bilingual pupils • school structures and routines   • the general school environment.

Attitudes

The attitudes of staff to young bilingual learners is critical. If teachers dismiss the pupil's home language and the degree of learning that this signifies then they are denying an important part of the young child's identity. A child's first language is part of his history, his relationships, his home, his community and his life experience to date. It is a powerful part of the child and must be accepted and welcomed by schools and teachers. If adults show respect and interest in children's community languages, children will feel that these are valued in the classroom. Children who are fluent in the use of one language at the age of 4 or 5 have accomplished a great deal and have demonstrated an amazing capacity to learn. Some children's knowledge of language will be even greater than this. Many children who begin school able to speak Turkish or Gujarati, for example, will probably also be aware of English. They will have heard it spoken in shops, on the television, in songs and on the radio and they may have noticed it in its written form in the environment. They may also be able to use more than one language at home depending on the person they are talking to or the situation they are in. This is a remarkable achievement and one that should be respected. Remembering this may help adults to avoid holding any unconscious lowered expectations about young bilingual children's potential as learners. Teachers do need to have positive attitudes towards bilingualism if they are to avoid damaging children's confidence as language learners. For bilingual children, the monolingual teacher is a symbol of the majority group and so the way in which a monolingual teacher acknowledges a child's first language is of crucial importance if the child is to feel positive about his identity and his ability to learn language.

School structures and routines

Schools which take the needs of bilingual pupils seriously have a number of procedures in place to facilitate their entry into school and to cater for their needs. These will be reflected in the school language policy and the way in which new parents and new entrants are welcomed. There may be a record of the names of children who share common languages and a list of interpreters which can be consulted by parents and staff if necessary. The school will also have considered the way in which arrangements can be made for interpreters when meetings with carers are arranged.

When bilingual children start school it is important to find out what each one knows, has had experience of and can do in languages other than English in order to plan to accommodate their individual needs. Bilingual learners are not a homogeneous group. Linguistically, socially, culturally and politically their lives and experiences are diverse and individual. They may operate along a continuum of language competences in the home and the community. With approximately 200 distinct language groups forming a significant part of the school population of Britain, many children are going to bring a wealth of diverse linguistic experience to school. The information concerning the children's linguistic background, the languages and dialects that are spoken at home, any previous schooling they may have received either outside or inside Britain and any additional schooling that they are receiving should be entered on their school record and consulted by all the staff who work with the children.

Good home–school links are important for the English language development of bilingual children. When parents understand and see the way in which bilingualism is welcomed in the school, they can support their children more effectively. So wherever possible information about the school, its policies, the curriculum and links between home and school should be available in community languages and given to parents when they first visit the school.

Bilingual parents can become involved in children's education at home and at school. Although the child's parents may not speak English fluently, they will be able to listen to a child as he reads a book and will be able to offer encouragement. They will also be able to tell or read stories to the child using his first language. In school parents may be willing to translate stories, rhymes, signs, labels, letters, notices and children's writing. They may share stories with children by reading, telling, writing or recording them. Some parents might like to teach songs to children or to record these on to tape. They might teach traditional forms of dance, sewing or games. In school parents might also write recipes, cook with the children, help in the home corner, work with children who are writing in community languages and accompany children on school visits. HMI (1990) comment that the help given by parents in producing bilingual resources for schools 'is important not only as a resource for learning but also for recognising the value of children's first language'.

School staff may take the opportunity provided by a bilingual community to learn some of the languages that are used in school, to use bilingual children's expertise to teach counting, greetings, rhymes and songs to the children and to adults or for children to read aloud in their home languages during assemblies. Teachers and parents might organize a language club at lunch time where the children could speak, read and write in their home languages. Children who attended could teach each other and teachers might use the club to learn from the children. All these structures will help to develop self-esteem among bilingual children and encourage all children to respect and appreciate the diversity of languages that exists.

The school environment

This aspect of provision is perhaps the easiest to arrange or change. Reflecting a real commitment to multilingual and multicultural education by representing the home, community and cultural experiences of children in the locality and in Britain today is perhaps the most straightforward aspect of provision. The availability of resources means that teachers only need to make careful selections of resources and ensure that these are used.

Home corners and role-play areas should contain resources that reflect different cultures, such as Chinese cooking utensils, a selection of dressing-up clothes from different parts of the world, including shorts and T-shirts, which are universal forms of clothing, and dolls with the skin tones and features of a variety of ethnic groups. Each classroom should contain games, jigsaws, books and other equipment with multicultural images. Positive images and artifacts from other countries and cultures should form part of displays around the school, as should alphabets, number charts, notices and posters in community languages. Teachers might normally include a repertoire of songs and games from other cultures in classroom activities and give children paints and crayons in all skin-tone colours to use in art sessions. School and individual teacher's curriculum planning should contain reference points which recognize the cultures and histories of all the children in the school.

Developing English in the classroom

Teachers know that regarding and supporting a child's home language is not enough. They are aware that it is important to develop bilingual learners' abilities in all aspects of English because it is   • a legal requirement on schools   • the entitlement of every child attending school in Britain   • the main medium of learning in school   • the way of gaining access to the National Curriculum   • the means by which learning is assessed in the National Curriculum   • a means of socializing with peers   • a vehicle for operating in a wider society   • vital, particularly in later life, for accessing institutional power and achieving social and political rights.

Teaching English to young children takes place within the context of good early-years practice. This begins with establishing what children can do. It is based on an understanding of what the learner brings to the task, giving children the self-confidence necessary for future learning, planning for each child's needs, building on each child's own interests, motivation and strengths, creating meaningful learning situations and helping children to develop their own purposes and strategies for learning. Working with these principles means that the teacher of bilingual pupils has three tasks: first, to recognize that knowledge of a language other than English is an asset; secondly, to support and value children's home languages; and, thirdly, to induct children into the fluent use of oral and written English.

The guidance on the teaching of English to Welsh-speaking pupils at Key Stage 2 in the 1995 National Curriculum orders provides a useful starting point for all teachers concerned with developing bilinguals. It directs teachers to begin with the experiences that each child brings to school and describes a continuous and progressive view of language development. It states that teachers will need to

- build on the English language experiences of the home and of the community at large;
- encourage pupils to transfer their skills in, and knowledge and understanding of, one language to the other;
- draw pupils' attention, in a structured and systematic way, to the similarities and differences between the two languages;
- assist pupils to acquire appropriate terminology that will enable them to discuss those similarities and differences purposefully;
- develop pupils' understanding of the social contexts in which the languages are used;
- provide a variety of reading material, *eg pupils' own work, the media, literature, reference books*, that will highlight these social contexts.

(DfE, 1995a, p. 32)

Organization

Successful teaching depends upon careful organization. Each class needs to provide a positive, secure environment for language learning. The teacher will be sensitive to and aware of the children's linguistic and cultural backgrounds and will create a climate of respect for all languages amongst the children. She will actively promote community and other languages by encouraging the children to use their first language in class, either in groups or individually and allocating some children to act as interpreters. The normal organization of the class will include activities that provide opportunities for the repetition of words and structures of English, practical activities and group work. The learning and teaching of bilingual pupils will be integrated into the normal routines of the class.

Group work is particularly important for children who are learning English. The practical nature of group work generally presents children with contextual and visual support which helps them to understand what they are required to do. Working with English-speaking children presents bilingual learners with a significant opportunity to learn English, as the English speakers in the group provide language models and act as role models for participation. Children want to interact with others and to do this they need to share a common language so, when they are working in groups with children who are using English, they will need, want and begin to develop a language that enables them to participate fully in the group. They will be encouraged to use language for expressing their understanding of activities they are involved in as well as for listening and responding to the contributions of others. The experience that children gain in using language in small groups may give them the confidence to talk in more formal settings such as class discussions. Teachers can support communication in groups by

- allocating sociable and helpful children to work with new children and initiate them into classroom and school routines;
- sitting newcomers with others who share the same first language;
- introducing and explaining tasks clearly before assigning children to groups;
- making the expected outcomes of collaborative work clear before children begin to work;
- ensuring that children often work in collaborative groups or pairs, particularly on activities that require children to talk and to use simple repetitive language;
- arranging for compatible personalities to work together; and
- sometimes having adults working alongside pupils to support their contribution to the group.

Developing oral language

Competence in oral language is signified in two ways: first, through understanding the communicative uses of languages and, secondly, through knowing and being able to use the system of the language, its vocabulary and its grammatical structures. Bilingual speakers will be familiar with the uses and purposes of language from their first language, but will have less familiarity with the system of the new language. Most children have a competent knowledge of the vocabulary and syntax of their first language by the age of 4 or 5 and after this age start to learn how to understand and express new and increasingly subtle meanings. As with first-language acquisition, bilingual learners will need lots of experience of listening as they learn the vocabulary and grammar of English. They may pass through a silent period while they focus on listening to and understanding what they hear. Although this is a silent period, it is an active time, since the words and word order needed for participation in conversations and discussions are being acquired. The silent period is perfectly normal and should not be interpreted as the child having language problems or learning difficulties (Ervin-Tripp,

1978; Krashen and Terell, 1983). The production of the second language emerges in stages. First, the child is likely to respond to others through non-verbal communication, next to communicate with single words such as 'OK', 'me', 'come' and 'see'. Gradually the speaker will begin to combine two and three words, saying such things as 'where go?', 'where go you?' and 'stay here'. These utterances will gradually become longer and show increasing understanding of the accepted word order of the second language, for example 'where you go?' Eventually the child will begin to use complete sentences and increasingly more complex discourse fluently. Throughout each stage the speaker is expressing meaning, but exact grammatical accuracy takes time to develop. Cummins (1984a) suggests that it may take up to two years to acquire face-to-face, context-supported oral communication skills and between five and seven years to use oral language competently in more abstract situations. Inaccuracies do not need direct correction, errors and misunderstandings need to be accepted as the prelude to greater accuracy which will develop as the learner listens and speaks more. Teachers may repeat and expand utterances as adults do with young children who are acquiring a first language. In this way they are signalling that they have understood and are presenting the learner with correct models.

Activities to develop oral language

In order to acquire the full range of skills that competent and confident language users have, the listener needs to understand what is being said and the teacher needs to ensure that the child understands. She can do this by providing visual and contextual support, concrete referents, practical demonstrations and by using eye contact, gesture and repetition in her own conversations, instructions, requests and questions. Speaking an unfamiliar language involves taking risks, risks of getting it wrong, of being misunderstood and of one's attempts being dismissed or ridiculed. Therefore the learner's confidence and motivation are crucial and depend on the teacher creating a positive learning environment.

For children at the initial stages of learning English, simple, structured and supported oral activities are helpful. Later children will be increasingly able to participate in all the daily speaking and listening activities in the classroom such as discussions, report backs, offering opinions and suggestions and working equally with their peers. The following list provides some examples of structured oral activities for use in the early stages of second-language learning: • mime games such as 'Simon Says' involving action and imitation • imaginative play with others, dressing up, the home corner and role play based on familiar stories • collaborative games involving naming and counting such as 'Pelmanism' • sorting, matching and labelling activities • describing activities such as using a feely box • working with others on practical tasks • carrying out tasks with others in the sand and the water • listening to stories in English • joining in retelling stories activities in a group • listening to and joining in with songs and rhymes • listening to class discussions • becoming acquainted with school routines by participating in social activities such as answering the register and accompanying others as message takers • participating in all the regular activities of the school.

The teacher will also look for opportunities to work on particular aspects of language with bilingual children. For example, it is quite common for inexperienced English users to say 'me like' and 'me no like' rather than 'I like' or 'I don't like'. Noticing this one day, a class teacher spent some circle times with the class talking about things they liked and things they did not like. After the discussions the children had a turn to name something they did like and one thing that they did not like. Each named item was preceded by the words 'I like . . .' or 'I don't like . . .' The teacher followed up these oral sessions by making two class books with the children. On each page she wrote the child's name followed by likes, or doesn't like. Every child then drew a picture of the appropriate item which they stuck into the book and this was labelled by the child and the teacher. The process of making these books and the use of the books were a way of teaching children about the structure of English.

Although the teacher will focus more on oral language development for the child who is new to English, because speaking, listening, reading and writing are all closely related many of the starting points and activities that are used will also support the development of reading and writing. Listening to stories familiarizes children not only with word order, vocabulary and pronunciation to be used in oral language but also with the visual aspect of letters and words and the structures of the language that are important for reading and writing. Stories are a particularly productive starting point for bilingual children as they provide visual support for understanding and can be returned to again and again by the child either alone or with others. Hilary Hester (1983) suggests a number of ideas for language activities suitable for all children, but for bilingual pupils in particular, that can follow on from sharing a story with children. The following list is based on some of her suggestions:

- Listening to familiar stories while looking at the book and using story visuals in the listening area.
- Making and labelling models arising from the story.
- Making and labelling collections of items related to the story such as a collection of clothes to accompany *How Do I Put It On?* (Watanabe, 1977).
- Re-creating the sequence of the story using pictures, oral retelling or writing.
- Using a set of sequencing cards based on the story to retell it.
- Making and playing a bingo game based on the story.
- Listening to the story again and following an illustrated and simply labelled map of a book such as *Patrick* (Blake, 1968).

- Making puppets of the characters in the story.
- Making story visuals to accompany a retelling of the story.
- Making a dual-language book of the story.
- Creating a new ending for the story.
- Making a book based on a book such as *Opposites* (Harrison, no date) or *The Baby's Catalogue* (Ahlberg and Ahlberg, 1982).
- Following up one aspect of the story such as investigating boats after hearing *Mr Gumpy's Outing* (Burningham, 1970).

Stories that are used in this way will be shared and used regularly. For this reason they need to be sufficiently interesting and of a high enough quality to bear being returned to and read many times.

Besides offering a way into language, stories also provide children with personal and emotional experiences that are important for their social development and for their learning in its widest sense. For this reason bilingual learners benefit from access to stories in the language they understand most easily. Wherever possible this should be provided through story-telling sessions and taped stories in home languages.

Developing reading

It is important to appreciate that for most bilingual children, literacy will be an established part of their home experience and others may be receiving some instruction in the written form of their community language at a community school. The majority of bilingual learners, like their monolingual peers, will already have insights into the purposes of reading, what it means to be a reader, the way in which written text works and the connection between oral and written language, and these understandings will provide a means of entry into reading in English. Verma (1984) found that many teachers did not appreciate this and commented: 'there is a general tendency to adopt a narrow view of literacy as the ability to read and write in English.' Research into reading attainment suggests that bilingual pupils are helped as readers when their home or community languages are valued and promoted in the classroom (ILEA, 1990a). The linguistic and cognitive gains that may develop from learning to speak more than one language are particularly enhanced when literacy learning takes place in two languages (Cummins, 1984b). So wherever possible children's reading development should be encouraged in their home language as well as in English.

Bilingual learners will approach learning to read and learn to draw on the same strategies for making meaning in much the same way that monolingual children do. However, their experience of another language system and their developing competence in English may influence the way they use these strategies and teachers may need to be aware of this in order to provide appropriate help and support and in order not to judge bilingual learners hastily or harshly as they refine their existing understanding of reading and develop their competence in reading in English.

The difficulties that bilingual pupils may have with reading English texts may occur at a number of levels and are associated with their experiences, not their difficulties with reading (Merchant, 1992). These include different understandings of the cultural context of particular texts, problems with the semantic system, unfamiliar syntactic structures and difficulties with the grapho-phonic representation of the English language.

Readers draw on the cultural familiarity of beliefs, knowledge, feelings, attitudes, behaviour and events expressed in a text when they read. In order to do this and to reconstruct the author's meaning the reader needs to be familiar with the culture in which books are set (Halliday and Hassan, 1985). British-born English speakers usually take western cultural contexts for granted when reading and since most books for young children are set in these contexts, adults are often not aware of the difficulties this may cause to children with a different repertoire of culture awareness and different levels of familiarity with British culture. In order to avoid problems that might be caused by unfamiliar settings and cultural assumptions the teacher might provide children with books that are set in a British context but have been written by bilingual writers. The experiences of these authors might match that of young bilinguals.

Readers draw on their prior knowledge of how texts work in order to make meaning. Their previous experience of stories, books and other written material helps them to recognize the significance of the phrases and words that are read and to make predictions about what they are reading. Bilingual learners may not always be familiar with the vocabulary that they encounter in books and they may need additional preparation and discussion before and after they read to help them to use semantic strategies and to ensure that they are understanding what is read.

The grammatical structure of the English language helps readers to predict words as they read. Inexperienced users of English may only have a partial understanding of the syntactic structure of the English language. For example, they may be more familiar with a subject-object verb sentence pattern, which is used in Panjabi and Urdu, than with the subject-verb object structure commonly found in English. Children who are unfamiliar with English syntax will only receive limited support from sentence structures. They might also be unable to judge the grammatical correctness of their reading and this will restrict their ability to correct their mistakes.

Readers use grapho-phonic information to complement the other strategies that are used when reading. With its alphabet of 26 letters representing about 44 distinct sounds and with its comparatively complex spelling patterns, English has a grapho-phonic system which can be difficult to learn. Some bilingual learners, for example those from Spanish-speaking backgrounds, may have too great an expectation of the alphabetical consistency of written language, while those familiar with ideographic text, such as Chinese-speaking children, may initially have a very limited awareness of sound–symbol correspondences. Emphasizing individual letter sounds and sound combinations when the child is just acquiring a vocabulary of common words and an awareness of pronunciation and intonation in English could be unnecessarily confusing. Introducing bilingual children to the use of phonics as a support for reading is probably best done incidentally and as the child's competence at oral language increases.

The cues which British-born English-speaking pupils draw upon when reading may not be immediately accessible to bilingual pupils. They will develop in time as their oral fluency develops and as their encounters with written language increase. For this reason they should participate fully in the reading curriculum in the class and should be introduced to reading and to books in the way that the teacher considers best for all children.

Activities and resources to develop reading

There is no evidence to suggest that specially designed language and reading programmes are more effective than the best of good practice when teaching young bilingual learners to read (Merchant, 1992). However as part of the normal reading curriculum, the following list of activities may be useful when planning for the needs of bilingual learners:

- Providing access to stories in home languages and in English through the use of dual-language texts including dual-language dictionaries as well as English books, to develop the children's awareness of language, stories and early reading material.
- Shared reading, group reading and individual reading sessions with adults in order to hear and see models of reading and the language of books.
- Developing familiarity with the sight and sound of the English language through looking at names, talking about print, playing language games, playing with words and sounds, singing rhymes and songs, listening to taped stories and listening to and watching story videos.
- Building up a sight vocabulary of words through reading and re-reading familiar stories.
- Making simple books containing repetitive language structures such as 'I like . . .' and 'I can . . .', writing counting books, individual dual-language dictionaries and books based on simple, familiar stories.
- Recognizing and valuing children's knowledge of other languages.
- Providing a rich and exciting reading environment.
- Emphasizing reading for meaning and enjoyment.
- Using materials that match the children's experience and understanding.

Selecting books for the multilingual classroom

There are many advantages in using real books rather than reading-scheme books with bilingual learners. The range, diversity and relevance of picture books are much greater than that available in scheme books, as are books which use natural oral language patterns. Well selected real books are more likely to contain stories that are rich enough to be told and listened to frequently and to be explored in detail. Some good-quality story books are also available in dual-language versions.

The following criteria may be helpful when selecting books for bilingual learners • the books should contain positive images of all children • the books should contain an interesting story and be worth while in themselves • the text should be predictable, contain repeated sequences of words and be easy for children to retell • the illustrations should enhance the understanding of the text • children should be able to identify with the events and characters in the books • they should contain simple grammatical patterns and an accessible vocabulary making them easy to read independently • they can be used as models for the children's own writing • bilingual versions are available • the books can be used for cross-curricular activities.

Not every book will match all the criteria listed above but books which meet some or most of the criteria are not hard to find. Books that have been used successfully in multilingual environments include *Dear Zoo* (Campbell, 1982); *Titch* (Hutchins, 1971); *What's the Time, Mr Wolf?* (Hawkins, 1983); *'Aah,' said Stork* (Rose, 1977); *Where's Spot?* (Hill, 1980); *The Hungry Giant* (Melser and Cowley, 1980a); *A, B, C, I Can Be* (Wilkins, 1993).

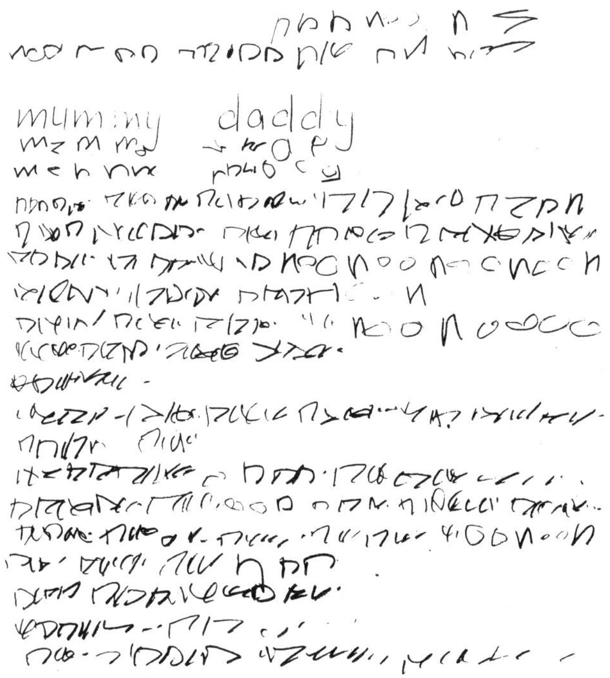

Figure 6.1   Noorah Bengali writing

Developing writing

Bilingual children's writing will follow the same pattern of development as monolingual writers. If there are differences these may be a result of children using their knowledge and experience of writing systems other than English and incorporating features of these systems into their writing. The writing in Figure 6.1, produced by a 4-year-old, probably reflects the child's familiarity with Bengali, a language he would have seen at home, and it demonstrates his understanding of the need to use a particular set of symbols and shapes when writing.

The samples of writing that follow represent the development of one bilingual pupil's writing during one school year in a Year 2 class. By September Sezgin had been in England for six months and had spent one term in the Year 1 class. Prior to coming to London he had attended school in Turkey. At first Sezgin was reluctant to write, his spoken English was developing slowly and he was unable to read alone either in Turkish or English; however by December he began to produce long pieces of writing. He drew on his memory of words that had been

Figure 6.2   Sezgin visit to a friend

Figure 6.3   Sezgin – sisters

introduced to the class through shared-reading and writing sessions and incorporated these into his writing. At this stage his writing was difficult to read and, although Sezgin was willing to read his writing back, his spoken English made it hard for the teacher to understand what Sezgin was trying to communicate. The teacher praised all Sezgin's efforts at writing and always commented on any words that she recognized. This gave him greater confidence in his ability to write and he began to write long stories using his reading books as a source for spelling. The example in Figure 6.2 is a story he wrote in February about a visit to a friend's house. Although it is not easy to read it indicates how Sezgin incorporated words displayed around the classroom into his writing. He was also experimenting with some spellings on his own, such as 'HES' for 'his' and 'WES' for 'was'. At this stage he was mainly using capital letters in his writing. Through reading and shared-reading sessions Sezgin became very aware of the features of text and words. The example in Figure 6.3 shows Sezgin using lower-case letters in speech bubbles as he introduces his three sisters to the reader.

The example of Sezgin's writing shown in Figure 6.4 was written in June. The class were writing their own reports. These were to be put in a booklet and were to be sent home along with the teacher's report. This extract contains Sezgin's comments about his learning in mathematics and English. This was a first draft. Sezgin was clear about the task and

Figure 6.4 Sezgin – report

communicates his feelings very effectively. Most of his spelling is correct and again he referred to books to find the correct spelling for many words. The writing shows the influence of Sezgin's spoken English on his writing; he omits some words such as 'and' and 'at' and inserts others such as 'a'. For words that he found difficult to write, such as 'addition' and 'division', he has used the mathematical notation but the meaning is clear. Sezgin was aware that the main purpose of writing was to communicate to an audience.

Throughout the year Sezgin had been included in all the literacy and language activities in the class. His teacher had expected Sezgin's oral competence in English to grow and she had encouraged him to read and write in English. Her interventions, discussions and suggestions had ensured that by the age of 7 Sezgin was well on the way to becoming a competent writer. Sezgin is not unusual. This case study typifies the sort of development one might expect from a confident child who understands the purpose of literacy.

Activities to develop writing

Bilingual children do not need tightly structured or special writing experiences in order to develop as writers. Like all beginning writers they need opportunities to write independently for a real purpose and for a real audience and should participate fully in the writing curriculum in the class. The list which follows contains some suggestions for writing that are appropriate for all children but because of their structure, they may be particularly useful for teachers working with young bilingual pupils. Bilingual children should

- write collaboratively with an adult or with another child as this provides support and models of writing in English for the child, as do shared-writing sessions;
- be encouraged to write in their preferred language as this enables the teacher to see what they know about the form and function of writing and enables the child to explore the act of writing;
- write stories based on familiar story books as this provides a simple structure for them to copy;
- write accounts of personal and class activities which follow a simple structure such as I went to . . . , I saw . . . , I bought . . . ;
- be encouraged to use the writing area in the classroom;
- be given help and guidance by adults writing beneath the pictures and writing produced in response to a task and through discussions about writing; and
- join in writing and illustrating activities leading to the production of big books.

Exploring language diversity

Examining the oral and written forms of different languages can help children to explore how languages work, the purposes for which language and different forms of language are used and be a starting point for work on knowledge about language and language study. Bilingual pupils' own languages and their implicit understanding of how language is used in different situations and with different people provide a valuable resource for exploring language, written and spoken, with all the class. The experience and understanding of language that bilingual children have will be of benefit to monolingual pupils' learning and may lead monolingual children to appreciate the skills of their bilingual peers. The LINC Project stressed the contribution that bilingual children can make to raising the linguistic awareness of monolingual English-speaking children in the classroom, an awareness which is beneficial for children's development as readers and writers.

Undertaking a project on languages in school has many benefits. The aims for such a project indicate what these might include. To • support bilingualism in the school setting • enhance self-esteem and self-image • generate respect for all cultures and languages • develop the cognitive, social and emotional gains of maintaining a first language • enhance the linguistic awareness of all pupils.

Work on a language theme might begin by exploring the languages, accents and dialects that are used by and familiar to the children in the class. The children may investigate and make an oral and written collection of greetings in all the languages of the class. They may then try to discover others. The collection could be recorded on tape and in written form and displayed in speech bubbles alongside photographs of the children. The children might select a language for the day or for the week and use the greeting of that language at registration time and at the end of the school day. Looking at community newspapers, posters and writing done by children and adults might result in a collection of written scripts which could be examined and compared. A collection of number systems might also be made. The children might each compile a language history profile to show how they use different languages and different forms of a language with different people. This might contain statements such as 'I speak to my brother in . . .', I speak to my teacher in . . .' The class might design a questionnaire to be used with other children in the school including items that elicit information about the different use and purposes of language. Questions might include such things as 'How do you speak to a shop-keeper?' or 'What language do you use with your grandmother?' When all the information has been collected it can be presented and displayed as a flow chart, poster, spider web or graph. A collection of songs, rhymes and games in different languages and from different cultures could also be made and used by the class. The children could teach these to one another. Bilingual speakers could be invited into school to share their language with the children and to teach them some words and phrases. They might also be able to add to or comment on the collections of greetings, songs, rhymes and games begun by the children. Books written in various languages could be examined and the information contained in all books, such as publisher, ISBN and date, compared. Traditional tales from different cultures and countries could be shared with the children and compared in order to discover common themes. Other books and stories could be examined for their portrayals of people, events and locations in the text and in the illustrations.

Describing a six-week language project in a West Midlands primary school, Mills (1993) shows how an apparently monolingual staff revealed themselves as a valuable language resource and were able to offer the pupils a number of valuable experiences of language diversity. The staff were able to teach the children • classroom commands in Bengali • Bengali greetings • French greetings and counting • German greetings and counting • songs in Glaswegian dialect • Polish greetings and counting • Urdu phrases • Welsh phrases and songs.

The staff were able to offer these language experiences to the children from their own experiences in the home, community, school, work and further study. Whilst not exaggerating the command of languages that monolingual speakers have, it is likely that the majority of adults will have some knowledge of accents, dialects and European if not other languages as a result of friendships, holiday and work experiences as well as the other life experiences mentioned above. By drawing on these and making them public it should be possible to discuss with children the positive aspects of knowing languages other than English, some similarities and differences between the forms of languages and when, and in what ways, different languages may be used.

The assessment of bilingual children

The assessment of bilingual learners is an area of concern for monolingual teachers in a number of ways. Some monolingual teachers feel that they may not be able to develop bilingual children's full potential since the children's lack of English may prevent the teacher having full access to the pupil's thinking and understanding. They may also be concerned about recognizing speech and language disorders, such as language delay and deafness in children who are developing fluency in English. Teachers are very aware that bilingual children are expected to reach the same levels of attainment as monolingual English speakers in their use and understanding of oral and written English and in all other areas of the curriculum. Achievement in the National Curriculum for English is assessed through English so children who are developing fluency in English at the age of 7 may not do as well in the English tests and tasks as children who began school with a fluent command of English. Whilst language support staff may provide translations of the Key Stage 1 tests and tasks, not every school has access to an adult who speaks the language of the children to be tested. This again might interfere with the assessment of bilingual children's learning.

These issues are difficult and there are no easy solutions. However when teachers are making their own assessments of children's learning, particularly at the end of a Key Stage, they might reflect upon their considerable experience and ability at observing and interpreting children's learning. This should give them some confidence as they collect evidence of children's language development and learning strategies. Teachers are also aware that assessment is affected by teacher expectations and children's confidence and so where both are realistically high teachers will be presenting children with the best possible opportunity to do well.

Conclusion

Bilingual pupils come to school with knowledge and experiences that are valuable and important. Schools and teachers that create learning environments which celebrate cultural diversity, recognize prior learning and provide for the full participation of bilingual learners in the English curriculum will be helping all pupils to grow in competence in all aspects of English.

Suggestions for further reading

Buxton, C. (no date) *Language Activities for Bilingual Learners*, Tower Hamlets Education Authority, London.
Hester, H. (1983) *Stories in the Multilingual Classroom*, Harcourt Brace Jovanovich, London.

Chapter 7

Language and gender

Introduction

This chapter examines gender differences in relation to speaking and listening, reading and writing. It considers the different learning styles and language behaviour of boys and girls and the ways in which adult interaction and the organization of the English curriculum affect what and how boys and girls learn. Each section contains practical suggestions for teachers who wish to implement an English curriculum that gives all children the opportunity to achieve their potential as learners and as users of language.

Why gender is an important issue

The world outside school affects children's perceptions of themselves in many ways. The hopes, expectations, treatment and interactions that are received from adults are often determined by a child's sex. Young children may be dressed in gender-specific clothing which indicates the type of behaviour that is expected of them as a girl or as a boy. For example, trousers and trainers give far more access to energetic play and physical pursuits than do skirts and flimsy sandals. Children are presented with models of appropriate play and other behaviour from TV advertisements, comics, magazines and books. The behaviour of the adults they see around them and in the media acts as a role model for children's aspirations. Through all these influences children become aware of what is expected from them as girls, boys, women and men.

Schools cannot be held accountable for producing gender differences but, as microcosms of the world, they may contribute to them by reflecting sex-stereotyped practices. School staff are role models for the children. Their expectations, attitudes, interactions and judgements about children may be linked to stereotyped beliefs about boys' and girls' learning and behaviour and their own particular views relating to gender. Decisions about school routines such as lining-up and uniforms may indicate that the staff distinguish between children on the basis of their gender. The organization of children within the classroom, the type and length of attention that is given to pupils, the choice of themes and the selection of resources may indicate regard for equality of opportunity for girls and boys or may reinforce the differences in behaviour and attitudes that are being learned outside school.

Language and literacy may seem to be a neutral part of the curriculum. The role of the teacher is to teach all children to listen, speak, read and write competently. However there is a growing body of evidence which suggests that language use and language competence at school are strongly gender differentiated (White, 1990; Whitehead, 1990; Swann, 1992). More boys than girls experience difficulties with reading and writing. Girls seem to read more books and to produce longer pieces of writing than boys in early-years classrooms. But the significance of gender difference does not end there. Researchers and writers are now suggesting that, since gender identity is constantly rehearsed and learned from what is said, what is heard, what is read and what is written, the language curriculum at school plays a major part in creating differences, not just in language development but in shaping the wider aspects of children's personal and social development: 'Language use contributes to the establishment and maintenance of gender identity. Making gender-appropriate reading and writing choices is part of learning how to behave appropriately as a girl or a boy' (Swann, 1992, p. 135).

These findings are significant for all those concerned with young children's development, if they agree that all children have the right to equality of achievement, that all children should receive similar educational experiences and that education should empower and widen the horizons and choices of all learners. Discovering that the English curriculum may be contributing to the difficulty of realizing these aims and supporting 'gender-related underachievement' (Minns, 1991) has prompted a great deal of reflection about the best ways to organize and implement an English curriculum that allows all children to fulfil their potential as learners.

Speaking and listening

Women and men and girls and boys use language in different ways. In comparison to men, women's vocabulary is characterized by a greater use of words related to domestic interests, of empty adjectives such as 'cute' or 'charming' and of intensifiers like 'It is *such* a good book' (Lakoff, 1975). Trudgill (1974) suggests that women tend to employ more prestigious dialects and more statusful accents than men. He also notes that the language of women often includes tentative and apologetic comments such as 'Is it possible . . . ?' or 'I was just wondering if . . .' They tend to avoid outright statements or, if they do state an opinion, accompany these with tag questions, such as 'Don't you agree?' In general women tend to ask more questions and to use language to maintain social interactions and to keep conversations going rather than to interrupt or argue (Crystal, 1987). They tend to use the more polite forms of language and tend to speak less in mixed-sex groups, two characteristics which have been seen as indicative of their social and linguistic insecurity (Montgomery, 1986).

These differences in language use are significant for teachers of young children. Teachers receive children who are products of a society that still, despite some changes, tends to characterize women as submissive and subordinate. By the time children come to school they have already learned how to speak in different ways according to their gender and their gendered identities lead them to use language in the classroom in different ways. They speak differently as a boy or as a girl, to boys and to girls and about boys and about girls. When they start school, many girls already seem to have learnt to expect to participate less than boys in classroom discussions whereas many boys expect to be listened to, to hold the floor and dominate during discussions (Jarmany, 1991). It has been suggested that teachers may reinforce this pattern by giving more attention to and interacting more with boys than with girls and as a consequence give boys more opportunities to participate in teacher-organized talk at school (Swann and Graddol, 1988). Children's gendered identities and their experiences and interactions in and out of school have implications for the way in which girls and boys will continue to learn about language, the range of purposes for language in which they engage and their growth in confidence as users of language. Since the teacher's aim is to encourage all children to participate equally in the oracy curriculum in order to extend their range of oral language experiences, use of key skills, awareness of standard English and understanding of language, she will need to take account of gender differences in oral language when planning the content and organization of the speaking and listening curriculum.

Gender differences in speaking and listening

Whilst there are always exceptions, some boys and men are quiet and diffident and some girls and women are confident and articulate. Some of the general differences between the oral language use of boys and girls in school that have been identified are that ● boys are more outspoken, assertive and confident ● boys are more likely to be openly disparaging about girls ● boys interrupt more ● boys take up more verbal time ● boys make longer verbal contributions ● boys may recall anecdotes in order to hold the floor ● boys use language to vie for status ● girls tend to defer to the ideas of others ● girls tend to gain more practice at listening than boys ● girls signify that they are listening to others ● girls respond to what has been said ● girls are better at taking turns ● girls speak more tentatively and with more need for approval ● girls take longer to become involved in discussions ● girls use language to draw out and include others.

Research evidence from the National Oracy Project (Norman, 1990; Swann, 1992) suggests that even teachers who are aware of these issues help to maintain and reinforce gender differences in language use by ● making distinctions between boys and girls for disciplinary or administrative reasons ● giving more attention and more time to boys' talk in discussions ● not noticing the disparity in number and length of oral contributions from girls and boys ● being more tolerant of behaviour such as calling out by boys, which helps them to learn how to take and hold the floor ● asking boys more demanding questions ● selecting topics that appeal to the interest of the boys ● permitting or arranging working groups which reinforce gender distinctions in behaviour and language use ● accepting rather than challenging the differences that exist in pupils' use of language.

Strategies to foster a gender-fair oracy curriculum

Girls and boys have different strengths and weaknesses as users of language. This becomes obvious when children work in single-sex groups. In all-girl groups the children are often keen to complete the task. They listen and respond to each other's contributions, are willing to negotiate and compromise and often manage to conclude with proposals that the majority agree with. In all-boy groups there can often be disagreement and argument, rather than a real consideration of other children's opinions. It is clear that girls and boys could learn a great deal from each other. Girls could learn to become more assertive and boys could learn to be better listeners and respondents. Before actively intervening with the children, teachers might want to observe the oral behaviour and strategies that children use in a number of different situations. It is likely that different combinations of children, different contexts, different topics and the presence and interactions of adults will affect the children's contributions and participation. Teachers might want particularly to observe how boys and girls communicate, collaborate and behave in groups, noting how they support and respond to one another. Teachers may also wish to reflect on their own use of language and their own behaviour. After observing the children and reflecting on practice, teachers might then wish to make some changes in their teaching style and classroom management in order to develop the aspects of oracy that the children lack. Teachers have found the following strategies useful when seeking to change established oral gender patterns:

- Selecting themes, resources, activities and organizational strategies carefully so as not to reinforce gender differences.
- Supporting the girls when they contribute to classroom discussions.
- Supporting boys as listeners in classroom discussions.
- Modelling non-stereotyped interactions in play situations such as the home corner, the hospital and the café.

- Intervening in mixed groups to counter stereotyped behaviour and allocating children to non-stereotyped roles, such as scribe for a boy and leader for a girl.
- Challenging stereotyped labels or behaviour and discussing this with the children.
- Ensuring that boys have the opportunity to engage in activities that will enable them to use the quiet, sensitive, caring aspects of their natures.
- Intervening when children regularly choose to work in single-sex groups by allocating children to mixed groups using sets of well matched single-sex pairings.
- Organizing all-girl groups or pairings in curriculum areas where girls appear to have less confidence, such as IT, science and construction, to ensure that girls experience success and to give them the confidence to hold their own in mixed-group settings.
- Establishing rules that allow equal access to resources for play, science and maths.
- Choosing girls to make oral presentations to the class and in assembly.

When appropriate teachers might discuss group work and the pupils' use of language in class with the class. Talking about talk and encouraging children to reflect on their own roles during small and large group discussions will heighten their awareness of language and may lead to the children compiling a set of rules for discussion times, such as 'Everyone needs to listen and to talk', 'Everyone has something interesting to say' and 'No one needs to shout'. Negotiating the ground rules for talk always involves a consideration of the different ways in which girls and boys use language and can make a positive contribution to effective group work.

Discussing equal opportunities with children in relation to the language of books, pictures, TV programmes and advertisements can be a useful way of helping children to reflect on gender and language. Brierley (1991) gives a very helpful account of a project intended to investigate children's perceptions of gender differences. Although this work was undertaken with 10 and 11-year-olds, the activities would be very suitable for much younger children. She began by using some of the activities suggested in the *Working Now* pack (Development Education Centre, 1989) which help children to examine their own perceptions of male and female roles. She then went on to ask the class to identify toys that would be appropriate for girls and boys. All the work was carried out in groups and ended with a class debate. Throughout the project the teacher was able to observe the oral behaviour and the attitudes of the children and these were discussed with them. This was a very productive way of examining gender-related behaviour at a level that was relevant and interesting to children and could make a good starting point for other practitioners.

Gender differences in reading

From the earliest stages of education girls seem to find books and reading more interesting than boys. In the main girls learn to read more quickly, with more ease and with greater success than boys. Boys read less from choice, form the majority of children with literacy problems and, later in their school career, perform less well in language-related subjects. A number of possible explanations for these differences have been suggested. General expectations about the behaviour of girls and boys may mean that reading is viewed as a more suitable leisure activity for girls than for boys. Girls are expected to read and to enjoy reading because it is a quiet, introspective pursuit rather than an energetic, physical activity. In the early years the reading curriculum is largely constructed around stories and although boys may enjoy stories as much as girls, the emphasis on stories may alienate some boys. Girls' and boys' reading interests and habits are affected by the models of adult readers they see and it is known that women read more fiction than men and that adult male readers tend to read information texts, often linked to their work or their hobbies. If boys do not see men reading fiction this may influence their interest in a story-based reading curriculum. The polarity of adult reading habits and the emphasis on story in the early years has disadvantages for girls as well as boys. For both sexes, much of their learning in their later school careers will depend a great deal on their ability to read a wide range of texts and to use information material successfully. Both boys and girls might benefit from an earlier introduction and greater use of information texts as they learn to read. A study of nursery classes and nurseries in Cleveland (Hodgeon, 1984) found that girls' interest and ability in reading is supported by the predominantly female culture of early years settings. The girls in the nurseries spent more time near their teachers and as a result had more access to stories and literacy activities and gained more experience of reading and books than the boys. The differences in attitudes and success at reading manifested by boys and girls seem to be linked to a number of cultural and societal expectations and norms which are beyond the control of the teacher. However, whatever the external causes for the differences in attitudes and achievement in reading, there is good reason to consider making some changes to some aspects of the reading curriculum.

Strategies to foster a gender-fair reading curriculum

In order to enhance the achievement of boys and girls there are a number of practical strategies that teachers may wish to consider employing. These include

- ensuring that there is a greater balance between fiction and information books in the reading material that is shared with and offered to children in the early years;

- using single-sex pairs or groups for group reading in order to support children in their least preferred choices of reading material; pairs or groups of boys might read stories together and all-girl groups might read information texts;
- keeping lists and records of the books that children read and reviewing their selection with them in order to provide books that match or extend their choices;
- using and displaying books which contain images of boys and men as readers;
- involving older boys, male teachers, fathers and male visitors in reading activities in the classroom;
- inviting male story tellers to school;
- creating play areas that have a literacy focus and where reading and writing are used by both male and female workers, for example a post office or a library;
- ensuring that children read in a variety of contexts including word processing and computer programs; and
- addressing gender issues with parents and making a positive effort to involve male carers in parent–teacher discussions about reading and in the home–school reading programme.

Gender differences in writing

Research in this area has revealed that boys and girls hold very different attitudes towards writing. Girls often enjoy writing, particularly imaginative and personal writing, while boys feel less competent at writing and prefer factual and technical writing. These views are not genetic. They are created by the institutional and societal examples that children see around them (Swann, 1992). As they continue in their school lives many boys, although good at writing, dismiss it, along with reading, in favour of mathematics, science or technology. They begin to pay less attention to writing and produce carelessly presented writing that does not do justice to their abilities. Girls are often expected to be better at all aspects of writing including handwriting and presentation. Many teachers still equate neat handwriting and length with girls' writing and exciting content in stories coupled with untidy handwriting in boys' writing. When children are planning and drafting their work, teachers often expect the boys to spend far less time in perfecting their work, while girls are expected to pay more attention to detail and take a greater length of time to complete the first draft, before producing the final copy.

As well as differences in attitude and presentation skills children's writing also reveals differences in content and style. Examining the content of what children write indicates how gender differences are rehearsed and reinforced through their own written words. Whilst teachers may be empowering pupils by teaching them to write confidently, the content of what is written and the way in which ideas are expressed in

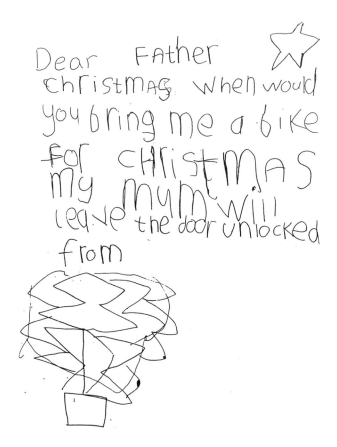

Figure 7.1   Letter to Father Christmas

writing may be limiting children's perceptions of themselves and their choices in the world. The pieces of writing illustrated demonstrate a number of gender differences in young children's writing.

The class were all writing letters to Father Christmas asking him to bring them a particular present for Christmas. Of the two letters reproduced in Figures 7.1 and 2, one was written by a girl and one by a boy. Perhaps readers would like to guess which one was written by Laura and which one by Robert. The first letter contains a direct request. It is straightforward and to the point, almost abrupt, as it simply ends 'from . . .' Interestingly it also refers to the mum as the one who remembers to do the social and domestic jobs at home. This was written by 6-year-old Robert.

Rather than containing a request, the second letter proffers an invitation to tea. It portrays a cosy domestic scene with the writer engaging in cooking and caring for others. Laura has not accomplished the task that

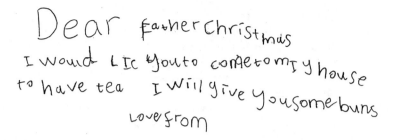

Dear Father Christmas
I would LIC you to come to my house to have tea I will give you some buns
Love from

Figure 7.2 Letter to Father Christmas

was set. She appears to have become so involved in her traditional female role that she is more concerned with correct social skills than with the purpose of the activity.

Both letters are well presented. It is clear that Robert is a good writer, but it is also clear that he is less concerned with correct letter formation, consistent use of lower-case letters and letter size than he could be, given his apparent ability. Laura's writing seems to be much more carefully presented.

If children tend to reproduce stereotyped norms when writing alone, might these change when boys and girls write together after discussing the plot, characterization, style and language of their stories? The next two stories were written collaboratively by mixed groups of boys and girls aged 5 working with the help of an adult scribe. As the starting point for the writing the children had been asked to use a stone or a rock from a display in the classroom. The stories were discussed and planned before a final draft was written on the word processor.

The Dinosaur Discovery by Abigayle, Adam and Vanessa
Once upon a time there was a red rock and a dinosaur saw it and thought it was a piece of beef. He picked up the piece of red rock and he took it back to Dinosaur Headland. He showed it to the other dinosaurs and they were fascinated. They all took a bite out of it and all their teeth fell out. A skeleton of a Brachiosaurus came along and it reminded them that it was a piece of red rock. A Europrofocepholus dinosaur took the rock back where it belonged. Every week the dinosaur went back to the museum to look at the red rock. It was put in the museum because it was a magic rock and it needed light so that it could glow.

The Stone and the Skeleton by Craig and Helen
There was once a stone in a cave and suddenly a skeleton popped out and we screamed. The skeleton was a magic skeleton. We picked up the stone and it changed colour. It changed from brown to blue to green and red. We threw the stone at the skeleton's head and his leg fell off. As he was a magic skeleton he used some of his magic to fix himself back together. He flew back into the stone and then we went home with the stone.

Although the children had complete freedom in what they included in their story, both groups chose to write a fantasy with elements of magic, adventure, violence and fear. In both stories the characters are male and active. The two girls contributing to *The Dinosaur Discovery* never thought to question this decision. Again in *The Dinosaur Discovery* Adam insisted that the correct names and spellings for the types of dinosaurs were included in the story. As Craig and Helen were planning the first draft of their story I asked them why they wanted to throw the stone at the skeleton and Craig replied that this was a good thing to do with a stone. I suggested that there might be other things that they could include in their story that were related to the stone, but Craig was adamant that he would throw the stone if he saw a skeleton and Helen agreed. As I observed the children working together it was clear that, in both groups, the boys took the lead in the discussions and in organizing the girls to make notes and plans. One might conclude that by participating in this activity the girls had the opportunity to write a story that was active and aggressive, was far removed from a domestic setting and without recourse to the consideration of motives or emotions. This was indeed the case, but I wonder how significant this experience was for them? As the boys were dominant in the discussions and as the stories were about male characters it is hard to judge how much ownership the girls felt over this writing. As I evaluated this exercise I also felt that the boys had missed out on a valuable learning experience. They had not explored the world of feelings, positive motives and gentle values; the potential contribution that the girls might have made to the writing was overlooked in the interests of excitement and combat.

These examples of children's writing were found in classes taught by thoughtful and aware teachers who were leading children enthusiastically towards the goal of control over the writing process. Structure, organization, coherence, presentation in all these stories is good, as were the children's attitudes towards writing and their understanding of writing as a purposeful and communicative activity. What the children seemed to have less control over was the content of what they wrote. In these examples, writing for all the children involved reproducing the attitudes and values they had learned as they grew up in a world that still differentiates between appropriate behaviour for girls and appropriate behaviour for boys. In their writing the children were expressing these values and, by committing themselves to paper, reinforcing these stereotypes both for themselves and for other children who might read what they had written. Even though the teachers of these pupils were concerned to promote equality of opportunity for the children they taught by the nature of the tasks they choose, their organization of groups and their interventions as the children wrote, writing still presented children with the opportunity to rehearse and reproduce what they have already learned about the roles and experiences of males and females in society.

Strategies to foster a gender-fair writing curriculum

When considering how to create a writing curriculum that will offer equal opportunities for girls and boys to achieve in all aspects of writing, the teacher may want to observe the children as they write. At the same time she might ask herself the following questions. Do boys spend less time on writing and do they consider it to be less important than other subjects? Do they rush the work and give less attention to style and detail? Are girls spending more time writing and concentrating more on handwriting and presentation? Do girls spend more time writing creative and imaginative pieces rather than technical or scientific scripts? She might want to reflect on the content of what the children produce to see if it reflects stereotypical ideas and values and to consider how these might be altered and perspectives widened.

If there are aspects of the writing curriculum that might benefit from change teachers might like to employ some of the following strategies:

- Emphasizing to all pupils that writing is an important part of the curriculum and that she expects high standards in all aspects of writing from all the children.
- Praising the boys for well presented writing.
- Encouraging the girls to take a chance with their ideas rather than allowing them to spend a long time on presenting a perfect copy.
- Creating a balance between imaginative, personal and factual types of writing that constitute the writing curriculum and ensuring that girls engage in factual writing, such as writing up experiments, and that boys have the opportunity for personal writing.
- Planning some shared-writing sessions in order to give girls and boys the opportunity to discuss suggestions and to challenge and justify ideas that are to be included in a piece of writing.
- Encouraging collaboration, to make sure that girls are listened to and that boys participate in groups without dominating.
- Organizing groups so that boys and girls get equal turns at suggesting ideas and making notes, reminding the boys that they have to listen and scribe and supporting the girls as they voice and justify their ideas.
- Selecting starting points for writing that challenge gender stereotypes and allow for the exploration of new perspectives.
- Positively discriminating when setting writing tasks by asking the boys to write a story that requires the central male character to be gentle and thoughtful and the girls to write a science-fiction adventure.
- Organizing different writing activities for each sex so that each group can respond differently, for example the girls may write the more powerful and controlling parts of the story and the boys the more descriptive and emotional parts.
- Considering all the messages that are contained in familiar stories that are read to and used with the children, for example discussing the intelligence that Red Riding Hood displays when she outwits the wolf.

- Monitoring what is written and analysing children's choices with them, raising gender issues where necessary.

Towards an unbiased English curriculum

In order for the strategies outlined in the earlier part of this chapter to succeed, there are some more general actions that the teacher might take when considering equal opportunities and English. These are outlined below.

Language awareness and use

We might be aware of how boy and girl pupils use language differently and we might be sensitive to the use of sexist language by pupils, but educators, as models for young children, may also need to be alert to their own and other adults' use of language. It is very easy to use words in a way that portrays girls as immature and incompetent and boys as rational or assertive. Adults can sometimes refer to boys who are behaving unacceptably as being like 'silly little girls'. They may be moved to sit or stand with the girls, as if this were a punishment. These references serve to highlight the distinctions between boys and girls and encourage boys to see female behaviour and company as incompatible with being a boy. Adults sometimes talk about children in ways that define the type of behaviour and characteristics that are considered to be the norm for each sex, labelling children in different ways according to gender. Quiet girls may be described as shy; quiet boys may be described as strong, silent types. Children who organize others may be called bossy if they are girls and leaders if they are boys. Girls' talk may be labelled as chat or gossip and boys' talk as loud or noisy. It is still common to hear references to 'the milkman', 'the postman' and 'the policeman', or to hear doctors spoken of as 'he' and nurses as 'she'. Some adults choose to use the word 'lady' rather than 'woman' because they consider it to be more polite, although it is very difficult to discover why they think this. One might ask why it is necessary to be more polite towards women than to men who are very rarely referred to as 'gentlemen'. It is easy to fall into this misuse of language when talking to children about the 'lollipop lady' or the 'dinner lady'. If adults' other efforts to reduce gender stereotyping in the classroom are to be convincing and effective then adult models of language use and behaviour must support these.

Resources

Over the past 20 years a great deal of attention has been paid to the stereotyped portrayal of female and male characters in children's books. Researchers have consistently found that, in both text and illustrations, women and men, girls and boys are frequently depicted in stereotyped and limiting roles. Because the visual and written images of books are part of the cultural patterning of children's lives and because readers are directly affected by and will reproduce in their own speech and writing what they see, hear and read, teachers need to continue to be aware of the influence that books may have on pupils. Fortunately there are now many authors and illustrators who are producing excellent books for young children which highlight the achievements of women and girls and illustrate the more creative, caring, responsible and sensitive qualities of men and boys. This makes the selection of new books that complement an anti-sexist approach to education much easier. However there are two areas where it is still not easy to find good resources. These are picture books that portray boys as readers and writers and information texts that represent and value the achievements and experiences of women and girls. Because classrooms do not just contain new resources it is often wise to read and appraise existing book stock and remove any material that may impede the aim of enhancing all children's learning. Changing the book provision in school does not necessarily change the attitudes and assumptions that people or children have and will not reverse the powerful process of socialization, but the careful selection of resources and awareness of the issues will prevent the school from reinforcing limiting stereotypes and open up avenues for potential change.

Themes

The English curriculum presents teachers with many opportunities for pupils to play an active role in exploring equal opportunities in general and those aspects of equal opportunities that may impede their success in English (Tilbrook and Grayson, 1990; Minns, 1991). The teacher might initiate a project where the children investigate the portrayal of women and men, girls and boys as readers, writers, workers and family members in books, resources and in the media. The children could devise questionnaires and interview pupils and adults in the class and school about their perceptions of appropriate types of reading and writing for females and males. They might also survey the reading material that is looked at and read by each sex in the class and follow this by asking adults about the reading materials and writing tasks that they engage in most. This activity might reveal whether there are gender differences in literacy beyond the classroom. Another activity might involve analysing the topics for writing chosen by their own and other classes to see whether there are differences between the writing of girls and boys and if so to find out what form those differences take. Analysing classroom and library books is a straightforward but often revealing activity. The headings listed below were used by one class to compile a useful data base of information about the books in their school:

- Title
- Author

- Publisher
- Year published
- Main character – girl, boy, woman, man
- The girls in the book are – brave, intelligent, kind, sensible, other
- The boys in the story are – brave, intelligent, kind, sensible, other
- The girls in the story are – silly, helpless, cowardly, other
- The boys in the story are – silly, helpless, cowardly, other
- Other comments

Examining and comparing old and new versions of fairy tales can often highlight aspects of gender stereotyping and encourage children to read and evaluate books attentively. The traditional Cinderella story might be compared with *The Paper Bag Princess* (Munsch, 1980), *Prince Cinders* (Cole, 1987) and *Petronella* (Williams, 1983). As a result of their investigations the children might write letters to publishers, authors and advertisers informing them of their findings. They could rewrite the stories changing the sex of some of the characters or describing different roles for the male and female characters. They might act out the changed fairy tales, giving 'The Three Little Pigs' an all-female cast, portraying Mother Bear in 'The Three Bears' as the biggest and the strongest of the bears and Goldilocks as a boy. The children could then be asked deliberately to change the way in which they portray female and male characters in their own writing. Such investigations and analysis might result in a more informed and conscious change in the children's own use of written language and awareness of literacy and gender issues.

Even if one does not choose to focus on a language and literacy theme such as the one described above, it is important to consider the scope of any theme that is selected and to avoid choosing themes that are obviously gender biased. Good themes are those which enable the teacher to present a balanced view of boys and girls, and men and women, provide for a balanced diet of imaginative and factual reading and writing activities and for which the available resources support non-stereotyped portrayals of both sexes. A theme such as 'Conquerors and Invaders' might be quite limiting, whereas themes such as 'Change', 'Patterns' or 'Ourselves' can be planned to have more immediate appeal to the interests of all pupils and provide more opportunities to explore issues of gender.

Gender in the English curriculum – two examples

The two examples which follow show how gender can affect the learning of young children. In the first example the teacher is unaware of the issues; in the second example the teacher has thought carefully about how she might avoid the potentially damaging effects of gendered responses and behaviour.

Example one

A Year 2 teacher was discussing possible titles for class books with the children. The children were all sitting in the book area of the classroom and the teacher was noting down the children's suggestions on a flip chart. He began the discussion by asking the children what their favourite television programmes were. A host of hands went up, mainly those of the boys. They suggested *Turtles*, *Thundercats*, and *Batman*. The teacher praised the children for so many suggestions and told them that these would be good starting points for their own stories. The mainly boy group that had volunteered the answers began to shout 'yeah' and raise their fists into the air. The teacher quietened the class down and then asked one girl what she would like to write about. The child did not answer and was questioned further by the teacher. Eventually she said *Blue Peter*. The class burst into laughter and one boy told her that *Blue Peter* was not a story and that it was boring. The girl said nothing. The teacher told the girl that *Blue Peter* might be a difficult starting point for a story and invited her to think again. The girl declined.

This example shows how one teacher attempted to stimulate his class into writing imaginatively. He believed that by beginning the class discussion with a mention of television programmes he would hold his pupils' attention and motivate them into wanting to write. The teacher succeeded in catching the attention of many of the children but the topics that were identified and the behaviour of some of the pupils excluded many other children. The teacher's choice of television programmes for beginning this work was misguided and led to a session which reinforced numerous gender and racial stereotypes. He had not considered the way that boys, girls, men and women are represented on television. When the teacher encountered shouts of *'Batman'* and *'Thundercats'* he simply saw this as a discipline problem, not as an assertion of the boys' power and competitiveness. The teacher's attempts to include the girl within the discussion led to her feeling isolated and threatened, hence her silence and refusal to answer any more questions. The teacher did not deal with the boys' response to *Blue Peter*. Instead he allowed the boys to intimidate her with their comments therefore isolating her even more. The example above was not a deliberate attempt by the teacher to differentiate between pupils according to gender. He had merely wanted to identify a starting point for writing that was relevant and familiar to the children. However he had not thought carefully about his starting point and even when many of the class were alienated by the discussion he did not rethink his strategies, stop the discussion or explore the issues with the class.

This example shows how and why teachers need to be aware of the content they select and the way in which they interact with pupils in the classroom. If teachers praise certain ideas and behaviour they are 'telling' the class what they feel to be good, commendable, exciting, important and so on. Similarly if teachers ignore or avoid particular issues that arise they may be silently reinforcing what the pupils already know.

Example two

A class of Year 1 children were discussing the care of babies as part of the their class theme, 'Ourselves'. A parent had come in to school to bathe her new baby and both the boys and the girls had been excited by this event. During the follow-up session, the teacher, who was aware of gender issues, had organized the class so that all the children could participate equally in the discussion. During the discussion the teacher put equal numbers of questions to the boys and the girls. She was careful to ask boys questions that involved thinking about the care of babies and to ask the girls about the more technical-questions aspects of childcare such as temperature and nutrition. As the discussion continued one boy put up his hand and said that he was fed up with letting everybody talk when he knew all the answers. He continued to complain, saying that it was not fair that everybody had to have a turn at answering when they didn't know what they were talking about. The teacher responded to this child by asking the rest of the class what they thought about his opinion. They told him that it was fair that everyone had a turn to speak. Later, when the children were asked to write about the discussion, the teacher made sure that the boy who had expressed his personal discontent worked with a group of children who sat with her. She made sure that each child in that group had an opportunity to speak and to make a written contribution to the class book. This example demonstrates careful and sensitive teacher intervention, rigorous planning and structuring of the oral discussion and attention to the organization for writing – all of which resulted in a productive and positive session for the class.

Conclusion

Gender-related underachievement and the part that language plays in defining gender-specific behaviour and attitudes are both complex issues. The causes of both are subtle and and multifaceted. Nursery and infant classes have a crucial role in presenting children with a view of the world which opens up choices and aims to overcome limiting and damaging attitudes. By aiming to free children from the constraints of gender, and taking positive steps to cater for the different needs of girls and boys as learners of English, teachers are helping to create opportunities for greater achievement across the curriculum for all the pupils they teach.

Suggestions for further reading

Swann, J. (1992) *Girls, Boys and Language*, Blackwell, Oxford.

Chapter 8

Difficulties in language

Introduction

This book has been written for the early-years teacher rather than the special-needs teacher and so this chapter cannot provide all the answers for successfully remediating all the language difficulties that might be encountered in school. Instead, the intention is to give guidance to teachers and students working with children who are making less than average progress in English. This chapter concentrates on difficulties, experienced by children and encountered by teachers, which affect children's progress in speaking and listening, reading and writing in the ordinary classroom. It should help teachers to review their own teaching, formulate appropriate expectations, plan programmes, consider ways of working and complement the work of external agencies when working with children in mainstream schools. All interventions with children who experience difficulties should be suited to the level the child has reached and form part of a regular, systematic and structured teaching programme that has clear and realizable aims for the child. Although some particular strategies are suggested for children with language difficulties, good language teaching and the way in which language is learned is the same for all learners and the good practice described in other chapters in this book should inform the teaching used for all children.

Fortunately only a small number of pupils, approximately 2% (Wade and Moore, 1987), experience severe learning problems which require a statement of special educational need. At the other end of the spectrum very able pupils, who comprise 2–3% of the population (Essen and Welch, 1990), may encounter learning difficulties since following the curriculum devised for the average members of the class may impede their progress rather than extend their learning. They too need to be recognized. Although the number of children in mainstream classes with sustained and severe difficulties is likely to be low, the DfE (1994) indicate that about one in five children may have learning difficulties at some time in their school career. As many children's difficulties will stem from immaturity rather than lasting special needs, it is likely that teachers of young children will encounter pupils who have some difficulties with speaking, listening, reading or writing. For all the children who deviate from the norm and for the teachers who work with them, difficulties in English can be a source of real anxiety.

The National Curriculum (DfE, 1995a) offers some guidance to teachers who are catering for children with difficulties by reminding us that all children progress at different rates and most children get over their difficulties quickly. It also emphasizes the importance of differentiated planning and careful classroom organization in order to cater for the cognitive and physical needs of all pupils:

> For the small number of pupils who may need the provision, material may be selected from earlier or later key stages where this is necessary to enable individual pupils to progress and demonstrate achievement.

> Appropriate provision should be made for pupils who need to use:
>
> - means of communication other than speech, including computers, technological aids, signing, symbols or lip-reading;
> - non-sighted methods of reading, such as Braille, or non-visual or non-aural ways of acquiring information;
> - technological aids in practical and written work;
> - aids or adapted equipment to allow access to practical activities within and beyond school.
>
> (*Ibid.*, p. 1)

For ease, difficulties in language are discussed in this chapter under the headings of speaking and listening, reading and writing. However this division is not meant to obscure the interdependence of these four processes. Oral language development facilitates and eases the process of acquiring competence in the written modes of language. If children lack reasonable proficiency in oral language it is often harder for them to achieve success in reading and writing. Children who find reading difficult may also encounter problems in their writing since their experiences with print may be limited. Success in one area is likely to contribute to developing competence in other language areas.

Speaking and listening

Fortunately many of the oral language difficulties that children present are linked to development and are outgrown as they mature. Others, such as hearing loss, can often be helped by technical means and thoughtful organization in the classroom. This section will examine some of the more common oral language difficulties and consider how the teacher can cater for these in the ordinary classroom.

Poor language

The problem of 'poor language' is one that worries many teachers. Teachers who describe children as having 'poor language' are not usually referring to children with sensory impairments or severe language disorders but are describing those children who, when they are at school, seem to find it difficult to ● listen attentively ● follow instructions ● articulate responses to questions ● speak clearly ● use standard English.

Teachers feel that children manifesting these characteristics are failing and will continue to fail not only in language but also in all areas of the curriculum, since spoken language is the main way in which teaching and learning is transmitted, understood and monitored at school. Teachers may refer to children identified in this way as having 'no language' or as 'hardly able to talk' and they may describe the home language experiences of such children as limiting.

The notion of a language deficit and the identification of language deficit as a language and learning problem may arise from a continued awareness of Bernstein's work in the 1960s and 1970s (Bernstein, 1971) and the attention that was given to it in the influential Bullock Report (DES, 1975). It may also arise from the very personal nature of oral language.

For all of us, our first and most familiar language forms are associated with our closest early relationships; they are intimately bound up with the models used by those who are close to us. Each individual's use of language represents his or her experience and the culture and values of his or her immediate society. Their use of language expresses who they are and where they are from historically, geographically and socially (Trudgill, 1974). Because each individual has a personal and emotional investment in oral language, his or her initial responses to others are strongly influenced by the feelings, assumptions, experiences and ideas he or she attaches to certain dialects and accents. This can lead to judgements being made about others that are based on personal rather than professional opinions. These can be damaging in the classroom. For young children who are very closely attached to their families and friends and who lack experience of themselves and the world, the way in which they and members of their immediate community use language constitutes a huge part of their identity. If we are not to damage children's self-image and self-esteem, it is important that we make any judgements about children's abilities in language sensitively and with professional understanding. To classify children as having 'poor language' implies judging not only that their language is deficient but also that their lives are similarly impoverished and that their ability to learn may likewise be limited. The teacher's attitude to the language use of the children in her care is crucial both to the development of children's personal confidence and to their willingness to take risks as they extend their language repertoire in response to new situations and new audiences.

In the 1980s two surveys of young children's oral language use at home were undertaken. The first by Wells (1984) investigated the home language of 128 children between the ages of 15 months and 5 years; the second undertaken by Tizard and Hughes (1984) examined the home language of 30 girls attending nursery school or nursery classes. Both groups of children were drawn equally from middle and working-class home backgrounds. Neither study found any evidence of the existence of a language deficit in working-class children. Out of the 156 children surveyed, 154 were found to be using language for a wide variety of functions and were exposed to a variety of language at home. Tizard and Hughes (*ibid.*, p. 160) concluded: 'the children who are said to enter school hardly able to talk are almost always children who can talk perfectly well at home, but are initially too ill at ease to display the full range of their verbal skills when they enter school.'

Some children may appear to be less articulate and attentive than is appropriate but, before making such an assessment, the teacher might want to discover how the child uses oral language in a number of situations and with a range of conversation partners. This would include talking to carers about the child's language use at home. Where there is evidence that the child's competence in oral language is poor in relation to normal development, then activities which enable children to use language in purposeful contexts and with real and supportive conversational partners should help to remedy this. The suggestions for group and paired work in Chapter 1 should form the basis of any oral language curriculum and will help all children to develop their competency in speaking and listening.

In addition, reluctant talkers might benefit from the following strategies:

- Enjoying the right to be quiet.
- Working and playing with a friend or partner with whom they seem to communicate easily.
- Talking or asking about a topic that they are really interested in.
- Recording oral contributions prior to group discussions which can be played back for others to listen to.
- Using puppets, toys, masks and role play to enable them to speak on behalf of someone else.

Adults often say that children cannot listen and they frequently blame the television for this. There is no evidence to suggest that children listen less well than they used to; they rarely seem to have a problem with hearing things that they want to or that adults would rather they did not hear. Children may have problems concentrating and listening in large groups for long periods of time. They may also stop listening if they do not understand or are not interested in what is being said. Teachers need to make sure that they do not speak for too long or about things that are removed from the experience of young children if they expect children to listen carefully. Teachers in the National Oracy Project (Norman, 1990) found that children were more attentive in classes where teachers limited their talk, did not repeat instructions and provided a good model of listening.

Reluctant listeners benefit from • discussion in small rather than whole-class groups • discussions that are relevant to their interests and experiences ● clear, brief teacher instructions ● compiling questions they want to know the answers to and asking these ● listening to taped stories ● seeing models of good listeners.

Hearing loss

Hearing losses may vary from those that are severe and only treatable by the use of a hearing aid to slight losses attributable to ear infections, impacted wax or glue ear. Children with undiagnosed hearing losses are sometimes labelled as inattentive or lacking in concentration. They do not appear to listen or to understand what they have to do and may withdraw into their own world or become troublesome in class. If a child manifests these sorts of behaviours or if the teacher suspects that a child is deaf, she should look for the following signs which are characteristic of those with a hearing loss ● does not respond when called ● hears name but little else ● misunderstands or ignores instructions ● frequently asks the teacher to repeat instructions ● watches faces closely ● frequently asks neighbour for assistance ● reluctance to speak ● speaks very softly ● speaks very loudly ● speech defect ● orally poor ● appears dull and is not making expected progress ● appears disinterested in class activities ● complains of ear ache ● discharging ears ● persistent colds and catarrh (adapted from Fraser and Chapman, 1983).

If a hearing loss is confirmed then the teacher needs as much information as possible about the impairment. It is helpful if she knows how severe the loss is, how much the child can utilize lip-reading skills and how the hearing aid works. She should also make a realistic assessment of the child's natural ability so that she neither under or over expects from him. All the staff in school who come into contact with deaf children need to be aware of them and need to be given basic guidelines for their interactions with them.

Deafness affects both communication and comprehension, but careful classroom organization may help the child with both these aspects of language. A quiet classroom will help the child to hear more easily. When the teacher is speaking the child should be close to the teacher and able to see her lips, face and gestures. The teacher will want to encourage the child's oral contributions and will be prepared to re-explain tasks and instructions to the child. She may encourage other children in the class to work with the hearing-impaired child, giving explanations and repeating instructions, and she may plan paired work for some tasks so that the child benefits from listening and speaking in a small group.

Speech disorders

Wade and Moore (1987) write that 75% of speech disorders are articulatory, that is, they involve the inaccurate production of phonemes. As an example the child might say 'tome' instead of 'come' or 'cool' instead of 'school'. Articulatory disorders may be linked with hearing disorders, physical abnormalities such as a cleft palate or immature development. Misarticulation frequently occurs as part of the normal pattern of speech development, most children acquiring 'normal' pronunciation by the age of 5 or 6. About 1% of 6-year-olds continue to have difficulties with accepted pronunciation and may benefit from the intervention of a speech therapist (Wade and Moore, 1987). If misarticulation persists the child may begin to avoid speaking and fail to gain the practice needed to extend his speech repertoire. He may also encounter problems with aspects of spelling and reading that draw on accepted pronunciation and phonic awareness. Intervention will involve the child in learning and practising the sounds that are mispronounced and it is helpful to the child if the teacher is aware of the programme that the speech therapist devises, so that she can help the child practise the relevant sounds and offer praise when these are pronounced correctly. Other speech disorders are largely those associated with language fluency and rhythm. Probably the most common of these is stammering, which is the involuntary distortion of speech rhythms.

For all children who have difficulties with speaking and listening the teacher should • give the child plenty of time to speak • not interrupt or finish what the child is saying • create safe situations in which the child feels comfortable about speaking aloud • encourage the child to relax when he is speaking • focus on the content of what is being communicated rather than the way the child speaks • accept and at times encourage brief responses • never force the child to speak.

Oral communication is vital in order to share ideas and listen to and learn from others. Those who have a speech or hearing disability are at a disadvantage both educationally and socially and do require the teacher's understanding and sensitive intervention in order to minimize and remediate the difficulties which they experience.

Reading

Children's failure to make good progress in reading is probably the area which causes early-years teachers the greatest concern. Even with high-quality teaching some children do not make sufficient progress in reading to enable them to gain satisfaction and success with books. These difficulties manifest themselves in a number of ways and some children may have several types of difficulty:

What sort of reading difficulty?
• Being unable to read.
• Not wanting to read.
• Not understanding what is read.
• Thinking one can't read.
• Not reading the texts provided.

What causes reading difficulties?

The following factors are often cited as contributing to failure at learning to read.

Physical factors • visual impairment • hearing problems • language delay or disorder • ill-health resulting in prolonged or frequent absence from school; *environmental factors* • high adult expectations and pressure • absence of books at home • unfavourable home circumstances; *school factors* • irrelevant materials • teacher expectations too high • teacher expectations too low • the purposes for reading not clear to the children • poorly organized reading programme • teachers responding negatively to children who are slow to start reading; *personal characteristics* • anxiety • lack of motivation • short attention span • poor self-image • not understanding what reading is for • general learning difficulties.

Before embarking on teaching a child who has difficulties with reading it is vital to explore the sort of difficulty the child has and the possible cause or causes of his difficulty. Any action that is then taken will be of most benefit to the child because it will be linked to what is wrong. Some causes may be corrected very easily. For example physical factors can often be corrected or helped by referring the child for a sight or hearing test. Physical problems do not mean that the child cannot or will not read, just that there are very tangible reasons why the child is experiencing problems. Environmental difficulties may be solved or at least helped by discussions with parents and carers about their expectations for the child and their own interest in reading. Home and school may then be able to work together at helping the child to become a reader. The absence of books at home need not prevent the child from learning to read; other forms of text, such as teletext, newspapers, etc., will probably have introduced the child to writing, but it may be that the teacher has to devote more time to ensuring that the child who lives in a home that has limited literacy provision gains as much experience as possible with books at school and learns about the purpose and relevance of literacy in his own life. Difficulties at home resulting in emotional trauma for the child may be temporary, such as those accompanying a separation or bereavement and again do not mean that the child has a problem in learning to read, just that there are problems that are making it hard for the child to concentrate on learning at the moment. It is useful if the teacher is aware of these circumstances so that she can alter her expectations in line with the present needs of the child as a learner.

If the teacher suspects that some aspects of the teaching programme are not helping the child to learn to read she can change these quite easily. She can ensure that all the children in the class are aware of the purposes for reading by her demonstrations of reading and her explanations about the uses of reading. Topping (1985) suggested that reading repetitive reading material and playing language games which are intended to teach children letters and words do not always make the purposes for reading clear to children and might not convince them that becoming literate is a worthwhile pursuit. The teacher might want to make sure that her reading programme consists of meaningful, intrinsically interesting activities which relate to literacy in the world outside school. She will want to provide the child with materials that are motivating, that are linked to the child's experiences and interests and that contain vocabulary and grammatical structures that match the reader's own use of language. She can consider whether the available texts help the child to make use of all the cueing systems that a reader uses. The books that the teacher provides are important since they are those that she approves of. Since books for inexperienced readers reflect their world, their experiences and their interests, the books that the teachers selects reflect how she perceives this. Classroom texts are a reflection of the teacher's attitudes and feelings about reading and about children. If the teacher offers the child beautiful books that have been chosen with care then the child is more likely to feel that the activity is valuable and that he is valued, and is more likely to want to be a reader.

Within the reading programme for the class the teacher may want to lay more emphasis on some of the following aspects, either to strengthen the overall programme or to help the individual with difficulties:

- Using big books for shared-reading times to teach children about reading.
- Including book making as a literacy activity.
- Having regular periods of silent reading.
- Making sure that children use the listening area to read and listen to tapes of familiar and new texts.
- Making and playing games based on books that children read.
- Emphasizing the value of reading at home to carers.

For the individual who is experiencing difficulties the teacher may want to set aside a time when she really listens to the child reading by perhaps carrying out a miscue analysis. She may want to know which reading strategies the child makes use of and those that he does not use. As the child reads she may ask herself, is the child reading for meaning? Does the child read on? Does the child go back and reread when he encounters difficulties? Does he self-correct? Can he use phonic strategies? Does he appear to have a sight vocabulary? This will help her to gain a much clearer picture of where the child's strengths and weaknesses lie. The results of this might lead her to alter the way in which she listens to the individual read. She might ensure that the child is given time to prepare the text before reading with an adult. She might make sure that reading sessions are long enough to spend time discussing the text both before and after the reading. She might encourage the child to select his own reading material so that it matches his interests. She might want the child to have experience with books that have little or no text. She may institute paired reading sessions for the child with adults or more experienced readers in school and at home. It is unlikely that the teacher will want to devise a special individual reading programme for children with difficulties that is different from normal good practice in reading. Poor readers do not just need an intensive diet of phonics or special reading books, they need to develop at all aspects of reading. What they may require are regular, systematic and sustained reading sessions and reading activities which cater for their weaknesses:

> There is no special mystique or methodology for pupils who have difficulties with reading. Time and effort spent with such pupils are the only factors likely to be repaid with increased interest and competence. Thus we can help best by diagnosing children's differing needs in reading and by adapting *the strategies we normally use* to meet them.
>
> (Wade and Moore, 1987, p. 95)

What follow are some strategies that may be helpful when the teacher has established a child's particular reading weaknesses. Using some of the ideas from this list might help teachers to cater for individual children's needs.

Practical suggestions to help with reading development

Semantic and syntactic cueing

● Reading taped books ● cloze procedure ● prepare texts and talk about the book, what it might be about, what will happen in the story, etc., before reading it ● talk about what has been read to develop understanding ● encourage guessing of words using the context ● encourage prediction when reading – what might happen next? ● set questions before the child reads ● shared writing in small groups ● make a story board of favourite books ● organize a treasure hunt around the classroom reading clues for meaning ● paired reading ● reading plays ● group reading ● reading with a partner ● using DEV TRAY alone or with a partner on the computer.

Grapho-phonic

● Play snap, matching and lotto games using single letters ● talk about words after shared-reading or individual reading sessions ● encourage the child to look at the ends of words as well as the beginnings ● play oral word games, such as 'I Spy', 'Odd One Out', etc., to develop phonic awareness ● sometimes use the books that are shared with the child to hunt for words that begin with or end with . . . ● build up a repertoire of rhymes and jingles, songs and jokes, which are enjoyed and learned by heart to develop awareness of language and sounds ● share entertaining books with simple rhyming texts such as those by Dr Seuss.

Establishing a sight vocabulary

• Help the child to make a book containing personally important words such as his name, family names, names of favourite toys or foods. Use this as a reading book and as a dictionary when writing   • make word and picture games such as pairs, lotto or dominoes using words from familiar and popular books; let children make the game   • sometimes use the books that are shared with the child to hunt for the word that says . . . • write out familiar rhymes and jingles for the child to read   • build up a stock of familiar books that contain simple, repetitive text for the child to read, such as *Peace At Last* (Murphy, 1980), *How Do I Put It On?* (Watanabe, 1977) and *My Cat Likes to Hide in Boxes* (Sutton, 1973).

General

• Demonstrate the purposes of reading print through displays of print, noticeboards and reading a variety of material in the classroom• provide plenty of opportunities for listening to stories   • involve parents in reading • use extra helpers to listen to reading   • match books to the child's reading ability and interests   • provide opportunities to retell and reread familiar stories using story visuals and tapes – children can make their own story visuals and word labels for these   • follow up silent reading times with a short discussion of books children have enjoyed   • blank out the bubbles in simple comic strips and ask the child to fill these in then read them – may need some support   • make reading and reading activities enjoyable and give the child praise for effort and concentration.

Self-esteem

Readers of this book will probably be very skilled and experienced readers and whilst 'knowing' that reading failure affects children's personal and academic lives, they may find it difficult really to understand the damage to self-esteem that the continued experience of reading difficulties may cause. It is salutary and sometimes illuminating to think of something which we as adults are not good at and then to consider • how we feel about that activity   • why we are poor at it   • what might make us better at it. By doing this we might be able to understand children's difficulties more clearly.

Despite being an experienced driver I am not very good at parking my car and even after arriving at my destination after a long, tiring journey can sometimes waste 15 minutes looking for an easily accessible parking spot which may be some distance away from where I want to be. How do I feel about this?   • I feel angry with myself   • I feel foolish and stupid   • I don't want anyone to watch me when I am parking   • I feel irritated with people who might see me and with those unknown people who have successfully parked their cars.

Why am I poor at parking? • When I learned to drive I didn't realize the importance of being able to park well • I then assumed that I would just learn how to do it • later I began to avoid situations where I would find it difficult to park • if I had a passenger who could drive I might ask them to park the car • I began to make jokes about my inability to park, to excuse myself and to conceal my frustration • I now begin every attempt at parking expecting to fail. What would improve my parking? Practice, encouragement and sympathetic guidance.

There are a number of lessons to be learned from this example. First, whatever I cannot do, in this case park a car, is not as central to my life as learning to be literate is to a young child. All children expect to learn to read, they see success at reading praised by adults in and out of school and know that it is a prized activity. When they have difficulty with reading not only may they feel they are failing at reading but also that they are failing as a person. Their failure is public. Children who are poor at reading are known to be so by all the members of the class and their failure is demonstrated every time they read aloud. As with the parking example, children who have difficulty at reading will avoid reading. They gain fewer reading experiences and as a result they will accumulate less knowledge about reading than their more competent peers. They will begin to distrust their own reading competence, become anxious about reading and they will not see themselves as readers; their self-confidence will falter. They may begin to withdraw increasingly from situations where they may have to read, not concentrate or attend to demonstrations of reading, appear unmotivated and even become disruptive during reading sessions in order to distract attention away from their reading failure. All this leads to them gaining even less practice and obtaining less guidance and support.

If any remedial programme is to succeed it is important to build up the child's confidence, allay his fears and remove the pressure so that the child feels he wants to learn and is secure enough to be able to take the risks that learning involves. For some children enhancing their self-esteem may be sufficient to enable them to succeed at reading. As Asher (1980) suggested, failure to learn to read often occurs not because children lack the physical or cognitive resources to succeed, but because they lose impetus and belief in themselves.

Ways to enhance children's self-esteem:

- Think through the learning experiences that are offered from the child's perspective.
- Organize activities to facilitate not impede children's sucess.
- Provide a safe environment where risk taking is possible and valued.
- Value the process of learning, not just the product.
- Build up the child's trust by being fair, straightforward, honest and courteous.
- Praise and encourage the child whenever the opportunity arises, making the reasons for your praise clear to the child.

- Provide learning situations (not necessarily to do with reading) which will result in success.
- Respond promptly and positively to work which the child does.
- Set clear and achievable goals for the child and let the child know when he has achieved these.
- Use language positively. Don't say, 'You aren't trying'. Say, 'I don't think that that is too hard for you. I think that you can do it'. Don't say, 'He's a problem'. Say, 'He's an inexperienced reader' (inexperienced readers improve as they gain more experience).

Ways to develop a positive self-image through literacy activities:

- Listen to what the child says about reading and texts, take this seriously, the child's views are important and enlightening.
- Make an 'I Can . . .' book with the child, containing simple sentences and pictures that demonstrate what the child can do.
- Use the child's interests to help him write his own material.
- Prepare all texts before reading.
- Compile data from books and magazines that interests the child.
- Listen to taped books.
- Make tapes based on books the child writes or the adult scribes for him.
- Praise the child's successes.
- Provide a wide variety of books at a simple level.
- Read books together that children with low self-esteem can identify with, such as *Willy the Wimp* (Browne, 1984) and *Willy the Champ* (Browne, 1985).
- Scribe a book he composes and use this as a reading book.
- Write a simple book for the child based on the child's interests or with the child as the central character.
- Write a letter to the child, for example 'You did some wonderful maths yesterday'.
- Let the child choose his own reading material.
- Ask the child to make up a story using wordless picture books.

Reading recovery

Reading Recovery is an intervention programme designed to provide support for young readers who appear to be struggling with reading but who have not yet experienced failure. One of the aims of the programme is to use early intervention to prevent reading difficulties from becoming established. It is open to those children who have made least progress in reading after one year at school and is taught by a teacher who has been trained in the Reading Recovery approach. Those children who qualify for the programme receive one-to-one teaching for half an hour each day for 12 to 26 weeks, in addition to the literacy teaching that is normally provided in their class. The reading and writing activities and the materials are carefully matched to the child's level of competence and needs.

During the sessions the teacher and child read together and build up a repertoire of familiar and well liked stories. These are used as the basis for reading and writing activities. Part of each session is spent examining familiar or relevant words and identifying letters, sounds, letter strings and links with other words. As the child becomes confident with the familiar texts unfamiliar but interesting texts are introduced and shared. The child is expected to do some independent writing in each session and this is used for work on sequencing, spelling and handwriting. By the end of the programme it is expected that the child will be reading at the average level for his class.

This programme was first begun in New Zealand in 1978 by Marie Clay and, in a later evaluation (Clay, 1990), she wrote that two-thirds of all the children who experienced Reading Recovery were able to continue to function at average levels for their group after finishing the programme. An evaluation of Reading Recovery in Britain (Sylva and Hurry, 1995) suggests that this programme provides an effective form of intervention with improvements in reading apparent one year after the programme had been completed. Unfortunately, because it is expensive in teacher time and training costs, it is not found in every school or every authority. However the characteristics of the programme – systematic, regular, intensive, structured and supportive whole-language teaching, matched to the needs and interests of the child – may be used to inform any remedial teaching that is planned for children with difficulties both within the classroom and in sessions undertaken by support teachers.

Dyslexia

Specific developmental dyslexia is a form of severe retardation in reading, writing and spelling that does not appear to be attributable to • poor teaching • lack of motivation • below-average intelligence • lack of opportunity or support for literacy at home • abnormal vision, hearing or physical health • resistance to normal teaching and remedial help.

The way in which it is manifested is often characterized by the following signs • an inability to recognize and name words • mispronunciation and omission of words when reading • an inability to integrate visual and auditory information and use phonics • omissions, bizarre spellings, reversals, mixed use of upper and lower-case letters, the right letters in the wrong order in words, words incorrectly ordered in written sentences • writing in English produced from right to left • an inability to sequence actions • left-handedness • speech disorders • reading and writing fails to develop normally.

In spite of there being a set of tangible traits associated with dyslexia it remains difficult to diagnose. In the first place not all these characteristics are present in all those who have dyslexia. For example as many as 50% of dyslexics may be right handed. The presence of these factors does not automatically impede normal reading development in all children and in fact many of these signs are characteristic of young children's early reading and writing. Whilst dyslexia is not seen as attributable to low IQ or unfavourable home conditions for literacy, there is no reason why these factors might not be present. The characteristics of dyslexia are conditions within, not external, to the child, and could be found across a range of abilities and environmental circumstances. Finally the diagnosis of dyslexia may be difficult because by the time the disability in reading is recognized other symptoms and compensatory strategies such as poor self-esteem, lack of motivation or deviant behaviour may have been acquired.

In practice it is often the size of the gap between IQ and reading age or reading quotient that predominates when deciding whether a child is dyslexic. This involves two assumptions both of which are open to question: first, the validity of IQ tests and, secondly, the existence of a strong correlation between reading and IQ. Using IQ tests to assess children may disadvantage those who are unfamiliar with tests, anxious in test situations or the less able who may well be dyslexic. IQ tests are often thought of as advantaging children who are articulate or who are used to problem solving. Additionally there need not be a perfect match or relationship between reading and IQ. We do not automatically assume that there is a link between IQ and ability in maths or science or art and there is no more reason to expect this relationship in reading:

> at any score point on a standardised intelligence test as many children 'over-achieved' in reading as 'under-achieved'. In other words although there *is* a correlation between intelligence level and reading attainment, this is only a rough and ready indicator and intelligence level is not a firm prerequisite of any particular reading attainment.
>
> (Cashdan and Wright, 1990, p. 144)

The diagnosis and identification of dyslexia remain difficult and it is a term that should be applied with caution. However its use can be positive. It can bring relief to carers when they are told that their child's difficulties are not due to laziness or stupidity, but to a neurological condition which demands special help and sympathy rather than pressure and disapproval. Children too can feel relief and welcome the term which appears to recognize their frustrating struggle with reading and writing. Their self-esteem may be restored and they may be in a better position to respond to making a fresh start at learning to read.

As for all children who are learning to read and write the special teaching that dyslexic pupils receive should be structured, systematic, intensive, regular and positive. The teacher's expectation should be that, even though improvement might be slow and in some cases minimal, there will be improvement and literacy will develop over time.

Success at reading for the child who has experienced difficulties

Success at reading will be different for every child and may be linked as much to a positive attitude towards reading as to successful performance.

The child who is interested in becoming a reader and who feels that he is a reader will make progress when his interest and efforts are supported. Teachers will have a number of particular aims for those children who experience difficulty at learning to read and their progress should be evaluated using these aims. The statements listed below represent the sort of aims that are important for all children but that have particular relevance to children who are not finding the path to literacy easy.

Successful readers ● make meaning from written texts ● read with intelligence, enjoyment and economy ● turn to books for information and enjoyment ● know how to select books for their own purposes ● use their knowledge of language and of the world when reading ● have developed reading strategies that with further use, practice and experience will enable them to grow in competence as readers.

Writing

Children who have difficulty with reading are often those who find writing difficult. The fewer experiences children have with print the less they will learn about its use and its conventions and the less they will benefit from the reciprocal benefits that occur when learning to read and learning to write develop together (Clay, 1991). For those children with combined literacy difficulties all the reading activities described in the previous section will also help to alleviate their writing difficulties. As difficulties with recording may affect the assessment of children's learning across the curriculum, it is helpful to remember that speaking and listening can provide an alternative means of learning and demonstrating learning for those children with literacy problems.

For less successful writers there is often little enthusiasm for the process. Writing is slow and painful and as a result they do less writing than their more successful peers. Because they engage less in the process, they receive less practice, less help and less positive feedback and begin to think of themselves as unable to write. This can result in an unwillingness to write. In order to be a successful writer it is necessary to know what writing is for and how it is produced. Children's difficulties in writing may be associated with understanding and interest in writing, the ability to compose or the ability to use the conventions of written language successfully:

What sort of writing difficulty?
● Doesn't want to write.
● Writes very little.
● Never completes a piece of writing.
● Poor spelling.
● Disorganized and repetitive writing.
● Poor punctuation.
● Can't read what was written.
● Poor handwriting.

Motivation

The sorts of difficulties which might appear under this heading are those where the child is reluctant to write, spends a great deal of time writing the date and the title of the piece of writing but little else, rarely completes a piece of writing or regularly produces one or two poorly transcribed sentences which even he has difficulty in reading back. With difficulties such as these it is first of all important to check that the child is aware of what writing is for, that he knows that it is a lasting means of communicating important, interesting information to an audience who would not otherwise be able to hear what the writer has to say.

Some classroom practices can conceal the true nature of writing from children, and teachers may want to check that they are not giving pupils poor messages about the nature of writing before they identify the child as having a problem. Classroom practices that may result in poor attitudes to writing include overemphasis on the transcriptional aspects of writing, 'one-chance' writing, the teacher as the only audience for writing in class, starting points for writing that are not relevant to the children and writing tasks in the classroom that are divorced from writing purposes in the real world. Often if these are changed and children can see that writing has a purpose and an audience who responds to what they have to say rather than what they do they will begin to write interesting and sustained texts. One way of demonstrating this to children is to find out what the child wants to say and scribing this for him in order to produce a text that he and his audience can read and respond to (Smith, 1994).

Composition

Difficulties with composition may be seen when children won't write, produce very short, incomplete or repetitive pieces of writing, present finished writing that is poorly structured or cannot read back what they have written.

If children have heard and participated in story sessions at school and shared stories at home they should be able to make up oral stories of their own. They will have some familiarity with the pattern and language of stories. Their reluctance to write may arise from lack of confidence in their own ability or their anxiety about spelling and handwriting. There are a number of ways in which the teacher can help children who have difficulties with composition. Writing which is modelled on known texts provides children with a familiar starting point and simple structure for them to follow (Smith and Alcock, 1990). Using stories containing a journey can be particularly good starting point (Smith, 1994), since these contain an easily recognizable and memorable structure. Children can first draw a sequence of pictures, a time line or a map which represent the events in the book and this pictorial representation can then be used to

This is Big Bear he is Cumphe
and hus. I like him. The man
at piddys shop gev him to me.
I play a lot with him.

Figure 8.1 Toy photo

sequence the writing. As children gain confidence in planning and rewriting known stories they can gradually be encouraged to work towards creating their own stories or relating their own experiences. Stories that make useful starting points for this activity include *Rosie's Walk* (Hutchins, 1970), *Patrick* (Blake, 1968) and *The Jolly Postman* (Ahlberg and Ahlberg, 1986). The teacher may set a limit on the number of events that are included in the retelling, asking the child to write about four people that the Jolly Postman visits or four things which Rosie passed on her walk. Telling the child that he can make a tape to accompany a story can also be a great incentive for reluctant writers. Other starting points for children who feel that they have no story to tell might include using a set of photographs of play resources in the class. These can be stuck into a book and accompanied by a brief written description by the child. The child might also make a catalogue of his toys using photographs or illustrations cut from mail-order catalogues (Figure 8.1).

Figure 8.2   Calum thank-you letter

   Scribing for a child will not only help him to learn about the process of writing but will give him the satisfaction of seeing that he can compose and may convince him that he does have a story to tell, particularly if the scribed story is made into a book and read by others. Asking a child to write an ending to a story that has almost been completed in a shared-writing session provides another means of support for the child who feels daunted by writing. The conclusion can be quite brief and may draw upon words that have been used during the shared-writing episode so these will be familiar to the child. The example in Figure 8.2 was written by 6-year-old Calum, a reluctant and careless writer, in collaboration with an adult. Seeing Calum playing in the office area in the classroom, the adult suggested that they write something together. Calum had previously spoken about his stay with his Aunty Pat and the teacher proposed that they write a thank-you letter to her. As the teacher and Calum shared the writing, Calum was impressed by the length of the letter, talked about his writing and asked about his spelling. He was eager to make some corrections as the writing shows. The next day Calum copied out this draft and the letter was sent. Collaborating on a piece of purposeful writing had been very motivating for Calum.

The child who is unable to read what he has written may not know that writing has a meaning and a purpose. When he writes he may simply be going through the motions of producing marks on paper. This child will benefit from demonstrations about the use of writing and from undertaking writing that has a wider audience than the teacher. The teacher could also help by talking to the child about the content before and as he writes and by writing the correct version beside the child's writing as soon as the writing is finished. In addition before the child writes but after the discussion about what will be written, the child can be given some of the key vocabulary that he will probably use thus giving the reader some clues to what has been written. Asking the child to draw a picture depicting the content of the writing before he writes will also remind the child about the content and give the teacher an idea about what has been written. If the teacher wishes she can discuss the picture with the child and together they can provide labels for some of the items in the picture. This provides another source of help and information for the child and the teacher. If children write at great length and cannot always read back every bit of their writing or if the length leads to repetitious writing the teacher will need to put a limit on the child's writing and work with him on planning and organizing writing. Children who write too much will also benefit from spending more than one session on writing – perhaps using the first session to plan and organize their writing and then returning to the plan later to write their extended version. This provides the incentive to remember what has been written and provides children with insights into the permanence of text and the process of writing.

Difficulties with transcription

Becoming a mature and confident user of the transcriptional elements of writing takes time and few children will move easily and speedily through the process. Indeed Moseley (1990) suggests that at any one time approximately 25% of children in a class of 30 will have problems with producing correct spellings. It takes over four years for children to become fluent if incomplete users of oral language and it would be reasonable to assume that it will take at least as long for children to become successful, albeit apprentice, users of the written language system, a system that can pose difficulties for many adult users. However some children may appear to be making very slow progress through the developmental phases of increasing competence and need extra forms of encouragement and help.

The transcriptional skills of spelling, handwriting and punctuation should always be taught in a meaningful context. As far as possible work on improving writing conventions should take place using writing that the child has produced. If secretarial skills are very poor or if the child is too reluctant to write because he feels inhibited by his transcriptional skills, scribing may provide the answer. The child will learn a great deal about how words are written, how letters are formed and how punctuation is used by watching an experienced writer. He will begin to understand the demands of writing such as planning, composing, drafting and taking the reader's role – all of which are useful for composition and transcription. The teacher's main aim should be to get the child to write. Once the child is writing something the teacher can to see the nature of the child's difficulties and work with him on these.

Spelling

Difficulties with spelling and handwriting may affect the content of what is written. Slow and less confident writers may may be limited to short words and simplistic ideas. They may be unable to catch their ideas in writing and put them on the page because they avoid unknown spellings or they are overconscious of the appearance of what they write. Scribing, brainstorming with the teacher to provide a short collection of words, using the word processor or introducing children to drafting may help with this difficulty as will general work on spelling, use of a dictionary and handwriting.

Some children seem to get stuck at the phonemic stage of spelling development and may only use sounds to help them write the initial letters of words producing, for example, 'CAD' for 'CAT'. For these children the teacher may first need to check that they do know the sounds and names of all the letters of the alphabet. Next she might, when writing correct versions of words, emphasize the ends of words by underlining these and discussing them with the child. She might also limit all her spelling interventions to a small, frequently used group of short words. Strategies which encourage children to see and remember important and often-used words, including the look, cover, write, remember, check approach, should also be used regularly.

If the child writes at length but his spellings are bizarre and the child himself experiences difficulty in reading back what he has written, the teacher may ask the child to limit what he writes to a couple of lines, but to think carefully about what he writes and to remember what he was writing about. The teacher may attend to this child as soon as the writing is finished, before the child has time to forget what he wrote, and provide a correct model immediately underneath the child's writing. This should be discussed and compared in detail to the child's writing.

Help can also be provided by putting commonly used words on a concept keyboard, providing the child with a short list of words for him to refer to when he is writing, encouraging him to compile his own personal dictionary and introducing him to the use of a simple dictionary. Good readers can be poor spellers since confident readers tend to read quickly focusing on the meaning of a text rather than the letters contained in each word. Although good readers will have the advantage of having more experience of print than inexperienced readers, they may need just as much help with spelling as poor readers.

Handwriting

For children with poor handwriting it is worth checking for any physical and locational factors such as posture, pencil grip, tension, space to write and paper position which may be inhibiting their writing. It may be that by changing these the child's difficulties will be eased. Some children with motor control problems or those who persistently reverse letters may need additional practice in handwriting. Activities such as pattern making incorporating letter strings and words, and drawing and painting using finger paints, big brushes and bold felt-tips may help. Computer programs that encourage children to form letters on the screen are available and these may be helpful for persistent reversals and difficulties with letter formation. Introducing children to the cursive forms for *b* and *d* may help when these letters are consistently reversed or confused as the cursive form emphasizes the differences between them far more than the print script does. Letter and letter-order reversals are not always indicative of a problem with writing since they are commonly noted in 'normal' apprentice writers but tend to disappear after two or three years of schooling in the majority of cases (Brown, 1990). Children who find handwriting particularly difficult may be motivated by using a word-processing package on the computer.

Punctuation

By the age of 8 it is probably too early to say whether a child is experiencing real difficulties with punctuation or whether he needs more time for his understanding and the correct usage to develop. However many children do seem to get stuck at the stage of connecting large sequences of writing with 'and'. Discussion about the limited use of 'and' in published texts, identifying alternatives and asking children to substitute full stops for 'and' may help.

Carelessness and overcorrectness

Some children, particularly boys, may grow careless in the presentation of their writing and others, often girls, produce pieces that are perfectly presented but very short. The teacher can address this issue by making sure that girls understand that they can use a rough draft in any way that they want to and emphasizing that initially content is more important than presentation in writing. The teacher may also want to make it clear to children who are habitually untidy, without good reason, that careless final drafts are unacceptable even if the content is good, since they are difficult for others to read.

Case study of John, a child making little progress in reading and writing

The following case study illustrates one child's literacy difficulties, the possible causes of these and the individual programme that was drawn up for him. It demonstrates how early systematic and thoughtful intervention can help to alleviate literacy difficulties.

John, aged 6, seemed not to be making progress in reading or writing. Although he appeared to be interested in books and was willing to write, he was not showing any inclination to read alone and took a very long time to complete any writing. When he shared books with adults he did not always seem to be paying attention to the overall meaning of the book, although if the book was read to him he was happy to talk about it after hearing the whole story. When he read alone he seemed to be concerned to read every word and used initial letters to help him make a guess at words that were unfamiliar. In writing he was able to use some letter sounds to begin words, but often his spellings, apart from the initial letters, were very difficult for others to read. He was always able to read back his own writing. This plateau in literacy had lasted for some time and when no progress had been made for nearly a term, was starting to cause the teacher some concern. John was slowly beginning to fall behind his peers in reading and writing and was not improving in line with his apparent ability.

The sorts of literacy difficulties that John was experiencing were limited motivation for reading and writing and not understanding what was read. There was no obvious physical, environmental, school or personal cause for these problems. The teacher concluded that John's lack of motivation was the problem and that this might have arisen because John did not appreciate the place of literacy in his life. Her aims for the reading programme she devised for John were to

- enable him to see the relevance of reading and writing,
- give him more control over the selection of reading material and topics for writing,
- work on visual strategies for word recognition and spelling,
- provide frequent and varied opportunities for him to gain practice at reading,
- ensure success and to praise any independent successes he might show.

The teacher knew that John had a good sense of humour and very much enjoyed drawing so she decided to use these as her starting point for working with him. She read a number of amusing books to the class, such as the 'Happy Family Series' (Ahlberg, 1988) and various joke books. She had made tapes of some of these books and placed them, along with copies of the books, in the listening area. She offered the books she had read to the children to read for themselves and particularly asked John if he would like to read some of the joke books. The whole class were invited to make a large book retelling the story of *Mrs Jolly's Joke Shop* (Ahlberg, 1988). John was asked to contribute some written and illustrated jokes to the book. These were short pieces of writing and because they were to be used for a class book it was important that the words were spelt correctly. As part of their research for the project the joke-writing group read and listened to the tapes, asked other members of the class for their favourite jokes and asked family members to write down jokes for school. The jokes that were written at home were read to the class, and since the humour of jokes very often depends on how they are delivered, they had to be read accurately and quickly. Any jokes that were not included in the class book were used to make small individual reading books for the class library. John became very involved in this project and became an avid collector and writer of jokes. His interest in reading and writing was rekindled and he appeared to see that one purpose for recording is to remember and that reading can recover what has been recorded. As many jokes rely on a simple formula, John encountered many repetitions of simple words, such as 'What do? . . . , What did the? . . . , Why did the? . . . , I say, I say, I say . . . , Knock, Knock, Who's there? . . . ', all of which were adding to his reading and writing sight vocabulary. After the project was over John continued to read the individual joke books and he and a friend made a tape to accompany the class version of *Mrs Jolly's Joke Shop*, an activity that required accurate reading and sustained involvement with text. As part of the project, when he was looking for jokes, John had examined a great many of the books in class. When he was asked to select books to read he was able to use his knowledge of what was available to select books that he thought would appeal to him.

This mini-project gave John's reading and writing development a boost and enabled the teacher to address many of her concerns about his progress. His successes also increased his own self-esteem; he had become an expert at telling, reading and writing jokes. The teacher pursued her aims for his learning during individual reading sessions, encouraging him to focus on the meaning of what he read, to guess at unknown words using the illustrations and meaning as a guide and to compare the words in books with words that he now knew and used in his writing. Through identifying John's needs and gearing her teaching towards her aims the teacher was able positively to intervene in John's reading and writing so that he was functioning at a level that was normal for his age and the class, rather than falling behind at a critical point in his development.

Conclusion

The sorts of difficulties that some children can experience in English are incredibly varied and can range from slight to severe. Some problems may best be tackled by consulting those with particular expertise in the area of special educational needs. However as long as children remain in the ordinary school the classroom teacher will have some responsibility for teaching children who encounter difficulties. This chapter has shown how careful planning, organization and analysis of the problem in order to adjust the curriculum to meet the needs of all children enable teachers to work productively with those who require additional support in their development as language learners.

Suggestions for further reading

National Oracy Project (1992) *Oracy and Special Educational Needs*, National Curriculum Council, York.

Smith, J. and Alcock, A. (1990) *Revisiting Literacy: Helping Readers and Writers*, Open University Press, Milton Keynes.

Wade, B. and Moore, M. (1987) *Special Children . . . Special Needs: Provision in the Ordinary Classroom*, Robert Royce, London.

Chapter 9

Involving parents

Introduction

The government emphasis on parents* as the consumers of education, specified in Education Reform Act (HM Government, 1988), has given parents the legal right to be involved in their children's education and to have access to information about education, schools and pupils. One of the criteria now used by Ofsted for judging the success of a school is the degree of satisfaction that parents feel with the school, which may be defined as how much they know about, are involved in and are supportive of the school and its curriculum. The educational rights that parents now have mean that there is probably even more need for schools to involve and inform parents and to address any concerns which they might express.

This chapter will outline how parents can and do contribute to children's learning and consider some ways in which schools can productively involve all parents in the language and literacy curriculum they offer.

The contribution of parents to language learning

Early-years educators have a long tradition of involving parents in the life and curriculum of the school and parental involvement is a significant and established feature of early-years education, particularly in the area of language and literacy. The part that parents can and do play in developing children's language learning is now widely recognized as beneficial to pupils and is so widespread that involvement in reading has been described as 'unstoppable' by Hannon (1989).

---

* *Who counts as a parent?* When we speak of parental involvement we no longer refer exclusively to biological parents. In keeping with this generally accepted and wider use of the term and to avoid repetition throughout this chapter, the word parent will mean those people who have parental responsibility for, or care for, pupils, and others who have a genuine and rightful interest in children's educational development and are in a position to make a positve contribution to it, such as grandparents, other relatives and siblings.

The benefits of active parental interest in education at home and at school have been demonstrated in a large number of studies undertaken over the past 20 years. The results of the work undertaken by Clark (1976), Tizard and Hughes (1984) and Wells (1986) have shown that parents do play a powerful and positive role in their children's learning before and outside school. They provide children with resources, literacy models and opportunities for learning about oral and written language as they involve them in everyday experiences at home. A survey undertaken by Hall *et al.* (1989) of more than 400 families showed that many parents do help children with writing at home without waiting for suggestions or support from schools – a finding that was probably fairly obvious given the large numbers of reading and writing work books that are published and sold in shops and supermarkets. The research reported by Minns (1990) gives a detailed picture of how parents of very young children spend a great deal of time sharing books with them. The initiatives which followed the Plowden Report (DES, 1967) such as the Haringey Reading Project (Hewison and Tizard, 1980) and the Belfield Reading Project (Jackson and Hannon, 1981) showed how additional practice in reading given to children at home enhances their competence at reading. These findings recognize the learning that parents encourage in the home, demonstrate that the majority of parents are keen to participate in children's education and suggest that maintaining and developing parental involvement can be educationally beneficial.

Ways of involving parents in language and literacy learning

Having a policy

Although encouraging parental involvement in the language and literacy curriculum is a familiar idea in primary and nursery education, practice often varies between schools and between classes in the same school. Parental involvement is most beneficial when schools have a coherent policy which is systematically implemented each year and throughout every class. Before embarking on a scheme to involve parents in children's learning, school staff need to have considered the potential advantages, pitfalls, support, resources and commitment that will be involved. This will necessitate having a clear policy which identifies the purposes of the scheme and the timing of events necessary to maintain and achieve its aims. If parents are to be invited to work with pupils in school or to listen to reading at home training will have to be provided by the staff. In order for teachers and parents to work together, it is important that all volunteer helpers in school are clear about what they are expected to do and that their work is carefully managed and explained by the class teacher. Schools will also need a coherent language policy which is understood by all the staff before involving parents, as inviting parents to participate in the language curriculum will lead to questions and queries which will have to be answered consistently by all staff.

The reasons for involving parents

If parental involvement is to be successful teachers need to be clear about what they want the partnership to achieve. The policy should contain a set of aims for parental involvement. These will act as a framework, helping teachers to decide on the contributions that parents are invited to make and the resources and activities which the school will have to provide in order to elicit and support these contributions. The following list contains a number of aims for inviting parents to contribute to the language curriculum at school and at home.

To enhance children's achievement in all areas of English by ● drawing on parents' knowledge of their child ● informing teachers about the child as a learner outside school ● smoothing the transition between home and school ● fostering mutual respect, understanding and openness between parents and teachers ● providing parents with information about the child's learning experiences at school ● inviting parents to support the work of the school in school and at home ● enabling children to apply learning in the world outside school ● extending the curriculum to include contributions from parents and members of the community ● giving parents advice and information about their child's progress at school.

Almost every child in the school is likely to benefit from parental involvement schemes, even when his or her carer does not play an active part. The involvement of some parents as volunteers in the classroom and the knowledge that some children receive a great deal of support at home may enable the teacher to organize her time or that of the volunteers to give more support to those children who may not be receiving a great deal of encouragement at home. In this way the interest of some parents can benefit all children, although one would always continue making efforts to involve all parents.

Ways in which parents can be involved

Their are many ways of involving adults and friends in the language curriculum at school and at home. The following list suggests ways of employing parents' oral and written abilities to help extend children's language learning.

Parents in school ● run the library ● run a school book club or shop ● talk to pupils while supervising activities ● lead activities such as cooking which involve talk ● teach games, songs and rhymes to pupils ● help with school drama productions ● tell stories to children ● encourage children to write in their mother tongue ● encourage children to read in their mother tongue ● act as a translator for parents and children • help children to use the computer for writing • make books with children • act as a scribe • listen to reading • contribute to children's records on entry to school and through parent conferences • act as an interviewee for children's questions during a theme.

Parents at home • reinforce learning begun at school, such as listening to reading • provide resources for learning at home, such as writing implements and books • record songs, rhymes and stories on tape • write recipes • write books for children • translate children's stories, published books, signs, labels, notices, letters and circulars • supply materials for use in school.

Initial considerations

Having established the purposes for involving parents, schools might need to consider their existing relationships with parents and their arrangements for communicating with them. Parents will be more ready to participate in the life and curriculum of the school if they feel comfortable in the school environment and valued by teachers. Schools may like to address the following questions when considering how to transmit positive messages to parents about relationships between them and the staff:

- Is the school environment welcoming to all parents?
- Are all visitors greeted and welcomed?
- Are there signs to direct visitors around the school?
- Is there a highly visible, attractive and up-to-date parents' noticeboard?
- Are parents' as well as teachers' preferences and needs, such as child-care facilities, considered when parents are invited into the school?
- Is there an established system of regular communications between school and home, such as a termly newsletter?
- Are the booklets that are available for parents well presented, accessible and jargon free?

In order to be actively and productively involved in children's education, parents need information about the school's way of working, what they can do and how they can do it at school and at home. The more they are aware of these the more confident they will be about participating in the life and work of the school. From the start of the child's school career parents can be given the message that education takes place at home and at school, that children's learning develops in a spirit of partnership between home and school and that it is important for both partners, parents and professionals, to be aware of children's learning experiences at home and at school.

Individual contacts between parents and professionals

During their initial contacts with the school, parents can be given information about the ethos, expectations and teaching practised in the school. Their early visits, the information contained in the school booklet and initial meetings with the head will provide some of this information. Parents may have their own expectations of schooling or of this particular school from their own school experiences, older children, friends or the reputation of the school. Initial meetings may be an appropriate forum to explore parents' existing knowledge in order to avoid later misunderstandings. Early meetings also provide schools with the opportunity to demonstrate the value they place on the learning that children bring to school. When parents are asked about their child's language abilities and interests, staff can make clear why this information is useful and how it benefits pupil learning at school. Involving parents in this way from the start acknowledges and values parents' intimate knowledge of their own children and signals that, although once children start school there is an important professional input to their learning, the contribution and knowledge of parents are still significant.

In *The Primary Language Record*, Barrs *et al.* (1988) suggest that there should be a 15-minute discussion between parent and teacher during the child's first term at school in order for parents and teachers to share their knowledge about the child. They give a clear set of guidelines which are helpful for setting up successful meetings between parents and teachers, suggesting that

- parents should be contacted personally through written invitations, conversations or phone calls,
- schools should offer day and evening times to suit parents' circumstances,
- once appointments are arranged they should be adhered to to minimize disrupting child care or other arrangements,
- interviews should take place in a private, comfortable area,
- if necessary the services of an interpreter should be arranged,
- parents should be clear that the purpose of the meeting is the educational welfare of the child,
- important and useful points should be recorded.

The discussion should focus on the child's speaking, listening, reading and writing experiences out of school, including his attitudes, language opportunities and interests. The meeting also provides the teacher with an opportunity to clarify any queries that the parent might have and should be the first of many regular meetings organized between parent and teacher to exchange information and discuss the child's progress.

Providing written information

Written information provides parents with something they can refer to and is a useful addition to oral explanations and requests. The following information was written for a first and nursery-school booklet and given to all parents on their initial visit to the school. The specific guidelines about encouraging children's reading at home were repeated in the school's home–school reading booklet.

Reading
All children have a daily reading time in school. They may read books, their own writing or the teacher's writing. They may read alone or in groups, aloud or silently. They also listen to stories. If you would like to know more about reading in school, please come in to see your child's teacher.

Children will bring reading books home each day and we ask all parents/carers to read to, listen to or encourage their child to do some quiet reading at home every day. We feel that the extra attention that parents/carers give to children is very helpful.

Helping Children with Reading at Home
You can help your child with reading in the following ways:

Read to your child
Read with your child
Listen to your child read aloud
Encourage your child to do some quiet reading.

All children enjoy listening to stories and all children need to have a go at reading. Whatever your child's ability s/he will benefit from a mixture of these activities.

Reading to Children
When reading to children talk about the pictures, what is happening, what has happened and what is going to happen in the book. This helps to develop the child's interest in books and understanding of stories.

Reading with Children
Sometimes you and your child might read a book aloud together. The child should join in with you when s/he feels confident. If the child attempts a number of words you can stop reading and let the child read alone. When the child stops reading you take over again.

Listening to Reading Aloud
If the child finds a word difficult there a number of ways that you can help:

Give the child plenty of time to work out what the word says
Encourage the child to guess what the word says
Ask the child to guess using the pictures for clues
Ask the child what word would make sense
Tell the child the word.

If the child uses a word which is different from that in the book, but one that does not change the meaning, don't correct this. The child is understanding what s/he reads and this is good.

If the word does change the meaning, ask the child if that word makes sense. If the child cannot guess the word tell it to him/her.

Quiet reading
All children benefit from looking at books and reading to themselves. Encourage your child to spend 5–10 minutes reading in a quiet place. You may want to ask the child what s/he has been reading about and whether s/he had any problems that you might be able to help with.

If you are not a very confident reader you can still help your child a great deal by looking at books together and talking about the story. The pictures will help. You can also listen while your child reads aloud. The child is still benefiting from practising reading. You may have an older child, relative or friend who can read with the child.

Please take care of books that are sent home, but if a book or folder is lost please tell the teacher so that a new book or folder can be supplied. There may be a small charge for lost books and folders.

We have a bookshop in school every Thursday afternoon. Parents/carers and children are welcome to buy books.

We all want children to enjoy and succeed at reading. If you have any queries about your child's reading please talk to your child's teacher.

This information was later explained at termly reading meetings organized by the nursery and reception teachers.

Other written information about language could be provided in a booklet or in letters, written by children for parents, describing the language work that they do in school.

Literacy meetings and workshops

Once a year schools may wish to hold a literacy curriculum evening to which all parents are invited. The focus could be on reading or writing or both. The aims of these evenings are to provide information about the school approach to the teaching of literacy, to give advice to parents about how to support their child's literacy development, to invite parents to participate in the school's home-reading or writing scheme and to invite parents to contribute to the language curriculum in school, either by coming into school or producing materials at home. At the beginning of the meeting the purpose and format of the session should be explained to all the participants.

Reading

The focus for a reading meeting might be to explain to parents why additional practice at reading outside school is important, to demonstrate how to do this and to explain the particular home-reading system that the school has devised.

Explaining the school's approach

To give parents a picture of what happens in school, teachers might explain ● the way that books are used in school ● the development of reading in the early stages ● the procedure for sharing a book with a child ● the reading experiences that all children receive.

Explaining the home–school scheme

The practical arrangements of the scheme might be explained, including the frequency with which children should take books home, the selection of books to go home, and filling in the record and comments card or booklet. Teachers might refer parents to the school's explanatory booklet about the scheme.

Providing guidance about how to listen to reading

The staff might talk parents through a list of guidelines for sharing books with children which could include the following suggestions:

- Sessions should be short, about 10 minutes is usually long enough.
- If possible read together about three times a week.
- Let the child sit close to you.
- Give plenty of praise.
- You don't always have to listen to reading aloud, you can read to your child.
- Encourage the child to guess at words that he can't read.
- Look at and discuss the illustrations.
- Talk to the child about the book.
- Do ask for advice if you have any queries or worries.

Videos such as the one produced by the Chiltern Consortium (1984) are very useful in demonstrating many of the points that teachers might want to make, or schools can make their own video of children reading in school. Teachers can also role play the wrong and the right way to hold shared-reading sessions at home.

For those parents who might find it difficult to share books at home with children, teachers can talk about the benefits of involving children in the daily literacy events of the home, such as shopping, using the teletext, reading street names and reading mail, such as postcards and letters, together.

Inviting parents to help with reading at school

At the end of the meeting a general invitation to help with reading in school might be issued. The staff might give some examples of how adults can contribute. Some parents may be able to stay and read to small groups of children first thing in the morning after bringing children to school. Very often these are women, which can, together with the preponderance of female staff in first and nursery schools, reinforce the idea that boys and men do not read stories. To counter this schools might want to make a particular effort to encourage male carers to volunteer. Bilingual parents may be able to read or tell stories in their first language. Parents who are able to read or tell stories on to tape help schools to reflect the linguistic diversity of the local community as well as extending the school stock of audio cassettes. There are many other ways in which parents can be invited to help with reading and some of these appeared on the list earlier in this chapter.

Writing

Below are suggestions for activities that could be included in a writing curriculum evening. Schools might like to select activities from this that would be most appropriate for their purposes.

How and why do we write?

Ask the adults, in pairs, to make a list of all the writing they can remember doing during the previous seven days. When the lists are complete ask how people wrote some of the things included on their lists. What was it written on? How long did it take to write? What was it written with? Was it written out more than once? If so, what was corrected on the second draft and how was it corrected? The answers to these questions should raise some interesting issues about the factors that affect how we write and the reasons for writing. At this point audience, purpose, style, transcription, composition and any other issues that emerge from the lists that the parents have generated can be discussed. Teachers can compare the range of writing that has been identified by the adults with the variety of opportunities for writing that are offered to children at school. They might then refer to the section on 'Range' in the Programme of Study for English.

The writing process

Talk to the adults about the process of writing. Use overheads of the children's writing to show how development occurs over time and to explain how writing is learned. Discuss how, when and why teachers intervene and correct children's writing.

Spelling

Give the parents a spelling test of ten commonly misspelt words. This should illustrate the point that spelling is a difficult skill for most people. The teachers can then explain that spelling needs to be learned and taught in a systematic way, not just corrected. The staff might explain the 'look, cover, remember, write, check' approach and any other methods that are used in school. Staff may like to illustrate this by 'teaching' the adults how to spell a word correctly.

Handwriting

Ask the adults to look at all the writing they have done so far during the evening and to consider whether it was uniformly neat, well formed and legible. Were there any crossing-outs in the spelling test? Did the neatness matter? If someone else was reading the writing would they copy it out? Follow this by discussing the school's policy on handwriting.

Asking adults to write

The parents can be asked to write a short description of the meeting for the children to read the next day. They should be given a time limit. Observe how the adults approach and carry out the task. Give feedback on what writers do when they write and what they need. Issues such as drafting, making mistakes, the value of collaboration and time should arise from this activity.

Writing a book

If children have been invited to the session ask the parents and the children to work together to write a book. The parents could write a story drawn from their childhood experiences. The children could illustrate the book. Again the adults should be able to see that writing is not straightforward. It calls for planning and drafting and it takes time to produce something for someone to read. The adults might like to continue and complete this activity at home.

Helping at home

Give parents some ideas about how they can help with writing at home in ways that will support the school's approach to writing. Providing children with resources for writing, including notebooks, pads and envelopes and allowing children to join in writing shopping lists, letters and greeting cards, are good starting points.

Helping at school

Explain and give examples of how adults can help with writing at school. Ask for volunteers.

Displays

As a backdrop to the meeting have displays of children's writing and the books that they have made arranged around the school. Display first drafts as well as the final piece of writing. Provide written explanations of the work. Some of these could be written by the children, and if appropriate link the writing that is displayed to the National Curriculum Programmes of Study.

Questions

Answer questions fairly and honestly. If teachers can convince parents of their commitment to and interest in children's progress it is likely that the parents will support the approach that is advocated by the school.

It is hoped that by the end of the meeting all the adults present will have remembered how hard writing can be, that it is rarely right first time, that sometimes ideas are hard to find and that neatness is not necessarily the most important part of writing. They may have gained some insights into the way that the staff of the school help the children to become successful and motivated writers.

Other ways of communicating with parents about language

One-off workshops or booklets will not sustain parental interest or reach every parent, so schools need to continue to send information and requests for help home and to plan a programme of literacy events each year.

The school newsletter might contain a regular invitation to parents asking for their help in school and might list some of the contributions they could make. Some schools notify parents of the themes that are being undertaken by classes each term and ask for offers of help in relation to the theme, such as talking to children about care of a baby, being interviewed by children about their own memories of school or bringing in items related to the theme for display and discussion. Specific invitations to help with class themes can also be written by the children. Other special literacy events to which parents can be invited, either as participants or observers, are book weeks and sales of second-hand books.

Schools might organize a language open day each year when parents are welcome to observe children at work in class and to look at displays of books and children's writing. They could also be invited to join in with the work in school that day. Teachers may produce a short booklet containing advice about book selection and the sorts of books to buy or borrow from the public library as well as a brief list of suitable titles. This could be distributed to parents at some point during the school year to encourage and sustain parental interest in literacy.

Some schools encourage parents to read with their children before they start in the reception or nursery class and encourage parents to borrow books for their preschool children as well as their children who attend the school. A selection of wordless picture books and stories for parents to read to young children may be established for this purpose. Schools may also wish to loan books about literacy to parents who wish to know more. Some useful titles include *Read With Me* (Waterland, 1988), *The New Read-Aloud Handbook* (Trelease, 1984) and *Babies Need Books* (Butler, 1982). As well as books some first schools and nurseries loan language games and equipment such as alphabet sets to parents to use with their children at home. Explanations about the use of the games can be given during workshop sessions with parents.

Conclusion

Parents and carers play an important part in children's language and literacy development. They can make a range of contributions in and out of school. When this is acknowledged and supported by the school the benefits to pupils and teachers may be even more significant. Involving and informing parents about the educational work of the school helps parents and professionals to respect each other and to reach shared understandings about children's learning. School schemes that involve parents in the language and literacy development of children can have a very beneficial effect on pupil learning. However these gains often accumulate over time and such schemes should be seen as long-term endeavours that need careful preparation and organization and that need to be sustained over time if they are to be truly effective.

Suggestions for further reading

Bloom, W. (1987) *Partnership with Parents in Reading*, Hodder & Stoughton, London.

Minns, H. (1990) *Read It To Me Now*, Virago, London.

Weinberger, J., Hannon, P. and Nutbrown, C. (1990) *Ways of Working with Parents to Promote Literacy Development*, University of Sheffield Division of Education, Sheffield.

Chapter 10

Assessment

Introduction

Although there are points in the school year when teachers make formal assessments of children's learning, there are rarely times when teachers are not assessing. They want to see signs of progress and monitor children's development in language frequently. Monitoring progress is a large and vital part of every teacher's role. This chapter begins by examining assessment in general and then describes a number of practical ways for assessing speaking, listening, reading and writing in the classroom.

The framework for assessment

Why do teachers assess?

Ideally there should be very close links between assessment and teaching. Assessment is 'an integral part of teaching and learning' (SCAA, 1995) and 'lies at the heart' of the process of promoting children's learning (DES, 1988b). Collecting and analysing information and evidence about children's achievements and experiences provides teachers and others with insights into what has been learned and how it has been learned, and enables teachers to understand more about the learning needs of the pupils they work with. This should lead to more effective teaching. As curriculum planning is informed by the learning needs of pupils, the more understanding teachers have about pupils as learners, the more closely they will be able to match planning and teaching to pupils' needs. In short assessment can help teachers to modify and enhance their teaching and can improve the quality of pupil learning.

There are other reasons for assessment besides providing the teacher with feedback about pupil learning and her own teaching. Assessment can ● form part of a record of progress ● provide a statement of current attainment ● be used to compare pupils ● measure progress ● be used to diagnose or confirm learning difficulties.

When should assessment take place?

Assessment can be formative or summative. Formative assessment occurs throughout a period of learning. During this time the teacher is concerned with collecting information about the progress and needs of the pupils and planning her teaching to ensure continued progress. Summative assessment records the achievements of pupils at the end of a phase of learning, such as a Key Stage. In order to make accurate judgements about children at the end of a phase of learning the teacher will consider the range of evidence that has been collected throughout the phase. Both formative and summative assessment are important since in both cases teachers will be able to use the outcomes in order to plan and accommodate the future learning needs of children.

Summative assessments for English at the end of each Key Stage of the National Curriculum are now a statutory requirement and should be based on a summary of teachers' assessments of children's levels of attainment and the results of the assessment tasks and tests. Teacher assessment is an essential part of the National Curriculum assessment arrangements and has equal status with the task and test results. As it is conducted continuously throughout each Key Stage of learning it takes account of progress as well as achievement in a range of contexts. The summary of teachers' assessments will therefore represent a broad picture of the child's strengths and weaknesses and complements the limited information about attainment levels provided by the tasks and tests. Although there is no statutory requirement to retain the samples of work which teachers use when making their formative assessments, SCAA (1994) suggest that keeping an annotated collection of work for each child is helpful for teachers when they are making their summative assessments at the end of a Key Stage. Many schools compile portfolios of children's work as part of their record-keeping system and consider this to be good practice.

The following illustrates the type of assessments that are made in English:

- *Formative* (daily, weekly, termly and yearly): marking and responding to work; record keeping; maintaining portfolios.
- *Summative* (at the end of a phase of learning): level descriptions; statutory tests and tasks; a summary of teacher assessment.

How is learning assessed?

Assessment of pupil learning requires the teacher reflectively to analyse her practice and make professional judgements about learning. Teachers should be supported in this activity by the school assessment policy, which should • outline clear learning objectives for each phase of learning • identify how and when children's learning will be assessed • emphasize the importance of using assessment to match work to the learning needs of children.

Children too can play a part in assessing their own work. Through discussions with their teacher they can review their own work and decide which pieces of work should be included in their portfolio and why. Parents, carers and other adults who work with the child may also contribute information about the child as a learner which is useful when assessing progress and achievement in a range of settings. In order to compile their formative and summative assessments teachers will elicit information from the following sources ● observations ● samples ● pupils ● interactions ● personal and school records ● school or LEA tests ● conferences ● parents/carers ● teachers ● responses to work ● checklists ● National Curriculum tests and tasks.

What is assessed?

Section 3.2 of the *Handbook for the Inspection of Schools* (Ofsted, 1993b) outlines three aspects of learning that should be monitored. These are progress in knowledge, understanding and skills, and attitudes. Understanding and skills include a developing ability to communicate ideas and information, pose questions and evaluate. Attitudes to learning including motivation, interest, concentration and co-operation. These are far broader than aspects of learning measured by the tests and tasks and require far more information than that which is provided by them. Teacher assessment is an essential part of an effective assessment process if teachers are to demonstrate children's progress in the way that Ofsted suggests.

Whom is assessment for?

There are a number of audiences for the assessments that are made in school. Teachers are perhaps the most immediate audience as they are in a position to act quickly on the results of their discoveries. Children will receive feedback from their teachers about their work and, if this is sensitively given and they are included in the evaluation process, they will benefit from the assessments that are made. Teachers will share their judgements about pupils with parents and carers, not only through the legal requirement of a yearly report but also at other times throughout the school year. This may be done formally at open evenings and informally if the teacher or parent wishes to ask about or discuss issues related to progress.

National government uses the results of assessments to keep a check on national standards and trends. They may use this information to support educational initiatives and research in areas where standards are not as high as is desirable. Local education authorities use the results from assessment procedures to monitor standards in their schools. They may also operate screening procedures in order to identify children who need extra help, often in aspects of literacy. All those who contribute to the life of the school will be concerned with the achievements of their pupils. They will want to keep track of the progress that children make over time and will want to ensure that standards are maintained or enhanced.

The assessment of language

Standards in English are probably monitored more closely than those in any other area of the curriculum, particularly in the early years of schooling. Success at reading, writing, listening and speaking is considered to be essential for every child. In order to assess each child's development in language appropriately, teachers need a thorough understanding of the way in which competence in speaking, listening, reading and writing develops. They need to remain aware of the long-term aims of development in language, which include enabling all children to become confident and critical users of language for their own purposes, and they need to make sure that the shorter-term goals which are assessed indicate progress towards the long-term aims. This is necessary if teachers are to avoid concentrating on skills and fragmenting the curriculum.

Most assessment is carried out by the class teacher. However, parents, carers and other adults who work with the children may offer further perspectives on their development in listening, speaking, reading and writing. In particular parents of bilingual children may be able to tell the teacher about the child's knowledge and understanding of languages other than English. Parents may talk about when the child chooses to read and write outside school, or if they have noticed a change in the child's attitude towards literacy. The next sections examine how the four areas of language are assessed.

Assessment of speaking and listening

Although children demonstrate other learning through talk this section will examine the assessment of children's use of speaking and listening in line with the requirements of the National Curriculum (DfE, 1995a) Programmes of Study and level descriptions.

The assessment of speaking and listening should begin by identifying what children can do rather than what they have failed to achieve. Indeed looking closely at talk can help us see children as effective communicators, and to realize that they are better at this than one might sometimes suppose. By the time they are old enough to embark on the statutory requirements, the majority of young children will already be able to do many of the things that are required by the National Curriculum in relation to speaking and listening. Because talk is not permanent it is important that teachers have a system in place which will enable them to capture moments which show a child using talk well. Since teachers are concerned with discovering positive achievements they will need to consider a number of factors, not necessarily related to oral ability, that may affect the quality of children's talk when they are undertaking assessments. These include ● the nature of the audience or listener ● the type of task that has been set to stimulate the use of talk ● the child's interest in and ownership of the task ● the child's previous experience of using speaking and listening during this sort of task ● the child's fluency in his home language as well as in English ● the child's gender and that of his partner or other group members ● the child's personality ● the composition of the group.

Teachers will also be aware that assessment is never based on single activities but on a range of evidence built up over time from a number of different situations in which children engage in different kinds of talk. Evidence from a variety of contexts is particularly important when assessing oracy since it is an area where it easy to make an unfair assessment by overestimating the confident, loud speaker in a group and underestimating quieter children who may be using speaking and listening effectively.

The aspects of speaking and listening which are monitored

The National Curriculum (DfE, 1995a) identifies three areas that should be taught and assessed at school. These are range, key skills and standard English and language study. Children are expected to grow in competence in using listening and speaking in a range of situations and for a variety of purposes. They are expected to develop the key skills of oracy, such as clarity, fluency and turn taking, while development in standard English and language study is signified by an increasing vocabulary and a growing ability to match their use of language to the situation and the listener.

In the level descriptions these indicators of competence are represented by phrases such as 'talk and listen confidently in different contexts' (Level 3, range), 'speak clearly and use a growing vocabulary' (Level 2, key skills) and 'beginning to be aware of standard English and when it is used' (Level 3, standard English and language study).

These are rather bald statements and do not do justice to the richness of curriculum provision needed to develop and assess communicative success in the classroom. For example in order for the teacher to gauge children's ability to 'listen carefully and respond with increasing appropriateness to what others say' (Level 2, skills), children will need to listen to other children as they play and work together and to listen to stories read by adults or on tape. They might demonstrate response by asking questions, commenting, interpreting, relating what they have heard to their own experience or acting on instructions. Assessing the appropriateness of response will involve children demonstrating confidence and sensitivity about when and how to contribute to discussions.

There are a number of features that teachers might look for to assess oral language, including ● what the child knows and understands about the way language works ● the ability to communicate one to one, in or to a small group, in or to a large group • the ability to communicate with known and unknown audiences • the appropriateness of language used in different circumstances • the ability to interest an audience • the ability to co-operate, to take turns and not to dominate • confidence • clarity • coherence • audibility • progression • range, variety and appropriateness of vocabulary • the ability to reason, argue and debate • the ability to summarize • the ability to listen to others in different situations, e.g. when playing, when working, during story time • the ability to use speech to project oneself into different roles • the ability to ask questions.

As well as providing teachers with a framework for the assessment of children's use of talk this checklist might be helpful when planning for speaking and listening activities and opportunities in the curriculum.

How and when speaking and listening are assessed

With speaking and listening, as with every other area of the English curriculum, it is helpful if teachers build up a record of children's achievements and progress over time. This will involve observing and noting children's spoken interactions within the normal classroom day. To facilitate this, it is useful for teachers to indicate in their weekly planning the activities that lend themselves to observations of children using talk in a variety of situations, across different curriculum areas and with a range of partners and audiences.

Within their observations teachers may want to record samples of children's talk using notes or a tape recorder as well as taking account of spontaneous examples of children demonstrating positive achievements as speakers and listeners. By having examples of children's successes over time they will have sufficient evidence on which to base their assessments and to provide information which may help with future curriculum planning and provision for children's individual needs. They will also have the information they will need when they are making a summary of each child's progress and achievements to pass on to the next teacher, share with other relevant adults or use for their assessment at the end of a Key Stage. In Wales there is currently a Key Stage 1 test for oracy, but there is no formal oral test or task for 7-year-olds attending school in England.

The assessment of reading

As with speaking and listening and with writing, most assessment of reading is formative and informs the teacher's day-to-day actions in the classroom. The teacher learns a great a deal about children's reading through normal classroom interactions and is able to give immediate feedback to children as she supports their use of all the written material in the classroom.

The aspects of reading which are monitored

The aim of teaching children to read is not just to produce children who can read but also children who want to read, who do read for their own purposes and who can learn from and evaluate what they read. To this end teachers will assess a great many aspects of reading. They will assess the child's competence and use of reading strategies, his attitude to reading, his choice of reading material and his understanding of and response to what is read. To discover whether the child is progressing towards these overall goals of learning to read the teacher will employ a number of assessment procedures.

Ways of assessing reading

Regular individual reading sessions

This is probably the most commonly used method of assessing pupils' reading. Discussing and sharing a book with a child can give the teacher a great deal of information about a number of the aspects of reading behaviour that she wishes to monitor. Often teachers maintain a record of these reading sessions in a notebook or file, allocating a number of pages for each child at the start of the year. In the example which follows the teacher has noted the books which Shippu has chosen, some of his reading strategies, such as his ability to remember some words and stories, his confident attitude to reading and the sort of support and teaching strategies she has given to him during the sessions and will continue to offer to him. In this extract these include working on meaning and graphophonic cues:

Name Shippu   **d.o.b.** 6.8.89   age 5 yrs 1 mth

Date	Book	Child's Strengths	Teacher strategies
13.9.94	Hairy Bear	Read well. Pointed to words. Confidently re-told story.	Discussed story.
19.9.94	Better Move on Frog	Remembered this well. Read many words alone.	Supported shared reading – needs more opportunities to read with others and with tapes.
23.9.94	Bet You Can't	Found this difficult – lack of narrative?	Discussed tidying up at home. Told story using illustrations. Looked for and talked about the 'bs' in the text.

This record, together the child's home-reading notebook containing a list of books shared at home and comments from other adults, would present a very full picture of Shippu's reading.

With more experienced readers the teacher's comments might refer to specific miscues, fluency and response to the text. Sharing books will always involve the child in some reading aloud, but children who are at the stage of reading silently may spend very little time reading to the teacher. The teacher can assess the children's growing competence through discussion and their retelling of the text, and reading only a short extract from their current book. Looking back at records at the end of a term or a year often reveals a very positive account of progress which is extremely useful when the teacher is writing records and reports.

Observations

Teachers can learn a great deal about their pupils as readers from observing them in a number of reading contexts. These contexts will include children

- listening to, telling or participating in stories in sessions led by an adult or shared with other children as in the listening area,
- browsing and choosing books to read for pleasure or use in class or at home,
- reading aloud alone, with adults or with other children during shared or group-reading sessions,
- reading silently either voluntarily or during quiet reading times,
- demonstrating incidental awareness and use of print,
- discussing books,
- incorporating literate behaviour or actions and words from stories into play.

Observations made of children in these situations will help the teacher to build up a full picture of *how the child reads* (with independence, with confidence, with interest, out of choice, in English or in another language); *when the child reads* (with others, alone, out of choice); *what the child reads* (published stories, books written by the class, information texts, dual-language texts), as well as providing an indication of some of the the child's strategies for reading.

The teacher may want to make a note of anything she observes that is particularly striking or that reveals a pattern in the child's behaviour and add this to the reading record. Alternatively the teacher may feel that there is some aspect of the child's reading behaviour that she would like to verify and so deliberately makes time to observe the child's interactions with books in a number of different situations.

Reading samples

Taking a reading sample is a very focused way of listening to a child read. It should be done about once a term (Barrs *et al.*, 1988) and results in a detailed picture of the child's reading strengths and strategies. It involves the child reading aloud a whole book or a substantial piece of text. This can be familiar or new to the child and may be in English or, if appropriate, in the child's heritage language. During the reading the teacher makes notes on the child's approach to text, his confidence, independence, involvement and enjoyment. The teacher also notes the range of strategies which the child employs, such as semantic, syntactic and grapho-phonic cues, and the balance between them as well as his use of prediction and self-correction. With less experienced readers teachers may be particularly interested in noting the child's use of book language, his ability to read the illustrations and awareness of print as well as skills such as directionality, one-to-one correspondence and the ability to recognize some words. After the reading the child is invited to talk about his response to the text and this gives the teacher further insights into the child's understanding and ability to evaluate what he reads. As a follow-up to the sample the teacher will make notes about the experiences and support that the child should be given to enable him to make further progress as a reader.

Reading conferences

During a reading conference a child is invited to talk at some length about himself as a reader and the books that he enjoys. Conferences should take place about twice a year (Barrs and Thomas, 1991). Preparation for the session may involve the child reviewing his own reading diary or looking back at the list of books he has read since September. As the child speaks the teacher may make notes which will be included in the child's portfolio. At the end of the session the teacher should read what has been written to the child and ask whether the child wants to change anything or has anything more to add. This form of monitoring children's interests, attitudes and knowledge about reading can begin in the nursery when the teacher acts as a scribe. Older children may well be able to write down their own thoughts about reading. This is a useful way of involving children in self-evaluation and enables them to make a real contribution to the assessment of their own progress.

Reading diaries

Children can keep their own lists of what they read. If these are kept in a personal reading diary there will be space for children to write comments about some of the books or authors they encounter during the year. If reading diaries are shared with adults they may respond to these comments. Reading them gives adults a useful insight into the child's tastes, range, understanding and responses to books.

Checklists

As a way of keeping track of children's early development in reading, some teachers like to fill in or refer to lists of signs which demonstrate children's growing competence in reading. They might include characteristics such as   • demonstrates an interest in books   • chooses to look at books   • is able to recognize his own name   • is able to retell a story using picture clues.

For more experienced readers teachers might want to see signs such as • takes over from adult when sharing a book   • is able to self-correct when reading   • is able to talk critically about what he reads   • enjoys silent reading.

Schools very often compile their own lists and make them appropriate to the age and experience of the pupils that they cater for. Even if checklists are not used as a record for each child, they can be a helpful reminder about the sorts of behaviours which indicate progress in reading development.

Miscue analysis

Miscue analysis (Goodman and Burke, 1972) is a very detailed and systematic method of listening to a child read. It is a diagnostic assessment

Miscue	Symbol	Example
Substitution	Cross out the word in the text and write in the substituted word	in the ~~corner~~ *cannon*
Non-response	Underline with dots	m̤o̤o̤r̤
Insertion	Write in the additions the child makes	In the *dark* wood ∧
Omission	Circle the word/s omitted	Across the passage (there) was
Hesitation	Insert a stroke when the child pauses for longer than is appropriate	there was a dark, dark / pussy
Repetition	Underline the repeated word	In the hall <u>there</u>
Reversal	Indicate with a curved line	shoes and socks
Self correction	Write in the miscue, then amend with a tick	~~Once~~ *One* ✓

Figure 10.1   Miscue notation

technique which can provide the administrator with insights about the reader and the whole reading process. It requires no special materials. The child reads a book or a passage of text containing about 150 words. This should not be too easy or too familiar since the child's miscues will provide the listener with information she requires about the child's reading. But neither is it necessary to make the reading frustrating or unnecessarily difficult. The teacher requires a photocopy of the text which the child will read, on which to note the miscues, although some teachers prefer to tape record the child's reading and fill in the miscues later. Before beginning the miscue analysis the teacher and child may discuss the book and the teacher may support the child as he reads the opening few sentences. The child will have been told that for most of this reading session the teacher will not provide the usual support and will only intervene if the child is really stuck. Once the child begins reading alone the teacher notes the miscues that occur using a consistent form of notation. Typical miscues and the symbols used to represent these are shown in Figure 10.1. The possible causes of the different types of miscue are summarized in Table 10.1.

In addition to noting the reader's miscues the teacher also observes the way in which the child reads, listening for the child's use of intonation, fluency and awareness of punctuation. After the child has finished the reading the teacher may ask the child to retell the story and ask about the child's response to what has been read. The analysis of the miscues, the teacher's observations and the child's summary and comments provide the adult with a full picture of the child's strengths and weaknesses as a reader. They indicate the strategies the child employs and his

Table 10.1   Miscue analysis

Miscue	Indicates
Substitution	If acceptable, e.g. 'steps' for 'stairs', generally indicates that the child is understanding what he reads. Fluent readers make substitutions when they are reading quickly and their eyes are ahead of their voice. If unacceptable, e.g. 'forest' for 'front', the child is not understanding what is read. Examine other strategies, e.g. use of initial letters, phonic and graphic cues. May be an over-reliance on strategies other than meaning
Non-response	Word or concept outside the child's experience. Child lacks confidence in making predictions
Insertion	Fluent reading, eyes ahead of voice
Omission	Fluent reading, when there is no interruption to meaning. Negative omission occurs when the reader does not recognize the word
Hesitation	Trying to decode the text. Trying to understand confusing syntax, style or meaning
Repetition	Uncertainty about the word or meaning. Trying to understand confusing syntax, style or meaning
Reversal	May indicate fluent reading, where the reader is adapting what is written into a form closer to familiar speech patterns, e.g. 'Martin said' rather than 'said Martin'
Self-correction	Understands that reading involves making meaning. Trying to make sense of the text

Actual Text	Michael's Reading
1 Once upon a time there	One ✓ ~~Once~~ upon a time there
2 was a dark, dark moor.	was a dark, dark <u>moor</u>.
3 On the moor there was	On the moor there was
4 a dark, dark wood.	a dark, dark wood.
5 In the wood there was	dark In the ∧ wood there was
6 a dark, dark house.	a dark, dark house.
7 At the front of the house	forest At the ~~front~~ of the house
8 there was a dark, dark door.	there was a dark, dark door.
9 Behind the door there	Behind the door there
10 was a dark, dark hall.	hill was a dark, dark ~~hall~~.
11 In the hall there were	hill In the ~~hall~~ <u>there were</u>
12 some dark, dark stairs.	steps some dark, dark ~~stairs~~.
13 Up the stairs there was	steps Up the ~~stairs~~ there was
14 a dark, dark passage.	pussy a dark, dark⎮~~passage~~.
15 Across the passage there was	Ae Act As ~~Across~~ the passage ⟨there⟩ was
16 a dark, dark curtain.	cat a dark, dark ~~curtain~~.
17 Behind the curtain was	cat Behind the ~~curtain~~ was
18 a dark, dark room.	a dark, dark room.

Figure 10.2   A Dark, Dark Tale

19 In the room was a dark,

20 dark cupboard.

In the room was a dark,

dark c~~upboard~~. **cup**

21 In the cupboard was

22 a dark, dark corner.

In the ~~cupboard~~ was **cup**

a dark, dark ~~corner~~. **cannon**

23 In the corner was

24 a dark, dark box.

In the ~~corner~~ was **cannon**

a dark, dark box.

25 And in the box there

26 was ... A MOUSE!

And in the box there

was ... A MOUSE!

Figure 10.2 continued

understanding of reading as an activity. After the analysis the teacher is then in a position to draw up an appropriate reading programme for the child. Figure 10.2 is an example of a miscue analysis undertaken with Michael, aged 5, reading *A Dark, Dark Tale* (Brown, 1981).

Analysis of Michael's reading

Michael uses grapho-phonic cues, relying a great deal on initial single letters at the beginning of words, for example when he substitutes 'forest' for 'front' and 'cannon' for 'corner'. Sometimes he looks beyond the initial letter and uses letter strings as with 'cup' for 'cupboard', 'hill' for 'hall', 'Ac' for Act' and 'As' for 'Across'.

Some of Michael's miscues are syntactically appropriate, indicating that he understands how language works, for example 'hill' for 'hall'. His awareness of book language can be seen when he self-corrects the opening word and when he inserts 'dark' in line 5.

He depends a great deal on the illustrations to help him read unfamiliar words. A large black cat is featured on the cover of the book and appears in many of the illustrations. This is never referred to in the text but it seems to influence some of Michael's substitutions, for example 'a dark, dark pussy' in line 14 and 'Behind the/cat' in line 17. The cat was the main character in Michael's retelling. In some cases the illustrations are misleading him and lead to inappropriate substitutions as in lines 23 and 24, 'In the cannon was a dark, dark box'. The previous page had shown a toy cupboard which could have contained a toy cannon.

Many of Michael's substitutions, repetitions and hesitations indicate that he is trying to understand what he is reading, for example 'step's' for 'stairs', line 12. He uses a combination of grapho-phonic, syntactic and picture cues to help him decode unknown words, but he does not use the narrative itself.

Michael's retelling was brief and indicated that he was distracted by the cat in the illustrations. There was little sense of story in his retelling, which was rather disjointed involving him in listing individual items rather than narrating a sequence of events.

Follow-up action

Michael approaches text confidently and believes himself to be a reader. Further experience with books and stories will add to this confidence. He is able to use grapho-phonic and pictorial cues well. He needs to be encouraged to think about the sense of what he reads, to use the context of words and sentences in books and to read on to the end of a sentence to help him tackle new words. He should be encouraged to think as he reads and to self-correct if he thinks that what he reads does not make sense. He would benefit from talking about his books before and after reading. Shared reading of big books, reading with tapes and group reading might also help Michael to read with more understanding.

Miscue analysis is time consuming for the teacher, but it is truly a 'window on the reading process' (Goodman and Goodman, 1977) and many teachers have found miscue analysis an illuminating experience. By administering one or two miscues analyses with average readers or children who seem to be experiencing difficulties in reading the teacher can gather a great deal of information that she can use with these pupils. She will also learn a great deal about the way she is teaching reading and the strategies she is emphasizing. It may be that this will lead the teacher to focus on other strategies with all the children she works with. Both the National Curriculum reading task at Level 2 and the examination of reading samples are based on miscue analysis.

Reading tests

In addition to the National Curriculum tests and tasks, schools and LEAs may administer reading tests to individual children, particularly those who are experiencing difficulty in becoming readers. They will use tests which they believe best suit the apparent difficulties the child is having. The best assessments that are undertaken for this purpose should provide information about • why the child is failing • the nature of the child's difficulties • the possible focus for the intervention – to make them useful to the teacher and the child.

Record keeping

The information about children's reading development that is gathered using all or some of the methods described in this section should enable the teacher to make a comprehensive, useful and informative summary of the children's reading development at the end of a term, a year or a Key Stage. These summaries should be included in the school records for each child as should the notes from reading conferences and samples. Alternatively summaries, conferences and samples may be included in children's language portfolios. The summaries may also be used on the reports that are issued to carers each year. With the addition of a level indicator they may be used as the teacher assessment required as part of the National Curriculum assessments, since the information they contain will indicate the breadth of children's reading experience, the key skills that are developing and their awareness and use of features of print as identified in the Programmes of Study.

The assessment of writing

The aspects of writing which are monitored

In writing the teacher is seeking to develop children's competence and enjoyment of writing as well as enabling them to discover personal reasons for writing. In order to plan what children need to learn each teacher needs to discover the existing writing competences, understanding and skills that the children have. The assessment of writing should be accompanied by reflection on the classroom practices that support children's learning in order to ensure that the curriculum provision and organization is enabling the pupils to learn what the teacher intends. Teachers have found the following questions a useful framework for assessing children's writing. Answers to the questions can be discovered through observation, discussion and analysis of writing as well as through pupil conferences.

Attitudes

About the child

What is the child's attitude to writing? Can the child identify his own reasons for writing? Does the child choose to write freely? Does the child become involved in his writing and sustain his involvement over time?

About my practice

Am I an enthusiastic writer? Do I convey this enthusiasm to my pupils? Do I provide a range of resources for writing for the children? Do I make provision for writing in play activities? Do I give children a variety of written activities with different purposes and audiences? What happens to finished writing? Is it praised, displayed, published or shared with others?

Content

About the child

Are the ideas expressed in writing equivalent or nearly equivalent to those expressed orally? Does the child use vivid, imaginative and appropriate language in his writing? Does the child organize his writing clearly? Can the child write in a variety of styles and formats?

About my practice

Do I respond to content and organization first when assessing children's writing? Are a range of writing styles and formats displayed around the classroom? Do I encourage children to 'have a go' at difficult or un-familiar spellings? Have I given children strategies for collecting ideas for pieces of written work, e.g. brainstorming, listing, etc.? Do I give guid-ance on ways of organizing and planning written work using drawings, diagrams, headings, etc.? Do I demonstrate all the processes involved in writing through shared-writing sessions? Do I encourage children to dis-cuss stories and to base some of their writing on familiar story structures?

Writing conventions

About the child

Does the child use visual and phonic strategies when spelling? Does the child make use of capital letters, full stops and speech marks in his writ-ing? Is the child's writing clear, legible and correctly formed? Does the child use grammatically appropriate structures in his writing, e.g. sus-taining the use of 'he' throughout a narrative written in the third person?

About my practice

Do I encourage children to look at and memorize words as part of my spelling policy? Do I encourage children to notice grammatical features in books during shared-reading and individual reading sessions? Do I en-courage children to reread their writing once it is finished? Do I correct handwriting errors in the presence of the child?

Ways of assessing writing

Teachers make frequent assessments of writing whenever children are engaged in written work, and long-term assessments of progress at the end of each term, each year and each Key Stage. Daily assessment takes place during the course of a writing activity. It is an integral part of the child's learning about writing rather than something separate. As part of the daily assessment process teachers will use a variety of methods including observation, response, discussion and analysis of the child's writing, involving the child in these procedures whenever possible. Assessing writing in this way provides the teacher with insights into the process of writing as well as the outcome of the activity, providing information about what the child knows as well as about what the child can do.

Observation

Observation involves listening to and watching pupils engaged in an activity. Sometimes observations are preplanned and may have a specific focus, or they may occur routinely as the teacher moves around the classroom offering support and checking on children's engagement with the task. Although teachers continually make observations about children's work and progress in the course of daily classroom activities, all children may not be observed equally. Quiet children may receive less teacher attention than children who have difficulties or those who frequently seek the teacher's help. In order to ensure that all children are observed over a period it might be necessary to draw up a schedule of observations. For instance, teachers may decide to observe one writing activity that will be undertaken by all the children over the course of a few days. The teacher will focus on each group of children as they work at this writing activity. Alternatively the teacher may identify two or three children to observe each day until all the class have been observed as they write. In addition there may be spontaneous and important moments of literacy learning that occur and that are observed. These may represent a significant step in the learning development of a particular child and may be noted or recorded by the teacher. Observations may reveal that bilingual pupils write fluently in their home language, incorporate features of scripts other than English into their writing or understand about the purposes of writing.

It may be useful for the teacher to have a loose-leaf notebook to use as an observation diary. Several pages in the notebook can be allocated to each child in the class. As the pages are completed they can be removed, analysed and placed in the child's record folder. One or two observations for each pupil should be recorded each term. As observations are recorded a picture of the child's development as a writer will be built up. If teachers look back on these observations they will be able to draw conclusions about the development the child has made and the support he needs.

The two observations which follow are of John and Glen, two Year 2 pupils. Each observation has been analysed to show the value of observational data in adding to one's picture of the child as a learner and in providing evidence for teacher assessments:

2/11/92 John
Tiny writing.
Does not use the page correctly.
Crosses out continually. Can only guess at first letters of words. Little knowledge of letter patterns. Words he knows 'the', 'and', 'we', 'put'. Common mistakes 'soc' for 'stories'. Does not know letter names. Reverses 'b' and 'd'. Can form letters correctly.
Doesn't want to write.
Finds it difficult to make the words make sense. Panics about work. Chooses because of difficulties to talk and not complete work.
Needs more opportunities to write for a purpose – short texts.

From this observation it is clear that John is having difficulties with writing and because he finds it difficult, he does not want to write. The teacher needs to find ways of making writing easier for John. If he is to make progress as a writer he needs to become interested in writing and to understand what it is for. He needs to gain some satisfaction from writing. The observation also indicates that some direct teaching of how to form *b* and *d* would be useful. The teacher might also begin to revise letter names with him and provide some activities that encourage John to look at how words are spelt. He needs to see how writers use the page and how writing is arranged.

The following observation, although primarily about Glen, also features John and gives further information about him as a writer when he is working collaboratively with a more able and enthusiastic child:

12/11/92 Glen and John
Glen asked if he could make a book about 'Mrs. Plug the Plumber'. Chose John to work with him.
He has now been working on the book for 2 days.

13/11/92
Glen and John read the book to the class today. They are extraordinarily proud of it.
Glen explained how they worked – planning together, writing a first draft together and then each writing a page of the final draft in turn. They also took turns with the illustrations. They needed to refer to the text to remind themselves of the details of the story.
They worked without any help from me on this project.

Although John has many difficulties with writing, when he is supported by a more able writer, he is able to sustain his interest in writing. Glen is able to work independently for long periods of time and is willing to collaborate with others. The second observation includes evidence of Glen fulfilling some of the requirements of the Level 3 descriptions for writing: 'Pupils' writing is often organised, imaginative and clear. The main features of different forms of writing are used appropriately, beginning to be adapted to different readers. Sequences of sentences extend ideas logically. Spelling is usually accurate.' (DfE, 1995a, p. 30). The second extract also shows how the work that the children have done fulfils many of the requirements of the Programme of Study for writing at Key Stage 1.

Although these are primarily observations of children writing, because all areas of the English curriculum overlap they also contain evidence of achievement in speaking and listening and reading. The two observations provide a rich picture of both children's strengths, weaknesses and learning styles. They provide the teacher with important information that could be missed if the teacher only referred to samples of work for her assessments. Reflection on these observations gave the teacher an indication of what to work on next with both children in order to meet their individual needs as developing writers.

Interactions

Interactions occur when teachers respond to pupils' writing, during writing conferences or during individual writing interviews which are held once or twice each term.

The most frequent interactions occur when children are engaged on their daily writing activities. At these times teachers are able to provide immediate help and support for the child. Before intervening it is important to ask the child to talk about what he has written and to ask him to read back what he has produced. When making a response to writing the teacher should first focus on and comment on the content, giving feedback about the positive aspects of what has been written and then provide the child with some form of teaching that is related to his stage of development and his immediate needs. The focus should always be on the writing and the teacher's response should be helpful and informative. It is not enough to say or write 'That's really good'. The teacher needs to say why the writing is good so that the child can incorporate the good features into his next piece of writing. Similarly if the writing could be improved the teacher needs to explain how this could be achieved. Ticks, crosses and general comments such as 'good' do not give children the information which they need to develop as writers.

Writing conferences provide opportunities for children to reflect on their learning and enable the teacher to provide the pupil with an input that is directly related to his needs. In this form of assessment the teacher will be asking questions and listening carefully to answers. She may be drawing out ideas and checking understanding. There may be a specific focus for the discussion that enables the teacher to check her observations or to explore an aspect of the child's writing behaviour more thoroughly.

Writing interviews involve pupils in the assessment process and help them to reflect on and understand what they have learned. Interviews often take place when the teacher is reviewing the child's writing profile. The child may be asked to select a recent piece of writing to be included in the portfolio or the teacher may ask the child to comment on one or all of the pieces of writing that have already been selected. Teachers can ask pupils how they think they can develop and improve their writing. As the child talks the teacher should note down what is said and include these comments in the profile. These comments may provide additional evidence for assessment and future planning.

Analysing samples

Another way to gain insights into a child's writing development is to analyse what the child writes. Collecting samples of writing every term and analysing them at one's leisure gives the teacher the opportunity to gain insights into children's progress as writers. The teacher may also add samples to the children's portfolios and use them as a starting point for discussions with children and carers. It is useful to collect one piece of writing from the beginning of the school year as this provides a baseline from which teaching can proceed and a reference point when assessing how much progress children have made over the course of a term or a year. The rest of the samples that are included should be drawn from a variety of starting points and curriculum areas and represent a variety of styles of writing, for example narrative, poems, notes, records and messages. First drafts as well as fair copies should be included to show how the child revises and corrects his work as well as how he has responded to suggestions from the teacher. Some of the writing may be selected by the child and accompanied by the child's comments.

Once a piece of work has been selected it should be dated and then analysed, using headings such as those which follow:

Context   This section might include notes about how the work arose, the purpose of the writing, the intended audience, the length of time the child spent on the writing and information about the child's previous knowledge or experience in this area.

Comment   This section is concerned with the strengths and weaknesses displayed by the child as a writer. The comments might refer to attitude, content and writing conventions as displayed in the piece of work. If plans and drafts are collected one might note the differences between the drafts and refer to the learning processes that the child has gone through between the first and final copy. It is always useful to look for positive points in children's writing and to ask oneself, what has the child attempted and achieved?

Ways forward   Under this heading the teacher might indicate the activities, experiences and work that might extend the child as a learner.

Figure 10.3 Imran – boys and girls

National Curriculum requirements A note could be made here of the Programme of Study requirements covered and the level descriptions reached in this piece of work. Although the primary focus of the analysis might be on English the piece of writing could have grown from another area of the curriculum and demonstrate learning in other areas.

The two samples of writing in Figures 10.3 and 4 are taken from the language portfolio of a 6-year-old pupil, Imran. Imran's first language was Urdu but at the time of this writing he was able to talk clearly in English. He enjoyed writing but tended to rush at his work.

Context This piece of writing emerged after the children had listened to the story of *William's Doll* (Zolotow, 1972). The children had been asked to think about the sorts of games that both girls and boys like to play.

Comment Imran writes easily and confidently. He had understood the task and responded appropriately. His response is in the form of a list. Imran frequently uses the same letters when he is writing. He does not yet see the connection between sounds and words. He was able to read back what he had written and the teacher wrote the correct version close to his words. Imran and the teacher talked about the letters that were common to both sets of writing. The teacher also talked to Imran about spaces between words.

Ways forward Imran needs to be encouraged to think before he writes. He needs to consider the initial letters of words and to become familiar

Figure 10.4   Imran – making a house

with the sounds and names of letters. Work on these aspects during shared reading and writing should help. He needs to gain practice at writing and to be praised for his positive approach to writing (see Figure 10.4).

Friday 6th December
How I made my home
First we got a box
Then we cut the door
Then we put the carpet
Then I me and Kevin finished.

Context   The class were working on the theme of 'Homes' and after listening to the story *Charlie's House* (Schermbrucker, 1992) had worked in pairs to make a home for Charlie. The writing was an account of how they had made their model. The children were going to copy out the writing to make explanatory notes for the display of model houses. The title was written on a flip chart for the children to copy.

Comment   This writing demonstrates a vast improvement since September. The writing is organized logically and well. Imran has produced a clear, factual account of his work with Kevin. It includes spaces between words and concludes with a full stop. Imran is beginning to be aware of the features of print. Many of the spellings approximate closely to the correct versions and words such as 'we', 'door' and 'put' are spelt correctly. There is evidence of attention to initial letter sounds and a greater variety of letters than in the earlier sample.

Ways forward Imran needs to continue gaining experience as a reader and writer. He needs to write for a variety of audiences to encourage him to take care with his writing. Perhaps he needs to be shown how to proofread his writing. He might also work with a response partner. The teacher needs to continue to draw Imran's attention to the details of print, including the use of upper and lower-case letters in text.

Checklists

Some teachers like to include checklists for writing in children's records. These sometimes take the form of a preprinted list or wheel of common behaviours seen as children's writing develops. As the child incorporates these strategies into his writing, the relevant box is marked. In practice checklists are usually ticked or coloured in twice a term. Some teachers make one mark when the child is beginning to use a strategy and a different sort of mark when the strategy is being used confidently and

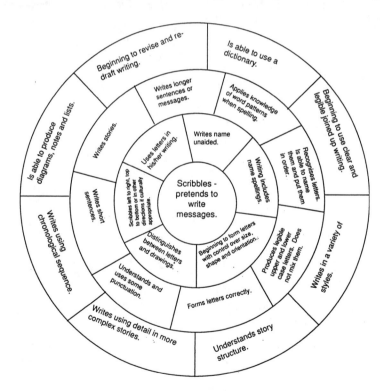

Figure 10.5 Checklist – writing

consistently. A sample version of a checklist for writing development is given in Figure 10.5. The items which have been included in this example could be changed or adapted to suit the needs of particular schools, classes, teachers and pupils.

Conclusion

The use and understanding of assessment and record keeping in school has changed considerably over the past few years. The National Curriculum and the statutory assessment requirements have made evaluation and record keeping a necessary feature of every teacher's daily work in the classroom. If assessment is seen as part of teaching and learning and if opportunities for assessment and record keeping are built into one's curriculum planning and classroom organization then they need not be seen as a burden but rather as an important part of the learning process for both children and teachers.

Suggestions for further reading

Barrs, M., Ellis, S., Hester, H. and Thomas, A. (1988) *The Primary Language Record: Handbook for Teachers*, CLPE, London.

Chapter 11

Planning a scheme of work for language

Introduction

Careful planning enables good-quality teaching to take place. Clear, detailed, well planned schemes of work ensure that all aspects of each subject are covered and that there is progression, balance, coherence and continuity in the curriculum that is offered to pupils. Schemes of work should have clear aims and contain activities that are sequenced and structured and allow for the acquisition, practice and consolidation of knowledge, skills and understanding. The activities should be appropriate to the learning needs of the pupils, paced according to age, differentiated according to individual need and flexible enough to be changed in response to evaluation.

As the Dearing Report (1993) noted, English teaching rarely takes place in isolation. It is usually integrated with and arises from activities in other curriculum areas. These provide speaking, listening, reading and writing with a context and a purpose. Consequently planning for English is usually located within planning for the whole curriculum. What is planned has to take account of a number of factors, including • the National Curriculum Programmes of Study (in England and Wales) • the whole curriculum • school language policies • the teacher • the needs of the pupils.

This chapter examines some of the general issues that affect planning, illustrates these with an example of a scheme of work for language in the early years and ends by describing some characteristics of a well planned scheme of work for English.

Factors that influence planning

The National Curriculum requirements for English

The learning experiences and activities that are planned and contained in a scheme of work will be far richer than the requirements specified in the

Programmes of Study for English. The National Curriculum outlines a list of desirable, logically sequenced aims for children's learning but states that the way in which these aims are achieved is left up to individual schools. However because the National Curriculum is a major influence on the range of experiences and the particular skills that need to be included in the teacher's planning, it is helpful to have a list of the National Curriculum requirements for English to hand when planning an English curriculum for early-years pupils. This can be referred to, to ensure that what one is planning meets the statutory requirements. It may also help to ensure balance in what is planned and progression and continuity in each individual's planning and between-year groups.

Whilst the National Curriculum may act as a framework, the goals that it contains need to be considered alongside the teacher's general and overall expectations for all the children she teaches. These will include ensuring that during the first years at school, all children's competence develops, that all children develop favourable attitudes to English, that all children make a solid start on speaking, listening, reading and writing in line with their potential and that all children experience the range, key skills and standard English and language study aspects of the curriculum.

Although 3- and 4-year-olds are legally exempt from the National Curriculum, the curriculum which is planned for nursery and reception classes is being increasingly influenced by the Programmes of Study at Key Stage 1. SCAA (1995) suggests that, although schools continue to have some discretion over when to start teaching the National Curriculum, they may wish to begin to cover aspects of Key Stage 1 with 4-year-olds in reception classes. The desirability of curriculum continuity between nursery, reception and Year 1 classes may well affect the degree to which the Key Stage 1 requirements influence planning for the under fives.

English within the whole curriculum

When planning a scheme of work for any subject the statutory requirements for the whole curriculum also need to be considered. The Education Reform Act (HM Government, 1988) stipulated that schools should provide pupils with a broad and balanced education which

- promotes the spiritual, moral, cultural, mental and physical development of pupils in school and in society; and
- prepares pupils for the opportunities, responsibilities and experiences of adult life.

(DES, 1989b, para. 2.1)

The subject orders of the National Curriculum form only part of the curriculum that is offered to pupils. The National Curriculum may be the foundation for much of the teaching and learning that is planned within the school but it is only part of the curriculum and should be augmented by religious education, additional subjects beyond the National Curriculum, cross-curricular elements and extra-curricular activities. Schools are expected to ensure that children develop an awareness and understanding of issues, explore values and beliefs including equal opportunities and develop communication, numeracy, study, problem solving, IT and personal and social skills. They are also required to promote children's self-knowledge, awareness of their rights and responsibilities of the society they live in and to foster interests which will help pupils to make productive use of their leisure time. Planning for each curriculum area needs to reflect aspects of the dimensions, skills and themes of these cross-curricular elements and, from time to time, offer pupils extra-curricular experiences. It is likely that the English curriculum will contain many of these aspects of the wider curriculum.

The teacher

When teachers plan they may consult the school language policy which might outline the agreed priorities for language learning for the children in the school, include details of school themes and indicate the nature of the learning experiences which should be planned for each year group including the under fives in nursery and reception classes. The curriculum co-ordinator may also influence what is planned for each class and provide information, guidance and support to the staff.

Teachers may have a number of documents to refer to as they are planning but they will still have a great deal of flexibility in deciding what will be learned in the classroom. The expertise and individual characteristics of each teacher affect what is planned, learned and taught. All teachers do not adhere uniformly to curriculum documents. They adapt, interpret and extend guidelines in line with their own understanding of each curriculum area and their awareness of the previous experiences, achievements, interests and current needs of their pupils.

Their own attitudes and values about the nature of learning, the school and particular subject areas along with their expectations about the children and their abilities are transmitted to pupils and affect their learning. In particular, each teacher's understanding of the principles of planning, knowledge of the locality, use of resources, teaching style and system of classroom organization and management will affect individual plans and schemes of work across the curriculum and for English. In these ways each teacher plans and mediates her own curriculum for the class.

Selecting and interpreting a theme

Most early-years practitioners plan children's learning around a cross-curricular theme. Themes are usually chosen for their relevance to children's lives and experiences. They enable teachers to make links with what young children are already familiar with before beginning to extend their learning. They also allow teachers to make cross-curricular links between different areas of the curriculum which help to reinforce children's understanding and lead to a wholeness and integration of the learning which takes place. At its best a theme should

- offer opportunities for new learning in all curriculum areas,
- reflect and acknowledge children's own interests,
- extend children's present understanding into new areas of interest,
- allow children to explore issues, values, beliefs, attitudes including equal opportunities,
- present opportunities for children to look at the experience of people outside themselves and to make connections between themselves and the wider world,
- develop pupils' concepts, understanding and skills
- contain possibilities for involving the local community and carers in the children's learning.

Most themes that are selected by teachers fulfil the criteria listed above if they are interpreted broadly. The skilful practitioner will be able to see new possibilities in almost every theme, even those that are returned to regularly.

Devising activities

All planning begins with a set of aims for developing children's learning. The teacher will have identified these as she begins to construct a scheme of work. She will also be aware of the stage of learning reached by the children in her class as she undertakes her initial brainstorm and constructs a preliminary topic web. The activities that the teacher generates around the title of the theme reflect her knowledge of suitable learning experiences for her class. As the initial brainstorm is examined and refined the teacher will be considering the best activities, out of all those that are possible, to match what the class as a whole needs to learn next. The final choice will indicate the teacher's understanding of the development of learning in each subject area, her understanding of how children learn, her awareness of cross-curricular reinforcement and her wish to present children with learning experiences that are coherent and complementary. To check that the activities represent a broad and balanced curriculum and a curriculum that is in line with the Programmes of Study, the teacher may list the activities under subject headings. At this stage the potential for covering each subject area, including English, within the theme will become clear. The teacher will be able to examine her planning to make sure that she has covered all four language areas and included activities to extend the range of children's learning, their command of key skills and their awareness of standard English and language. The teacher can then see whether the activities that she has devised are in line with her original intentions for the pupils' future learning. Are they matched to the current abilities of the class and will they ensure progression? Will she be able to use these activities as starting points for every child and still ensure that she is offering appropriate levels of challenge to each pupil? Are the reading, writing, listening and speaking experiences complementary? Is what has been planned flexible enough to incorporate any ideas the children may have or interests they may develop as the theme unfolds?

Organizing the activities

The activities which are devised will reflect the teacher's teaching style and her system of classroom management. They are likely to involve the children in active, first-hand experiences. Different activities will probably require different forms of organization such as co-operative group work to encourage collaborative learning as well as opportunities for the children to work independently. The teacher will have thought about the demands of the activities, her role as a provider of information and instruction and as a facilitator of children's own discoveries and how these may require whole-class, group and individual inputs. Sequencing the activities will involve including time and opportunities for children to reflect on what they are learning. Play activities will have been included in the planned curriculum, with the intention of developing and reinforcing the children's learning since play helps children to explore and represent their new learning in different ways. In order that the classroom organization runs smoothly and is conducive to learning it will be physically arranged to enable children to have easy access to all the resources they will need and the environment will stimulate initial and continuing interest in the theme. Careful forethought about the implications of the plans for organization and resources is likely to lead to an atmosphere of order and calm in the class and a much greater likelihood of the aims of the activities being realized.

A scheme of work for language in the early years

What follows is an illustration of planning for English in the early years. It may be helpful to those with less experience in curriculum planning or to those who are anxious about planning an integrated English programme. Apart from being designed for young children this example is not age specific; most of the activities are capable of being differentiated according to learning need and developmental level. An example of differentiation is given at the end of the theme.

Select the theme

This may be partly determined by school guidelines, a particular curriculum focus, the needs and interests of the pupils or available resources.

The theme that has been selected as the starting point for this example is that of 'Homes'.

Establishing aims

The aims that the teacher identifies should be appropriate to the learning needs and the interests of the children, extend but not repeat previous experiences, ensure that there is progression in learning and be suited to the theme. In this case the aims for the children's learning during the period of learning covered by the theme are to

- extend the pupils' knowledge of their own homes,
- promote understanding and appreciation of the many sorts of dwellings that are homes,
- become aware of the environment and the locality,
- appreciate and understand the contribution of all those who live in and work for our homes,
- promote collaboration, sharing and respect for each other,
- develop autonomous and independent work habits,
- enhance achievement in all curriculum areas through the planned activities.

Identify the aims for each curriculum area including English

The aims for the children's learning in English in this example are to

- practise asking and answering questions confidently,
- gain confidence when addressing large audiences,
- read print in the environment,
- produce books that they and others will read,
- explore factual writing through reading, using and making information books,
- practise planning, drafting and revising writing.

Brainstorm ideas for activities across the curriculum

In the initial plan the teacher may think of as many ideas for activities as she can. These may cover every curriculum area.

Identify the English activities

The teacher may look back to her aims for developing language and identify any activities in her initial plan that are particularly suited to realizing these. The following list contains a number of activities suited to the development of listening, speaking, reading and writing that might emerge from this theme (those marked with a single asterisk, see 'Link the plans with the Programmes of Study' below; those marked with double asterisks, see 'Differentiation' below):

- What jobs do people do at home?
- Who contributes to our homes – consider occupations.
- Can women be builders, window cleaners, etc.?
- What are houses like in other parts of the world?
- Patterns – house numbers, building materials.
- Interviewing visitors and other children and staff about their homes.
- Homelessness.
- Likes/dislikes about my home.
- Lists of items to be found in different rooms in the home.**
- Drawing and labelling items around the house.**
- Individual books in the shape of the child's home to include drawings of each room and list of items to be found there.*
- What makes a building a home?*
- My room.*
- My home.*
- Four places in my home that are special to me.*
- Make a tape of a guided tour around my home.*
- Making a *Homes Dictionary*.
- Make an ABC frieze based on items in homes.
- On my way home I see . . .
- My map showing my journey to school, my friend's home, where I play, the school, places I go to, places that are special to me.
- Words that begin with *h*, words with the same spelling pattern as 'home'.
- Addresses.
- Construct a data base containing information about the children's homes.
- Retell the story of *Miss Brick the Builder's Baby* (Ahlberg, 1981b) and *Mrs Plug the Plumber* (Ahlberg, 1980).
- Make up other titles and stories for the series, for example 'Miss Pat the Painter'.
- Make figures and props for use in the listening area with the books and tapes of the different versions of 'The Three Little Pigs'.
- Make a large reference book about 'Homes' towards the end of the theme containing information selected by the children to show others what they have discovered.

(Although these activities have been listed under the heading of English, it is obvious that they will lead to or follow on from activities in many other areas of the curriculum.)

Checking the scheme

At this stage it is helpful to check whether the planning is developing in the direction that was intended. It might be appropriate for the teacher to ask herself: Do these activities fit in with the Programmes of Study? Will they realize the aims outlined earlier? Which activities will best enable these aims to be realized? Will anything need to be added? Should anything be discarded?

Link the plans with the Programmes of Study

Many schools now expect teachers' plans to make overt links between their plans and the National Curriculum Programmes of Study. The teacher might also want to make her own links between the four areas of English. In this example, the activities marked with an * and listed below form a sequence, cover all four language areas and are particularly related to some of the statements in the Programme of Study for English (for those marked with double asterisks, see 'Differentiation' below):

- Lists of items to be found in different rooms in the home.**
- Drawing and labelling items around the house.**
- Individual books in the shape of the child's home with each page used to draw a picture of one room in the home and facing this a list of items to be found there.*
- What makes a building a home?*
- My room.*
- My home.*
- Four places in my home that are special to me.*
- Make a tape of a guided tour around my home.*

As the teacher I might envisage these activities taking place in the following way. After discussions about what makes a building a home the children will draw and label or make lists of items in their home. It might be most appropriate to begin with their own room or a space that is special to them. I would like them to make a first draft and a best copy to be included in their individual reference books about their home. As the books are made the children will make tapes to accompany the books. These will be in the form of a guided tour of their home and they will be shared with others in school and at home.

This sequence of activities directly links with the Key Stage 1 Programme of Study for English and the following example shows these connections:

> During the course of the activities undertaken in this theme the children will be given opportunities to [at the beginning of the sequence of activities] talk for a range of purposes including exploring, developing and clarifying ideas; describing events, observations and experiences (speaking and listening, range, 1a).
> practise the conventions of discussion and conversation (speaking and listening, key skills, 2a)
> indicate thoughtfulness about the matter under discussion and use talk to develop their thinking and extend their ideas (speaking and listening, key skills, 2b)

[During the follow-up activities] learn to use reference materials and examine and use the structural devices for organizing information (reading, key skills, 2d)

consider the characteristics and features of different texts (reading, standard English and language study, 3)

understand the value of writing as a means of remembering, communicating, organizing and developing ideas and information; write independently on subjects that are of interest to them (writing, range, 1a)

write in different forms including notes, lists, captions, and records (writing, range, 1c)

write confidently; experience the different purposes and functions of written language; write independently (writing, key skills, 2a)

plan and review their writing, assembling and developing their ideas on paper and screen individually and in collaboration with others (writing, key skills, 2b)

experiment with and practise using capital letters, full stops and question marks (writing, key skills, 2c)

increase their known spelling vocabulary; use dictionaries to locate words; discuss misspellings and words (writing, key skills, 2d)

practise conventional ways of forming letters; develop an awareness of the need for clear presentation in order to communicate meaning effectively (writing, key skills, 2e)

apply their understanding, drawn from oral language knowledge and use, of word choice and word order in writing (writing, standard English and language study, 3a)

[During the taping activity] talk for a range of purposes including reading aloud (speaking and listening, range, 1a)

talk and present work to different audiences including friends, the class, the teacher and other adults in the school (speaking and listening, range, 1b)

speak with confidence, make themselves clear through organizing what they say; take into account the needs of their listeners (speaking and listening, key skills, 2a)

consider how they communicate with others, particularly in more formal situations (speaking and listening, standard English and language study, 3a)

read their own writing to the teacher and to others (reading, range, 1a).

Although plans should indicate connections with the National Curriculum, it is unlikely that they will require the detail given in the illustration above. The intention of this list is to demonstrate how a careful selection of activities made on the grounds of educational worthwhileness will satisfy the National Curriculum requirements without any difficulty.

Selecting resources

If the teacher is satisfied with what she has planned she will want to begin to consider how she is going to implement the activities. This stage might begin by identifying some of the resources that will be useful for the theme and the activities.

Stories

On The Way Home (Murphy, 1982); *Gregory Cool* (Binch, 1994); *The Three Little Pigs* (Blegvad, 1980); *The True Story of the Three Little Pigs* (Scieszka, 1989); *Coming Home* (Waddell, 1991); *Jafta The Homecoming* (Lewin, 1992); *Charlie's House* (Schermbrucker, 1992); *Through My Window* (Bradman, 1986); *Miss Brick the Builder's Baby* (Ahlberg, 1981b); *Have You Seen Who's Just Moved In Next Door To Us?* (McNaughton, 1991); *Mrs Plug the Plumber* (Ahlberg, 1980); *Our House on the Hill* (Dupasquier, 1987); *Piggybook* (Browne, 1986); *The Village of Round and Square Houses* (Grifalconi, 1989); *Mum's Strike* (Ritter, 1988); *Moving* (Zola, 1983); *Moving Molly* (Hughes, 1991).

Poems and rhymes

A House is a House For Me (Hoberman, 1978); 'There Was An Old Woman Who Lived In A Shoe (traditional); *The House that Jack Built* (Stow, 1992); *Secret Places* (Huck, 1993).

Information books

Bricks (Cash, 1988); *Houses and Homes Around the World* (Karavasil, 1983); *A, B, C, I Can Be* (Wilkins, 1993); *Inside My House* (Webster, 1994); *A Turkish Afternoon* (Bennett, 1983); *Housework* (Tanner, 1992); *Our New Home* (Bennett, 1990).

Visual resources

- Collections of photographs of houses in the locality and beyond
- for-sale details from estate agents • a collection of building materials • pieces of materials used for home furnishing and decorating
- tools used for DIY and jobs around the home • *Working Now* (photographs and activities for exploring gender roles in the primary classroom, DEC, 1989) • *Doing Things in and about the Home* (24 black and white photos of activities in the home, Trentham Books, 1983) • *Phototalk Books* (ILEA, 1984).

Audio resources

- Make or buy tapes of some of the stories, rhymes and information books to be used in the theme • blank cassette tapes for the children to record interviews, stories, guided tour, etc. • commercial tape of *The Three Little Pigs* by Tony Ross produced by Weston Woods, 1986 (see Appendix).

IT resources

- Albert's House • MOVING IN • data base program • concept keyboard with key words for the theme • ALLWRITE or a straight-forward word-processing program.

People

● A plumber, builder, carpenter, cleaner or electrician for the pupils to interview ● an older member of the community who can describe changes to homes and services.

Visits

A walk around the locality to look at homes, building materials, road names, numbering systems, shops selling goods for the home, clues about the ages and changes to homes that have taken place, clues about services provided for homes.

Play and role-play resources

● Resources to set up an estate-agents office or a home or a building site ● construction kits ● small-world equipment, the dolls' house, furniture ● sand, water, clay.

Ordering the activities

Having established that there are sufficient resources available to make the scheme and the activities viable, the teacher will want to consider how and in what order the activities will be introduced to the children. The answers to some of the questions that follow may influence her decisions about the sequence that is planned:

How much access do I have to a computer? When shall I invite the visitor into class? What preparation will the children require for this? When shall we take the walk around the locality? Will I want the children to make drawings, rubbings or take notes when we do this? How could the theme begin? Will I set up a starter display? How will the initial activities be introduced?

What might follow on? What displays will emerge? How and where will the children record their work? What will happen to finished work? How will the theme end? Could the children present their learning to the rest of the school in an assembly? Will we hold an exhibition of the work that the children have done?

After answering these questions the teacher will probably be able to produce a sequence of work for the period to be covered by the theme. She will probably have a clear idea of the activities that will take place in the first week and will know how the theme will begin.

Organization

If the activities are to be successful and if there is to be enough time for the teacher to incorporate important and necessary routines such as reading with children, quiet reading times and story sessions, the way the classroom is organized and managed is crucial. Children should have easy access to resources and be familiar with working independently. Areas of the classroom which support speaking, listening, reading and writing will already have been established. The class will be used to working collaboratively, be aware of alternatives to using the teacher as the only resource and will know what to do when they finish an activity. The children will know that if the teacher is busy, reading with a child or teaching a group, then they should seek help elsewhere or carry on with another activity until the teacher is free.

It is also important that the teacher has thought carefully about her own daily use of time, her teaching inputs, the demands that each activity will make on her and how the children will be grouped for each activity. On some occasions some English activities may be taught or carried out with the whole class, for example story sessions, discussions and shared reading and writing of big books. The beginning and end of the day might be used for class teaching. The start of the day is often a good time to introduce a new topic or activity to the class. Explanations can be given about the work that is to take place that day and the teacher can reiterate routines and the expectations that she has. Some teachers write the list of the day's activities on a flip chart before the children come into class and refer to this list as they talk to the class at the beginning of the day. This is a useful device as not only does it provide the children with a means of remembering what they are expected to do that day but also provides the class with purposeful reading practice and demonstrates a real use for writing. The beginning and final class sessions each day may also be used to review work and for individuals and small groups to share their working experiences with the class. Talk in this context is given a real purpose and audience.

Evaluation

Regular and systematic evaluation through observation, interaction with pupils, analysis of their work and pupil evaluations of their own learning enables the teacher to consider the appropriateness of the curriculum which she is providing, to see whether her aims are being realized and to make judgements about the nature and quality of pupil learning. Daily and weekly monitoring enables the teacher to be responsive to all the children's individual learning needs. The teacher will be expecting the children to achieve some if not all her aims for the period of learning. She will be looking for demonstrations of progress in learning in areas such as skills, understanding and knowledge. She will also be expecting children to progress as effective learners who are developing positive attitudes to learning and growing in perseverance, motivation and confidence. If these signs of progress are not evident it may be that, after reflection, the teacher needs to adapt the aims, activities or organization contained in her planning until she creates an environment in which every child can develop.

A summary of the planning process

Establish your priorities for this period of learning
- Consider the needs and interests of the pupils.
- Select a theme.

Brainstorm the activities
- Will these activities enable you to achieve your general aims?
- Are they relevant to the children's interests and learning needs?

Identify the English activities
- Do the activities fit in with the Programmes of Study?
- Do the activities offer scope for a broad, balanced curriculum which matches the children's learning needs and your aims?
- Will the activities lead to continuity and progression in learning?
- Will the children understand the personal relevance of these activities?

What resources will you need?

How will you organize the teaching and learning? Sequence the activities
- How will the theme begin?
- How will the theme end?

How and when will the children's learning be evaluated?

Differentiation

Planning needs to take account of the different needs and abilities of all the children in the class. The teacher may expect all the children to undertake some activities but expect different outcomes from different individuals. Alternatively she may present similar tasks in different ways to children who need less or more support. The two activities marked with a double star in the activities list, 'Lists of items to be found in different rooms in the home**', 'Drawing and labelling items around the house**', have the same aims. They are intended to encourage children to use writing to convey information and to see how writing can be used to recollect and remember. Less experienced writers may find it helpful to draw the items in their rooms before writing the names of the objects. Between the drawing and the writing the teacher can discuss the items with the children, talk about some of the words which the children will require and, if appropriate, remind them to refer to words on classroom displays or in books if they wish to when they write their labels. The drawing and writing might be done straight into the child's individual book, with the drawings serving as a draft and planning aid. More experienced writers may be able to write a list as a first draft, order this list using alphabetical order and then revise some of their spellings before making a final draft of this list in their 'Home' book.

Planning for the under fives

All early-years children need opportunities to play, talk, interact, experience and investigate at their own pace as they learn. These are some of the characteristics of good early-years provision. However children in the nursery or 4-year-olds in reception classes will be expected to do less recording and will engage in more play and oral activities than older children. For very young children there will be more opportunities to engage in large-scale, collaborative, imaginative and construction activities out doors, more emphasis on role play, greater exploration of materials and collections associated with the theme and more involvement in collaborative games that have been selected or made for the theme. The teacher will do most of the recording in the form of shared writing to produce large books for the class, although the children will have the opportunity to write in their individual books. Implementing the curriculum for the under fives will be different in pace and contain a different balance of activities from that designed for 5–8-year-olds, but many of the suggestions given earlier in this chapter will be appropriate as starting points.

The following description is taken from a week's work for the nursery on the theme of 'Homes'. The focus for the week is to be moving home. The children have heard the story *Moving Molly* (Hughes, 1991) and looked at the book *Our New Home* (Bennett, 1990), and some of them have shared their own experiences of moving with the class. The story will be read to the whole class again. The teacher's intention is to ask the children to consider how the nursery home corner can be moved from its present position to a new location in the classroom. All the furniture and inhabitants of the home will actually be moved later in the week. What jobs will have to be done and how should the move happen? These are the issues for the children to think about, discuss and solve. The children move on to the other activities in the nursery, drawing an item from the collection of building materials, providing a written label for their previously painted home picture, sharing the book *Moving Molly*, making a collection of items for the kitchen using pictures cut from catalogues, engaging in imaginative play outdoors in an area that has been resourced as a building site and playing a lotto game which asks children to match different sorts of homes. All these activities are supported by discussion between the children and the available adults. The teacher positions herself in the writing area with a small group of children and asks them to think about how the class will move the home corner. Suggestions from the children might include wrapping up some of the small items in newspaper, taking the dolls to the new home in the prams, making sure the dolls have access to milk, moving the large items in a truck. As the children make their suggestions the teacher writes them on a flip chart. She will repeat this activity with all the children in the class over the next two days and using the flip chart share each group's ideas with the class. In their home-corner play it has been suggested to the children that they incorporate activities such as making notes and phone calls in preparation for the move. On the day of the move the classroom assistant takes photographs of the children packing, moving the dolls and animals and packing the truck. More photographs are taken as the children arrive at the new home. These will later be used to make a large book written by the teacher recording the event. Before the new house is furnished the teacher intends to discuss how the new area can be made into an attractive home. Does it need decorating? Where will the kitchen be? Can we make a separate bedroom for the dolls? The suggestions made by the children will be incorporated into activities on subsequent days. This brief description is intended to highlight how English activities, drawn from the starting points listed earlier, may be incorporated into the nursery curriculum and used to develop young children's speaking, listening, reading and writing competences.

Problems and anxieties

In spite of clear plans and smooth, established organization, students, newly qualified teachers and even experienced practitioners can find it difficult to meet the listening, speaking, reading and writing needs of all the pupils in their classes. For example, since the advent of the National Curriculum Key Stage 1, teachers seem to spend less time listening to children read – a fact which causes them a great deal of concern (Campbell and Neill, 1994).

Some of the problems which teachers identify when discussing the difficulties of implementing the English curriculum include • time • the competing demands of other curriculum areas • meeting the needs of those children who need additional support in English • increased parental expectations • large classes • maintaining a balance between the four language areas • keeping up to date with books for children.

These are realistic anxieties but they are not insurmountable. Conscientious practitioners may well find that they are doing more work on English than they think and that they are worrying too much.

To help allay these anxieties teachers might survey their curriculum planning, classroom routines and organizational strategies to consider the daily and weekly opportunities which are provided for children in English. This may reveal that routines such as registration, story sessions and displays provide children with demonstrations about reading and writing. Group work, play and role play engage children in listening and speaking as well as offering literacy opportunities such as note making or reading and writing in role. Sharing poems and jingles and having fun with words may be providing children with information about the phonic aspects of language and fostering positive attitudes to English. As children use the listening, reading and writing areas in the classroom they will be gaining experience in language. Writing and reading will accompany many activities across the curriculum, for example reading a maths problem and recording answers to it or reading the instructions on the computer screen and using the keyboard. Finally children will be borrowing books from school to read at home and gaining experience of browsing, discussing and selecting books in addition to the practice they receive when they read to others.

After recognizing what they do in relation to English, teachers may ask themselves what they do not do. What aims are they not achieving? To discover ways of doing more they will need to examine their organization, the amount of time they spend working with individuals, groups and the class, the balance between the amount of time they spend on management and interactions about learning. Can the teacher see at a glance those who are involved in their work and those who are not? How are other adults used in the class? How are resources stored? Would the activities run more smoothly if resources were collected and prepared in advance of the theme? Would the day run more smoothly if resources were prepared at the start of each day? Do the children need to be clearer about the teacher's expectations about how they work? In order to achieve one's aims for English and provide more time for the teacher or time for the children to pursue activities it might be necessary to change some aspects of organization.

The characteristics of a well organized programme of work

- It has clear and realistic short and long-term aims for pupil learning.
- Use is made of routine times such as registration to foster children's learning.
- Evaluation and assessment of teaching and learning are built into the programme through systematic and regular record keeping.
- Space inside and outside the classroom is used well.
- The teacher is aware of the needs, interests, attitudes and experiences of the pupils.
- Planning is detailed and includes reference to how and when reading with children will occur each week, when reading conferences will take place and when and with whom specific work on spelling, such as 'look, cover, remember, write, check' will take place.
- The classroom atmosphere is calm, orderly and quiet.
- All those who work with the class have been involved in the planning and are clear about the aims of the activities and the teacher's approach.
- The teacher sees herself as the biggest resource in the classroom and organizes all the other factors which affect learning, such as equipment, people, the children and space, in order to realize her aims.

In a well organized and productive learning environment children are meaningfully engaged in learning activities which they perceive as interesting and relevant. They move between a balance of challenging and more straightforward tasks about which they receive and give feedback. The format of the activities and careful thought about differentiation enables all pupils to succeed. In planning the tasks the teacher has taken account of the amount of teacher support that will be required and the availability of resources. She has made her expectations about the activities clear and has deployed other adults well.

Conclusion

Planning is supported by the school and national guidelines about the curriculum and these can provide teachers with a useful framework. However, effective individual planning begins with reflecting on the expectations, aims and activities that are appropriate for 3–8-year-old pupils. It relies on the teacher's understanding of how children learn and what they need to learn. It is influenced by planning in other curriculum areas and by the cross-curricular links that the teacher makes. It depends on the teacher's knowledge of subjects, organization and management. Planning and implementing a scheme of work successfully demands that teachers use the full range of their professional knowledge and skills in order to guide and extend all children's achievements.

Suggestion for further reading

McFarlane, C. (1991) *Theme Work*, Development Education Centre, Birmingham.

Chapter 12

A policy for language and literacy in the early years

Introduction

This chapter presents the reader with a sample language policy for the early years, in which parts of the earlier chapters of this book are summarized. The policy is not intended to be prescriptive but offers a model or a starting point for anyone engaged on writing or maintaining a language policy in school. Some sections of this chapter have been written with the person who has responsibility for overseeing the English curriculum in mind, notably the sections giving suggestions about formulating a policy, but all readers should find it useful as the sample policy provides a framework for teaching English in the early years.

Developing a policy

Why have a language policy?

All schools are expected to have written policies which cover each area of the curriculum. Policies should guide the practice of those who work with pupils in school, providing them, the governors and others with a statement of teaching aims and intentions. HMI (1990) have found that clear policies combined with effective curriculum leadership have a strong, positive effect on the quality and standard of pupil achievement in English. Policies are helpful for a number of reasons. They can ● support professional confidence ● establish overall aims and ways of working ● ensure progression and continuity for pupils ● ensure consistency of approach throughout the school ● aid planning ● provide guidance and starting points for new members of staff, students and supply teachers ● help with the management of the curriculum ● be used by individual teachers to review their own practice ● lead to staff development ● provide a coherent explanation of practice for parents, governors, inspectors and visitors • affect the allocation of resources • affect the allocation of time and space.

Even the act of embarking on policy making, writing or review is helpful as this can • provide an opportunity for the school to review and develop its curriculum • identify what is happening currently and indicate areas for development • provide an opportunity for staff to pool their expertise and knowledge.

Above all a language policy should enable teachers to address and answer successfully the question, *how can I teach English effectively?*

What is a language policy?

A language policy is a document that deals with the learning, use, teaching and assessment of the four areas of language: speaking, listening, reading and writing. It may also consider the role of language in other areas of the curriculum and the contribution that work in such subjects as drama and IT can make to children's developing competence as language users.

A policy might contain • a statement of principles • a statement of aims • a summary of key points • curriculum guidelines for each area of language • sections indicating the development of learning within each language area • implications for classroom organization and management • a section on record keeping and assessment • examples of successful practice • a resources and reading list • an indication of how the policy is to be monitored and evaluated • examples of children's work.

Formulating an effective language policy

It is the responsibility of the language co-ordinator to ensure that the school has a language policy document, that all the staff are familiar with it and that they adhere to its guidelines. In order to foster successful practice in language teaching and to ensure that the policy is implemented fruitfully, the co-ordinator's role is likely to include the responsibilities listed below:

- Developing the teaching and learning of language throughout the school.
- Supporting staff in the area of language.
- Maintaining, implementing and developing the policy.
- Managing and organizing resources.
- Identifying staff-development needs in language.
- Liaising with colleagues in other local establishments from which and to which pupils transfer.
- Monitoring standards of learning and teaching.

If a new policy is to be written or if the current policy and practice in the school is being reviewed there are a number of stages before, during and after the writing of the policy which will contribute to successful changes in practice. Initially the language co-ordinator will want to assess the existing situation in school, including current practice, the approaches that are used, existing resources and any new ideas that might be profitably employed in school. In conjunction with the headteacher she will signal to the whole staff that writing, updating or working on the language policy is going to take place and will seek to secure the interest and commitment of all staff to a review of practice. One way of doing this might be to consult with the staff and ask them to analyse their own practice and to identify their own issues or concerns in order to draw up an agenda for meetings. The agenda should indicate a time scale for the review and the outcomes which are expected. The first meeting might focus on the positive aspects of the English curriculum in school. Subsequently there might be meetings for staff to discuss such topics as the aims of teaching language, catering for the needs of all children, identifying indicators of progress, the involvement of parents and carers, the record-keeping system, or how to interpret the requirements of the Programmes of Study. The co-ordinator may devise discussion sheets to prompt thinking and to encourage the staff to find solutions to problems which have been identified. A prompt sheet used for examining how and when standard English might be learned and taught is illustrated below. This could be adapted for any aspect of the English curriculum:

What do we do about
Standard English – oral?
How?   **When?**   **Why?**

What could we do about
Standard English – oral?
How?   **When?**   **Why?**

What do we do about
Standard English – written?
How?   **When?**   **Why?**

What could we do about
Standard English – written?
How?   **When?**   **Why?**

Before the policy is written, staff might be asked to examine their own practice in relation to one area or several areas of English. They might survey and record the speaking, listening, reading and writing experiences of two pupils over the course of a week in order to undertake a curriculum audit of English and to establish whether there is a balance between the teaching of the four modes of language. A survey such as this might reveal the variety of experiences that children receive or the use that is made of resources in the classroom and indicate examples of good practice that can be shared amongst the staff as well as highlighting areas requiring development.

After investigating the present situation it is usually appropriate for the staff to devise a strategy for change. New ideas and approaches may be trialled at this stage, before they are incorporated into the school's future practice and policy. During this time the co-ordinator will play an active role in monitoring, acknowledging and supporting positive changes in practice. She will ask the staff for feedback and take account of their opinions and needs. She will deal with inconsistencies and where necessary provide additional experiences and staff-development sessions. As the review continues, the language co-ordinator may also wish to evaluate, sort and catalogue existing resources and to think about new resources that may be needed to support any changes in practice.

All the staff need to be given ownership of the new or revised policy by making a contribution to it. To this end the language co-ordinator might organize drafting groups to work on different sections of the policy. Giving the groups guidelines on deadlines, length and headings is useful as is sharing the drafts among the staff. This provides all the staff with the opportunity to review, understand and be committed to the policy.

Once the policy has been written it should be distributed to all the staff who work with the pupils, including volunteer helpers and lunch-time assistants. It should also be given to governors and to LEA personnel. The information it contains should be disseminated to parents and carers through open evenings and workshop sessions. Other local schools who contribute or receive pupils from the school should be aware of how the school teaches English and might be given copies of the policy or invited to meetings at the school. Visitors to the school, such as students and advisers, should be provided with a copy of the policy.

Innovations in practice are not always easy and the co-ordinator may have to ensure that the policy is adhered to despite such factors as staff changes, lack of money and parental criticism, particularly in the early stages. Later the policy will become a framework allowing scope for interpretation and flexibility. An effective language policy is not static. It will change in response to classroom practice, teachers' experience, discussion with colleagues and continuing staff development. As teachers implement the policy they will be learning and redefining its guidelines for themselves. As the staff become familiar with the policy and experience for themselves its implications for their role and their management of the children's learning, new needs will be identified.

The co-ordinator and the staff may need to maintain a sense of proportion about the successes and failures of the policy. At regular intervals they may need to take a dispassionate look at how it is working and as a result will evaluate, revise and update the policy by sharing and adding to the examples of good practice and the list of resources and reading. They will make sure that the policy is a useful working document which represents an agreed basis for classroom practice, that it relates to the individual characteristics of the school, enables the best use to be made of expertise, resources, equipment, time and space and is used to plan and implement a successful language curriculum throughout the school.

A sample language policy

Principles

This policy outlines the approach to the teaching and learning of English at [school]. It should be used by all those who contribute to the development of the pupils' language in school:

> We believe that children learn best when they take an active part in their own learning, when they are aware of the reasons for what they are learning and when they are supported in their learning. When young children begin school they will already have learned a great deal about speaking, listening, reading and writing. By using a developmental approach to language we use the children's previous experiences and their proven capacity to learn in order to devise an English curriculum that meets their needs, extends their learning and enables all pupils to achieve their potential. English is taught in the context of a broad, balanced curriculum and is guided by the statutory requirements of the National Curriculum.

All teaching is informed by the general principle that learning should enrich the lives of all learners.

Overall aims for the teaching and learning of English

- To develop pupils' abilities to communicate effectively and confidently in a range of formats including oral and written standard English.
- To develop pupils' capacities to listen with understanding.
- To enable pupils to be enthusiastic, responsive, knowledgeable and critical readers.
- To encompass all aspects of the Programmes of Study and levels of attainment as required in English by the National Curriculum orders (DfE, 1995a).
- To provide opportunities for pupils to use IT to facilitate and extend their learning in speaking, listening, reading and writing.
- To enable pupils to use and apply their competence in one mode of language to extend and develop their competence in one or all other modes.

A summary of the key points contained in this policy

This policy contains the agreed aims for the teaching of the speaking, listening, reading and writing curriculum at [school]. It outlines the sequence of development in each area of English and makes some suggestions about the classroom organization, resources and activities that will encourage learning. It contains sections on the school library, work with the under fives, bilingual learners, children who experience difficulties, equal opportunities, assessment and record keeping and parental involvement. Lists of resources for language and examples of good practice are attached to the policy.

Speaking and listening

Aims

To enable all children to

- feel confident and valued when they express themselves through the spoken word,
- respect and value all languages,
- learn through discussion with others,
- listen to, evaluate and respect the opinions of others,
- become competent listeners and speakers.

The development of speaking and listening

Speaking and listening are important for learning and as a means of communication. All children start school with considerable oral ability but may still lack experience at using language in certain ways. Teachers will build on what children can already do but will extend the children's competence as oral language users by developing their abilities in the following areas:

- Taking account of the needs of listeners. Assessing the listener's understanding and knowledge; needing to be more explicit in certain situations and with certain audiences.
- Talking in front of large audiences.
- Turn taking in large groups.
- Answering the teacher's questions which may be phrased in school language.
- Participating purposefully, using reasoning and discussion techniques, in collaborative classroom tasks.
- Using different styles and forms of language appropriate to particular situations such as telling jokes, participating in a debate or giving reasons and step-by-step explanations.
- Organizing what is said.
- Acquiring and using a more extensive vocabulary.

Organization for speaking and listening

The effectiveness of teachers, and other adults in school, in extending the oral development of young children is related to • their own understanding of the value of talk • their attitude to talk • planning for talk • organization for talk • the choice of classroom activities • their own use of language.

Talk has equal status with other aspects of the English curriculum and speaking and listening activities should be considered and included when planning schemes of work. Group work is an effective way of encouraging children to listen and to use language for different purposes. The teacher will also need to support children's talk through sensitive and well timed dialogue and questions. Planning for talk in a range of formal and less formal situations will encourage children to use different dialect forms, including standard English, in appropriate contexts.

Resources for speaking and listening

These include listening areas, story sessions, whole-class discussion times, collaborative group work across the curriculum, role play, games, computer software, the use of story props and reading activities.

Reading

Aims

To enable all children to

- understand the purposes for reading and learning to read,
- develop confidence in their ability to read and to see themselves as readers, regardless of attainment,
- become voluntary users of books for pleasure, interest, information and the extension of experience,
- be able to read fluently and competently from a range of material,
- draw upon a variety of reading strategies in order to make sense of print,
- become critical and discerning readers who are able to evaluate the written word.

The development of reading

During their early years at school children are expected to develop from dependence to independence as readers. Independent readers are those who combine fluency and accuracy and who make sense of and respond to what they read. Children's development as readers will be supported by hearing and sharing books with adults and other children, having time to browse in the book corner, talking about books and practising reading. Learning to write will support learning to read, giving children further experiences with and insights into print. As they engage in all these experiences children should be encouraged to apply a wide range of strategies to their reading and to read a range of book and non-book texts.

Organization for reading

Opportunities for reading are provided during individual, group, paired, class and silent-reading sessions in each class. Daily organization of activities should take account of the need to provide opportunities for pupils to have sustained periods of reading every day. The children will also gain practice in reading during shared-reading sessions using enlarged texts, shared-writing sessions, and during activities arising from curriculum areas other than English which require children to read instructions and explanations. Story-reading and story-telling sessions occur each day and provide a valuable opportunity to introduce children to the power and use of books. Listening to audio tapes and reading the books which accompany these give children positive experiences with texts. Every class is allocated a weekly session in the library which can be used for sharing books and for borrowing books. Teachers should make sure that as many children as possible take books home each day to share with their parents.

Resources for reading

A well chosen range of good-quality picture books, poetry, song books, traditional tales, stories, novels, reference books, non-fiction, big books and books made by children and adults in school is available in classrooms and the library. Books are available in English, other languages and dual-language versions. Each class has a collection of core books which are used in conjunction with enlarged texts, audio tapes and group-reading sessions. These have been selected to cover the likely reading level of each class and are used to provide a framework for reading.

Audio tapes, story props and computer programs should be used to foster the development of reading. A selection of reading resources is exchanged between classes once a term to ensure that children experience a variety of books and stimuli for reading each year. Books and other resources are regularly updated and added to. It is an important professional responsibility for all teachers to familiarize themselves and keep up to date with books and other resources that are available for children.

The school library

The school has a well stocked library containing a large collection of fiction and information books. It also houses books written by children, additional sets of core books, group readers, audio tapes, story props, language games and pictures. Library resources can be used by the children and they should be introduced to the library system and organization. Resources may also be borrowed for class use by the teacher. Sets of core books may be borrowed to supplement classroom stock. Teachers should plan for the use of the library for book-sharing sessions, to help pupils to learn how to use the library and to give children access to the library resources. At the end of themes which have necessitated borrowing library stock resources should be returned so that they can be used by other classes. Suggestions for additions to library and class resources should be entered in the the stock book located in the library.

Writing

Aims

To enable all children to

- use the knowledge and understanding of writing that they bring to school,
- develop a positive attitude towards writing,
- understand the reasons for writing and for learning to write,
- understand that writing conveys meaning,
- write for a variety of audiences and in a variety of styles,
- become competent and fluent writers.

The development of writing

When children start school they are given opportunities to demonstrate what they know about writing. Teachers work with what the children are able to do. The children are asked to read back what they have written and are given correct models of writing which are compared with their own versions. As the children's writing becomes more readable the teacher may begin to focus on one or two aspects of transcription, for example word spaces or the correct spelling of one or two words. As children grow in competence they are expected to write more and to write and redraft their work, paying attention to organization, use of language, purpose and audience. Transcription is never emphasized at the expense of discussing the choice of words, detail, organization and structure of what has been written. As a general aim children are expected to progress in writing in accordance with Programmes of Study and level descriptions for writing. It is unwise to attach levels exactly to particular ages of children, but most 7-year-olds are expected to produce writing that shows achievement at Level 2 or above.

Organizing for writing

When only one or two groups are engaged in writing at one time, it is easier for the teacher to give support for each child's writing needs. Occasionally there may be times when all the class is writing at the same time, for example during a special book-making project. For some writing activities children may be organized in collaborative mixed-ability groups and pairs. Shared writing with the whole class or with groups of pupils is a useful way of demonstrating all the processes that are used when writing. It can be used to introduce young children to the conventions of print, and older children to ways of planning, drafting, and redrafting. The organization for writing should always complement the nature of the task.

Writing for different purposes and different audiences

Writing at school should always have a purpose that is made clear to the children. Writing activities should cover the range of uses for writing that exist, including personal, factual, expressive and imaginative. Children should be encouraged to make notes when carrying out practical tasks and to produce labels and captions for the classroom. Wherever possible children's writing should have an audience that goes beyond the teacher, such as older and younger children, children in the class, family members and audiences outside the school.

Resources for writing

Writing should be portrayed as a purposeful, everyday activity. In the classroom children should experience a print-rich environment with displays of lists, greeting cards, notes, letters, name labels, self-made books, registers and notices. In order to participate fully in a range of writing activities and become successful and competent writers children will require resources, such as pencils, writing pens, thick and thin felt pens, crayons, chalks and pastels. Typewriters and word-processing facilities should also be available for pupils to use. Pupils should learn that different implements are more suitable for particular sorts of writing, for example thick felt pens for writing notices, writing pens for final drafts and pencils for first drafts. Children should be provided with note books, class-made books, card, different sorts of paper and first-draft books for writing. These resources should be available in the writing corner, the home corner and alongside interactive displays. As children become more proficient at writing they should be provided with dictionaries and thesauruses and shown how to use these. Final copies of writing should be place in the finished work tray for discussion with the teacher, before being displayed or stored in the children's writing folders. Erasers should never be used when children are writing.

Transcription

Aims

To enable all children to

- be independent and confident users of written language,
- communicate the meaning of what is written efficiently,
- draw from a range of strategies when spelling,
- develop dictionary and reference skills.

Spelling

Spelling is only one part of the writing process. It is not the most important part and should not be overemphasized. Children should be encouraged to consider the look of words and to have a go at spelling when they are writing. The teaching of spelling should arise from what children write and be linked to individual children's needs. Spelling is taught during shared-writing sessions, through word games and by the 'look, cover, remember, write, check' method. Reception and Year 1 children should have access to simple dictionaries and word banks, while Year 2 and 3 children should begin to use more sophisticated dictionaries and thesauruses.

Handwriting

Handwriting is only one aspect of writing. All children need to learn to write legibly, fluently and with reasonable speed. To this end children need to be shown correct pencil grip and letter formation. Help with handwriting should be given as children write. Not every piece of writing children produce needs to be perfect, but teachers should emphasize attention to good presentation when they are writing final drafts. All final drafts should be written with writing pens. When demonstrating writing to left-handers, teachers should use their left hand and be alert to the difficulties that left-handed children may have. If necessary special provision should be made for left-handed writers. Children in Year 2 and Year 3 who are forming their letters correctly should be introduced to a simple from of cursive script. The teacher's own writing should always provide a good model for the children.

Punctuation

The correct use of punctuation is an advanced transcriptional skill. Children should not be pressed into using punctuation before they understand what it is for. Discussions about punctuation should arise during shared-reading and writing sessions. These will help children to recognize its function in writing. When children begin to incorporate punctuation into their own writing the teacher may wish to include this as a topic for discussion in writing conferences or with the class.

Other issues

Language in the nursery

Three and four-year-old pupils are exempt from the National Curriculum Programmes of Study. However the first of the general aims of the National Curriculum for English is one that will be shared by all teachers and will influence their planning for language throughout the school: 'English should develop pupils' abilities to communicate effectively in speech and writing and to listen with understanding. It should also enable them to be enthusiastic, responsive and knowledgeable readers' (DfE, 1995a, p. 2).

In the nursery opportunities for speaking, listening, reading and writing will be planned for children. Indoor and outdoor play, group work and collaborative activities as well as discussion times and adult involvement in activities will provide occasions for the development of speaking and listening. Story sessions using enlarged texts as well as other books should introduce children to the pleasure and purposes of reading and writing. The nursery has a well resourced library area which is used by the children for browsing and borrowing. Story tapes and books should be available in the listening area. Imaginative play areas should contain appropriate literacy resources and adults should enter into children's play to provide models of how these resources are used. All children are expected to explore and enjoy reading and writing during their time in the nursery. Close liaison with carers will enable nursery staff to match language and literacy experiences to the children's needs and to extend the knowledge, skills and understanding children already have.

Writing and reading

Good readers are not automatically good writers. However, as children gain more experience of print through reading, it is likely that their writing will improve. As young children gain more experience of print and books they will learn about written language. Attending to the details of print in reading will help children with the transcriptional elements of writing, such as knowledge about letters, presentation and spelling. Reading will also provide children with ideas for their own compositions as well as awareness of the structure and organization of writing.

Bilingual learners and English

Wherever possible children's development as listeners, speakers, readers and writers in community languages should be supported. Tapes and books in home languages should be available in every class. Initial and continuing meetings with parents should provide teachers with information about children's experiences in language and this should be used to guide the teacher's provision for English. Children who are fluent or literate in a language other than English should not be discouraged from speaking, reading or writing in languages that are familiar to them. This will not prevent them from developing as competent users of English. Support teachers may be available to work with bilingual children. Monolingual pupils should be encouraged to value languages other than their own.

Children who experience difficulties with English

Children who are making less progress in speaking, listening, reading or writing than one might expect should be brought to the attention of the language co-ordinator and the headteacher. Support staff may be allocated to work with these children. The language curriculum should be the same for all children and careful attention to differentiation of outcome or presentation and to organization should make this possible.

Equal opportunities and English

Teachers should ensure that the language activities they present to children should be appropriate to the needs and interests of girls and boys. Particular attention should be paid to the needs of both sexes as speakers and listeners, to the resources that are used for reading and to one's expectations about the content and presentation of writing.

Assessment and record keeping

Most assessment takes place as the teacher works with and observes the children each day. More formal evidence of assessment forms part of the language and literacy record for each child. Teachers should collect samples of children's reading and writing, and should keep records of observations, conferences and comments from parents and other teachers who work with the children. Wherever possible children should be involved in assessing their own language development. Children's assessments should be included in their language record. Judgements about children's work may refer to the National Curriculum Programmes of Study, the needs of the child and suggestions for the child's future language development. At the end of Key Stage 1 teachers should make a summary of children's progress in language which refers to the level descriptions in the National Curriculum for English (DfE, 1995a). Year 2 pupils are assessed using the standard assessment tasks and tests and their results are added to their records.

Parents and language

We value the experiences of language in its written and oral modes that children bring with them from their homes and communities. Making links and sharing information between home and school has a beneficial effect on children's learning and to this end parents are encouraged to participate in the work of the school and in their children's language development through • parents' evenings and reports • regular parent consultations and discussions • informal discussions • a home–school reading programme • curriculum evenings • invitations to parents to make contributions to the language curriculum in school.

Parents are provided with information about their child's language development during parent discussions held each term and a written report which is sent home towards the end of the school year.

Support available to implement this policy

Further information and guidance about the teaching of English is available in the first instance from the language co-ordinator. Other people who may be able to provide support include the assessment co-ordinator, the special-needs co-ordinator, support teachers, nursery and playgroup co-ordinators and LEA advisers. A number of other professionals such as speech therapists may be called upon when appropriate. Please consult with the language co-ordinator if you feel you would like to discuss issues with outside agencies.

Monitoring and evaluating the policy

Each year the effectiveness of the provision for English throughout the school is reviewed. A short report written by the co-ordinator is discussed by the staff and suggestions for future action are agreed. These are used to inform the school development plan. Monitoring is undertaken with regard to the school's aims for each area of English. The yearly review will be attached to the reference copy of the policy document.

Areas for future development

This section could refer to areas of known weakness such as the need to build up stocks of information books for younger children or the need for staff-development sessions on organizing for speaking and listening. It should identify future developments and give an indication of when and how these will be addressed.

Examples of practice

Samples of records and reports, brief accounts of activities, successful schemes of work and ideas gathered from staff-development sessions and courses could be included in this section.

Resources and reading list

Lists of core books, dual-language books, computer software as well as names and telephone numbers of contacts for book weeks or translations might be included in the resources section of the policy. The reading list could include books that were consulted when the policy was written, a list of language books available in the staffroom and other books that teachers have found or might find useful for their teaching.

Examples of children's work

Samples of work illustrating aspects of the level descriptions in the National Curriculum for English, demonstrating appropriate teacher intervention or depicting progress over time might be usefully included in this section.

Conclusion

A language policy cannot contain all the knowledge, activities and strategies known and used by every teacher in the school. But it can give guidance to staff and insights for other interested parties into agreed ways of developing children's language. All who work in the school should be familiar with the policy and teachers should use it to plan and inform their practice and to ensure continuity, progression and success for pupils.

Suggestions for further reading

HMI (1990) *The Teaching and Learning of Language and Literacy*, HMSO, London.
HMI (1991) *The Teaching and Learning of Reading in Primary Schools*, HMSO, London.

Appendix

Sources of information about books and book resources for young children

---

Books for Keeps, 1 Effingham Road, London SE12 8NZ tel.: 0181–852 4953. Book and cassette reviews and articles about authors and books published by the School Bookshop Association.

Children's Literature in Education, IBIS Information Services Ltd, Waterside Lowbell Lane, Colney, St Albans AL2 1DX.

Federation of Children's Book Groups, 23 Constable Drive, Bradwell, Great Yarmouth NR31 9RA tel.: 01493 652712. Publishes book lists, information leaflets, newsletters and the magazine *Books For Your Children*. Provides advice and information about books to parents, schools, libraries, hospitals, publishers and playgroups.

Front Line Books, 1 Newton St, Piccadilly, Manchester M1 1HW tel.: 0161–236 3112. A large community bookshop with a large collection of imported and difficult-to-find children's books.

Letterbox Library, Unit 2D, Leroy House, 436 Essex Rd, London N1 3QP tel.: 0171–226 1633. A mail-order bookclub specializing in non-sexist and multicultural books for children. Publishes quarterly catalogues and newsletters. Representatives throughout England and Scotland.

Magi Publications, 55 Crowland Ave, Hayes, Middlesex UB3 4JP tel.: 0171–387 0610. Publishes a number of dual-language texts and dictionaries for children. Texts available in Bengali, Chinese, Greek, Gujurati, Hindi, Punjabi, Turkish, Urdu and Vietnamese, all with English.

Mantra Publishing Ltd, 5 Alexandra Grove, London N12 8NU tel.: 0181–445 5123. Publishes dual-language books and tapes; largely specializes in Asian languages.

Poetry Library, Royal Festival Hall, South Bank Centre, London SE1 8XX tel.: 0171–921 0664. Houses a collection of poetry for children for reference and loan; provides information and courses for teachers.

Roy Yates Books, Smallfields Cottage, Cox Green, Rudgwick, Horsham, West Sussex RH12 3DE tel.: 01403 822299. Lists and supplies every dual-language text in print.

School Bookshop Association, 6 Brightfield Road, Lee, London SE12 8QF.

School Library Association, Liden Library, Barrington Close, Liden, Swindon, Wiltshire SN3 6HF. An advisory and information service; also provides practical guidelines on developing school libraries.

Signal, The Thimble Press, Lockwood, Station Road, Woodchester, Stroud GL5 5EQ. Journal containing reviews and articles about books and authors.

Soma Books, 38 Kennington Lane, London SE11 4LS tel.: 0171–735 2101. Sells and distributes titles from Indian publishers.

Tamarind, PO Box 296, Camberley, Surrey GU15 1QW tel.: 01276 683979. Publishes fiction and educational texts. All have black children as the main characters.

Weston Woods Studios Ltd, 14 Friday Street, Henley-on-Thames, Oxford RG9 1AH tel.: 01491 577033. Produce a large number of cassettes, videos, slides and filmstrips that accompany well-known books for children.

Young Book Trust, Book House, 45 East Hill, London SW18 2QZ tel.: 0181–870 9055/8 and The Scottish Book Centre, 137 Dundee Street, Edinburgh EH11 1BG tel.: 0131–229 3663. Houses a store of information about books for children. Produces videos featuring interviews with children's authors and sells a *Bookweek Handbook.*

References and further reading

Ahlberg, A. (1980) *Mrs Plug the Plumber*, Puffin Books, Harmondsworth.
Ahlberg, A. (1981a) *Mrs Lather's Laundry*, Puffin Books, Harmondsworth.
Ahlberg, A. (1981b) *Miss Brick the Builder's Baby*, Puffin Books, Harmondsworth.
Ahlberg, A. (1988) *Mrs Jolly's Joke Shop*, Puffin Books, Harmondsworth.
Ahlberg, A. and Ahlberg, J. (1988) *Mrs Wobble the Waitress*, Puffin Books, Harmondsworth.
Ahlberg, J. and Ahlberg, A. (1978) *Each Peach Pear Plum*, Kestrel, London.
Ahlberg, J. and Ahlberg, A. (1980) *Funnybones*, Picture Lions, London.
Ahlberg, J. and Ahlberg, A. (1982) *The Baby's Catalogue*, Puffin Books, Harmondsworth.
Ahlberg, J. and Ahlberg, A. (1986) *The Jolly Postman*, Heinemann, London.
Aliki (1986) *How a Book is Made*, Hippo, London.
Anderson, R.C., Hiebert, E. and Wilkinson, I.A.G. (1985) *Becoming a Nation of Readers: The Report of the Commission on Reading*, National Academy of Education, Washington, DC.
Arnold, H. (1982) *Listening to Children Reading*, Hodder & Stoughton, Sevenoaks.
Asher, S. (1980) Topic interest and children's reading comprehension, in R. Spiro, B. Bruce and W. Brewer (eds) *Theoretical Issues in Reading Comprehension*, Lawrence Erlbaum Associates, Hillsdale, NJ.
Ashton-Warner, S. (1963) *Teacher*, Secker & Warburg, London.
Baddeley, G. (ed.) (1992) *Learning Together Through Talk: Key Stages 1 and 2*, Hodder & Stoughton, London.
Barnes, E. (1994) One collar, two sleeves . . . ? *Language and Learning*, June/July, pp. 9–11.
Barrs, M., Ellis, S., Hester, H. and Thomas, A. (1988) *The Primary Language Record: Handbook for Teachers*, CLPE, London.
Barrs, M. and Hester, H. (1991) Bilingualism in recession. *Language Matters*, no 3, p. 1.
Barrs, M. and Thomas, A. (eds) (1991) *The Reading Book*, CLPE, London.
Bennett, J. (1979) *Learning to Read with Picture Books*, The Thimble Press, Stroud.
Bennett, N., Desforges, C., Cockburn, A. and Wilkinson, A. (1984) *The Quality of Pupil Learning Experiences*, Lawrence Erlbaum Associates, Hillsdale, NJ.
Bennett, O. (1983) *A Turkish Afternoon*, Hamish Hamilton, London.
Bennett, O. (1990) *Our New Home*, Evans, London.
Bernstein, B. (1971) *Class, Codes and Control, Vol. 1*, Routledge & Kegan Paul, London.

Binch, C. (1994) *Gregory Cool*, Francis Lincoln, London.

Bissex, G. (1980) *GNYS AT WRK: A Child Learns to Write and Read*, Harvard University Press, Cambridge, MA.

Bissex, G. (1984) The child as teacher, in H. Goelman, A. Oberg and F. Smith (eds) *Awakening to Literacy (The University of Victoria Symposium on Children's Responses to a Literature Environment: Literacy before Schooling)*, Heinemann, London.

Blake, Q. (1968) *Patrick*, Picture Lions, London.

Blegvad, E. (1980) *The Three Little Pigs*, Picture Lions, London.

Bloom, W. (1987) *Partnership with Parents in Reading*, Hodder & Stoughton, London.

Bradman, T. (1986) *Through My Window*, Little Mammoth, London.

Bradman, T. (1988) *Wait And See*, Little Mammoth, London.

Bradman, T. (1990) *In A Minute*, Little Mammoth, London.

Brice-Heath, S. (1983) *Ways with Words: Language, Life and Work in Communities and Classrooms*, Cambridge University Press, Cambridge.

Brierley, L. (1991) A climate for frankness in classroom talk with top juniors. *TALK: The Journal of the National Oracy Project*, Summer, no. 4, pp. 27–31.

Brown, E.N. (1990) Children with spelling and writing difficulties: an alternative approach, in P.D. Pumphrey and C.D. Elliott (eds) *Children's Difficulties in Reading, Spelling and Writing*, Falmer Press, London.

Brown, R. (1981) *A Dark, Dark Tale*, Scholastic, London.

Brown, R. and Belugi, U. (1966) Three processes in the child's acquisition of syntax, in J. Emig, J. Flemming and H. Popp (eds) *Language and Learning*, Harcourt, New York.

Browne, A. (1984) *Willy the Wimp*, Magnet, London.

Browne, A. (1985) *Will the Champ*, Magnet, London.

Browne, A. (1986) *Piggybook*, Magnet, London.

Browne, A. (1988) *I Like Books*, Julia MacRae Books, London.

Browne, A. (1993) *Helping Children to Write*, Paul Chapman Publishing, London.

Bruner, J. (1984) Language, mind and reading, in H. Goelman, A. Oberg and F. Smith (eds) *Awakening to Literacy (The University of Victoria Symposium on Children's Responses to a Literature Environment: Literacy before Schooling)*, Heinemann, London.

Bukiet, S. (1989) *Scripts of the World*, Mantra, London.

Burningham, J. (1970) *Mr Gumpy's Outing*, Puffin Books, Harmondsworth.

Burningham, J. (1977) *Come Away From the Water, Shirley*, Jonathan Cape, London.

Butler, D. (1982) *Babies Need Books*, Penguin Books, Harmondsworth.

Buxton, C. (no date) *Language Activities for Bilingual Learners*, Tower Hamlets Education, London.

Campbell, J. and Neill, S. (1994) *Curriculum Reform at Key Stage 1*, Longman, London.

Campbell, R. (1982) *Dear Zoo*, Puffin Books, Harmondsworth.

Campbell, R. (1990) *Reading Together*, Open University Press, Milton Keynes.

Campbell, R. (1992) *Reading Real Books*, Open University Press, Milton Keynes.

Cash, T. (1988) *Bricks*, A. & C. Black, London.

Cashdan, A. and Wright, J. (1990) Intervention strategies for backward readers in the primary school classroom, in P.D. Pumphrey and C.D. Elliot (eds) *Children's Difficulties in Reading, Spelling and Writing*, Falmer Press, London.

Cazden, C.B., Cordeiro, P. and Giacobbe, M.E. (1985) Young children's learning of punctuation, in G. Wells and J. Nicholls (eds) *Language and Learning: An Interactional Perspective*, Falmer Press, Lewes.

Chapman, G. and Robson, P. (1991) *Making Books*, Simon & Schuster, London.

Chiltern Consortium (1984) *Partners in Reading*, Wall Hall, Aldenham, Watford.

Clark, M.M. (1976) *Young Fluent Readers*, Heinemann Educational, London.

Clay, M. (1975) *What Did I Write?* Heinemann Educational, London.

Clay, M. (1979) *Concepts of Print: The Early Detection of Reading Difficulties*, Heinemann Educational, Auckland.

Clay, M. (1990) The Reading Recovery Programme, 1984–1988: coverage, outcomes and Education Board district figures. *New Zealand Journal of Educational Studies*, Vol. 25, no. 1, pp. 66–70.

Clay, M. (1991) *Becoming Literate: The Construction of Inner Control*, Heinemann, Auckland.

Cole, B. (1986) *Princess Smartypants*, Picture Lion, London.

Cole, B. (1987) *Prince Cinders*, Magi, Hayes.

Crystal, D. (1987) *Child Language, Learning and Linguistics* (2nd edn), Arnold, London.

Cummins, J. (1979) Linguistic interdependence and the educational development of bilingual children. *Review of Educational Research*, Vol. 49, pp. 222–51.

Cummins, J. (1984a) *Bilingualism and Special Education: Issues in Assessment and Pedagogy*, Multilingual Matters, Clevedon.

Cummins, J. (1984b) Mother tongue maintenance for minority language children: some common misconceptions. *Forum 2*, ILEA, Languages Inspectorate, Spring.

Dale, P. (1987) *Bet You Can't!* Walker, London.

Dearing, R. (1993) *The National Curriculum and its Assessment (The Dearing Report)*, HMSO, London.

DES (1967) *Children and their Primary Schools (The Plowden Report)*, HMSO, London.

DES (1975) *A Language for Life (The Bullock Report)*, HMSO, London.

DES (1988a) *Report of the Inquiry into the Teaching of the English Language (The Kingman Report)*, HMSO, London.

DES (1988b) *National Curriculum Proposals for English for Ages 5 to 11 (The Cox Committee Report Part 1)*, HMSO, London.

DES (1989a) *English for Ages 5 to 16 (The Cox Report)*, HMSO, London.

DES (1989b) *National Curriculum: From Policy to Practice*, HMSO, London.

DES (1990) *English in the National Curriculum (No. 2)*, HMSO, London.

Deshpande, C. (1988) *Five Stones and Knuckle Bones*, A. & C. Black, London.

Development Education Centre (1989) *Working Now*, DEC, Birmingham.

DfE (1994) *Special Educational Needs: A Guide for Parents*, HMSO, London.

DfE (1995a) *English in the National Curriculum*, HMSO, London.

DfE (1995b) *Information Technology in the National Curriculum*, HMSO, London.

Donaldson, M. (1978) *Children's Minds*, Collins, Glasgow.

Dupasquier, P. (1987) *Our House on the Hill*, Puffin Books, Harmondsworth.

Ellis, G. and Brewster, J. (1991) *The Storytelling Handbook for Primary Teachers*, Penguin Books, Harmondsworth.

Ervin-Tripp, S.M. (1978) Is second language learning like the first? In E.M. Hatch (ed.) *Second Language Acquisition*, Newbury House, Rowley, MA.

Essen, J. and Welch, J. (1990) *Survey of Provision for Able and Talented Children*, NAGC, Northampton.

Farquhar, C. (1987) Little read books, *The Times Educational Supplement*, 8 May.

Fernald, G.M. (1943) *Remedial Techniques in Basic School Subjects*, McGraw Hill, New York.

Ferreiro, E. (1986) Literacy development: psychogenesis. Paper presented at World Congress on Reading, London.

Ferreiro, E. and Teberosky, A. (1983) *Literacy before Schooling*, Heinemann Educational, Portsmouth, NH.

Flint, D. (1993) *China*, Simon & Schuster Young Books, Hemel Hempstead.

Fraser, B. and Chapman, E. (1983) Children with sensory defects in schools. *Special Education: Forward Trends*, Vol. 1, no. 4, pp. 37–41.

French, F. (1991) *Anancy and Mr Dry-Bone*, Frances Lincoln, London.
Furchgott, T. and Dawson, L. (1977) *Phoebe and the Hot Water Bottles*, Fontana, London.
Ghandi, N. (1990) *Sari Games*, André Deutsch, London.
Goddard, N. (1974) *Literacy: Language Experience Approach*, Macmillan Educational, London.
Goodman, K.S. (1972) Reading: the key is in the children's language. *The Reading Teacher*, March, pp. 505–508.
Goodman, K. and Goodman, Y.M. (1977) Learning about psycholinguistic processes by analyzing oral reading. *Harvard Educational Review*, Vol. 47, no. 3, pp. 317–33.
Goodman, Y. and Burke, C. (1972) *Reading Miscue Inventory*, Macmillan, New York.
Gorman, T., White, J., Brooks, G. and English, F. (1989) *Language for Learning, a Summary Report on the 1988 APU Surveys of Language Performance*, HMSO, London.
Goswami, U. and Bryant, P. (1990) *Phonological Skills and Learning to Read*, Lawrence Erlbaum Associates, Hove.
Graves, D. (1983) *Writing: Teachers and Children at Work*, Heinemann Educational, London.
Grifalconi, A. (1989) *The Village of Round and Square Houses*, Picturemac, London.
Griffiths, R. (1993) *Games*, A. & C. Black, London.
Hall, N., Hemming, G., Hann, H. and Crawford, L. (1989) *Parental Views on Writing and the Teaching of Writing*, Department of Education Studies, Manchester Polytechnic, Manchester.
Halliday, M.A.K. and Hassan, R. (1985) *Language, Context and Text*, Oxford University Press, London.
Hannon, P. (1989) How should parental involvement in the teaching of reading be evaluated? *British Journal of Educational Research*, Vol. 15, no. 1, pp. 33–40.
Harrison, J. (no date) *Opposites*, Health Education Authority, London.
Hawkins, C.J. (1983) *What's the Time, Mr Wolf?* Heinemann, London.
Hester, H. (1983) *Stories in the Multilingual Classroom*, Harcourt Brace Jovanovich, London.
Hester, H. (1990) *Patterns of Learning*, CLPE, London.
Hewison, J. and Tizard, J. (1980) Parental involvement and reading attainment. *British Journal of Educational Psychology*, no. 50, part 3, pp. 209–15.
Hill, E. (1980) *Where's Spot?* Puffin Books, Harmondsworth.
HM Government (1988) *Education Reform Act*, HMSO, London.
HMI (1990) *The Teaching and Learning of Language and Literacy*, HMSO, London.
HMI (1991) *The Teaching and Learning of Reading in Primary Schools*, HMSO, London.
HMI (1993) *The HMI Report on the Implementation of the Curricular Requirements of the Education Reform Act English Key Stages 1, 2 and 3: Third Year, 1991–92*, HMSO, London.
Hoberman, M.A. (1978) *A House is a House For Me*, Picture Puffin, Harmondsworth.
Hodgeon, J. (1984) *A Woman's World?* Cleveland Education Authority and the Equal Opportunities Commission, Manchester.
Hoffman, M. (1991) *Amazing Grace*, Frances Lincoln, London.
Hoffman, M. (1993) *Henry's Baby*, Dorling Kindersley, London.
Holdaway, D. (1979) *The Foundations of Literacy*, Ashton Scholastic, London.
Huck, C. (1993) *Secret Places*, Greenwillow Books, New York.
Huey, E. (1908) *The Psychology and Pedagogy of Reading*, Macmillan, New York.
Hughes, S. (1991) *Moving Molly*, Red Fox, London.
Hulme, K. (1985) *The Bone People*, Hodder & Stoughton, London.
Hutchins, P. (1970) *Rosie's Walk*, The Bodley Head, London.

Hutchins, P. (1971) *Titch*, Puffin Books, Harmondsworth.

Hutchins, P. (1976) *Don't Forget the Bacon!* Picture Puffin, London.

ILEA (1979) *Language in the Primary School*, ILEA, London.

ILEA (1984) *Phototalk Books*, Harcourt Brace Jovanovich, London.

ILEA, Research and Statistics Branch (1990a) *Reading Experience of Pupils: Validation Survey of Reading. Scale 2 from the Primary Language Record* (RS 1285/90) ILEA, London, March.

ILEA (1990b) *Language and Power*, Harcourt Brace Jovanovich, London.

Jackson, A. and Hannon, P. (1981) *The Belfield Reading Project*, Belfield Community Council, Rochdale.

Jarman, C. (1993) *The Development of Handwriting Skills* (2nd edn), Simon & Schuster Education, Hemel Hempstead.

Jarman, J. (1994) *The Jessame Stories*, Mammoth, London.

Jarmany, K. (1991) Considering gender differences. *TALK: The Journal of the National Oracy Project*, Summer, no. 4, pp. 23–26.

Johnson, A. (1989) *Tell Me A Story, Mama*, Orchard Books, New York.

Johnson, P. (1990) *A Book of One's Own: Developing Literacy through Making Books*, Hodder & Stoughton, London.

Karavasil, J. (1983) *Houses and Homes Around the World*, Macmillan, London.

Kemeny, H. (ed.) (1990) *Talking IT Through*, National Council for Educational Technology, Coventry.

Klein, G. (1986) Resources for multicultural education, in R. Aora and C. Duncan (eds) *Multicultural Education: Towards Good Practice*, Routledge, London.

Krashen, S.D. and Terell, T.D. (1983) *The National Approach: Language Acquisition in the Classroom*, Pergamon, Oxford.

Kress, G. (1994) *Learning to Write* (2nd edn), Routledge, London.

Lakoff, R. (1975) *Language and a Woman's Place*, Harper & Row, London.

Lewin, H. (1992) *Jafta The Homecoming*, Hamish Hamilton, London.

Lloyd, E. (1988) *Sasha and the Bicycle Thieves*, Heinemann, London.

Loban, W. (1976) *Language Development: Kindergarten through Grade 12*, NCTE, Urbana, IL.

Mackay, D., Thompson, B. and Schaub, P. (1970) *Breakthrough to Literacy*, Longman, London.

Mahy, M. (1991) *Keeping House*, Hamish Hamilton, London.

Mallet, M. (1992) *Making Facts Matter: Reading Non-Fiction 5–11*, Paul Chapman Publishing, London.

Maris, R. (1983) *My Book*, Picture Puffin, London.

McCracken, R.A. (1971) Initiating sustained silent reading. *Journal of Reading*, Vol. 14, no. 8, pp. 521–83.

McCullagh, S. (1969) *One Two Three and Away!* Hart-Davis Educational, St Albans.

McFarlane, C. (1991) *Theme Work*, Development Education Centre, Birmingham.

McNally, J. and Murray, W. (1968) *Key Words to Literacy* (2nd edn), Schoolmaster Publishing, London.

McNaughton, C. (1991) *Have You Seen Who's Just Moved In Next Door To Us?* Walker, London.

Meek, M. (1982) *Learning to Read*, The Bodley Head, London.

Meek, M. (1988) *How Texts Teach What Readers Learn*, The Thimble Press, Stroud.

Meek, M. (1991) *On Being Literate*, The Bodley Head, London.

Meek, M. (1992) Literacy: redescribing reading, in K. Kimberley, M. Meek and J. Miller (eds) *New Readings: Contributions to an Understanding of Literacy*, A. & C. Black, London.

Meek, M., Warlow, A. and Barton, G. (1977) *The Cool Web: The Pattern of Children's Reading*, The Bodley Head, London.

Melser, J. and Cowley, J. (1980a) *The Hungry Giant*, Story Chest Large Read Together Books, E.J. Arnold, Walton-on-Thames.

Melser, J. and Cowley, J. (1980b) *Mrs Wishy Washy*, Story Chest Large Read Together Books, E.J. Arnold, Walton-on-Thames.

Merchant, G. (1990) Teachers' perceptions of linguistic diversity, in C. James and
P. Garrett (eds) *Language Awareness in the Classroom*, Longman, London.

Merchant, G. (1992) Supporting readers for whom English is a second language,
in C. Harrison and M. Coles (eds) *The Reading for Real Handbook*, Routledge,
London.

Mills, J. (1993) Language activities in a multilingual school, in R.W. Mills and J.
Mills (eds) *Bilingualism in the Primary School*, Routledge, London.

Minns, H. (1990) *Read It To Me Now*, Virago, London.

Minns, H. (1991) *Language, Literacy and Gender*, Hodder & Stoughton, London.

Montgomery, M. (1986) *An Introduction to Language and Society*, Routledge, London.

Moon, C. (1988) Reading: where are we now? In M. Meek and C. Mills (eds)
Language and Literacy in the Primary School, Falmer Press, Lewes.

Moon, C. (1994) *Individualized Reading* (25th edn), Reading and Language Information Centre, University of Reading, Reading.

Morris, J.M. (1974) *Language in Action: Resource Book*, Macmillan Education, London.

Moseley, D.V. (1990) Suggestions for helping children with spelling problems, in
P.D. Pumphrey and C.D. Elliott (eds) *Children's Difficulties in Reading, Spelling
and Writing*, Falmer Press, London.

Munsch, R.N. (1980) *The Paper Bag Princess*, Scholastic, London.

Murphy, J. (1980) *Peace At Last*, Picturemac, London.

Murphy, J. (1982) *On The Way Home*, Picturemac, London.

Naidoo, B. (1994) *Trouble for Letang and Julie*, Longman, Harlow.

National Oracy Project (1992) *Oracy and Special Educational Needs*, National Curriculum Council, York.

National Writing Project (1989) *Responding to and Assessing Writing*, Nelson,
Walton-on-Thames.

National Writing Project (1990) *Perceptions of Writing*, Nelson, Walton-on-Thames.

NCC (1989) *English Non-Statutory Guidance*, NCC, York.

NCC (1990a) *English Non-Statutory Guidance*, NCC, York.

NCC (1990b) *The Whole Curriculum*, NCC, York.

NCC (1993) *National Curriculum Council Consultation Report: English in the National
Curriculum*, NCC, York.

Neate, B. (1992) *Finding Out About Finding Out: A Practical Guide to Children's
Information Books*, Hodder & Stoughton, London.

Nicoll, H. and Pienkowski, J. (1975) *Meg's Car*, Heinemann, London.

Norman, K. (1990) *Teaching Talking and Learning in Key Stage One*, National Curriculum Council, York.

Ofsted (1993a) *English: Key stages 1, 2 and 3: Third Year, 1991–92*, HMSO, London.

Ofsted (1993b) *Handbook for the Inspection of Schools*, HMSO, London.

Onyefulu, I. (1993) *A is for Africa: An Alphabet in Words and Pictures*, Frances
Lincoln, London.

Ormerod, J. (1981) *Sunshine*, Picture Puffin, Harmondsworth.

Ormerod, J. (1986) *Joe Can Count*, Walker, London.

Palmer, S. (1991) *Spelling: A Teacher's Survival Kit*, Oliver & Boyd, Harlow.

Pappas, C.C. (1986) Exploring the global structure of children's 'information
books'. Paper presented at the Annual Meeting of the National Reading Conference, Austin, TX, 2–6 December, quoted in Mallet (1992).

Perera, K. (1987) *Understanding Language*, National Association of Advisers in
English, University of Manchester, Manchester.

Peters, M.L. (1985) *Spelling: Caught or Taught? A New Look*, Routledge, London.

Peters, M.L. and Cripps, C. (1980) *Catchwords: Ideas for Teaching Spelling*, Harcourt Brace Jovanovich, London.

Phillips, M. (1990) Educashun still isn't working. *Guardian*, 28 September.

Potter, F. and Sands, H. (1988) Writing and the new technologies in developing children's writing, in D. Wray *et al.* (eds) *Bright Ideas Teacher Handbook*, Scholastic, Leamington Spa.

Pragoff, F. (1989) *Opposites*, Victor Gollanz, London.

Raynor, K. and Pollatsek, A. (1989) *The Psychology of Reading*, Prentice-Hall, Englewood Cliffs, NJ.

Read, C. (1986) *Children's Creative Spelling*, Routledge & Kegan Paul, London.

Redfern, A. (1993) *Practical Ways to Teach Spelling*, Reading and Language Information centre, University of Reading, Reading.

Reid, J.F. (1974) *Breakthrough in Action: An Independent Evaluation of 'Breakthrough to Literacy'*, Schools Council/Longman, London.

Ritter, M. (1988) *Mum's Strike*, Magi, Hayes.

Roberts, D.L.R. (1990) *The People Who Hugged Trees*, Rinehart International, Schull, Republic of Ireland.

Rose, G. (1977) *'Aah,' said Stork*, Picturemac, London.

Rubin, A. (1980) A theoretical taxonomy of the differences between oral and written language, in R. Spiro, B. Bruce and W. Brewer (eds) *Theoretical Issues in Reading Comprehension*, Lawrence Erlbaum Associates, Hillsdale, NJ.

Rumelhart, D. (1985) Toward an interactive model of reading, in H. Singer and R. Ruddell (eds) *Theoretical Models and Processes of Reading*, International Reading Association, Newark, DE.

Sardegna, J. (1994) *K Is For Kiss Good Night*, Doubleday, New York.

Sassoon, R. (1990) *Handwriting: The Way To Teach It*, Stanley Thornes, Cheltenham.

SCAA/DfE (1994) *Key Stage 1 Assessment Arrangements 1995*, SCAA, London.

SCAA (1995) *Planning the Curriculum at Key Stages 1 and 2*, SCAA Publications, London.

Schermbrucker, R. (1992) *Charlie's House*, Walker, London.

Scieszka, J. (1989) *The True Story of the Three Little Pigs*, Puffin Books, Harmondsworth.

Scullard, S. (1986) *Miss Fanshawe and the Great Dragon Adventure*, Macmillan, London.

Seuss, Dr (1963) *Dr Seuss's ABC*, Collins, Glasgow.

Shelley, M. (1990) *Telling Stories to Children*, Lion, Oxford.

Shook, S., Marrion, L. and Ollila, L. (1989) Primary children's concepts about writing. *Journal of Educational Research*, Vol. 82, no. 3, pp. 133–38.

Simeon, L. (1989) *The Streetwise Kid*, Blackie, London.

Simeon, L. (1992) *Marcellus' Birthday Cake*, Mantra, London.

Singer, H. and Ruddell, R. (eds) (1985) *Theoretical Models and Processes of Reading*, International Reading Association, Newark, DE.

Smith, B. (1994) *Through Writing to Reading: Classroom Strategies for Supporting Literacy*, Routledge, London.

Smith, D. and Cassin, S. (1990) *At Home*, Collins, London.

Smith, F. (1971) *Understanding Reading*, Holt, Rinehart & Winston, New York.

Smith, F. (1977) Making sense of reading and of reading instruction. *Harvard Educational Review*, Vol. 47, no. 3, pp. 386–95.

Smith, F. (1982) *Writing and the Writer*, Heinemann Educational, London.

Smith, F. (1983) *Essays into Literacy*, Heinemann Educational, London.

Smith, J. and Alcock, A. (1990) *Revisiting Literacy: Helping Readers and Writers*, Open University Press, Milton Keynes.

Somerfield, M., Torbe, M. and Ward, C. (1983) *A Framework for Reading: Creating a Policy in the Primary School*, Heinemann, London.

Southgate, V., Arnold, H. and Johnson, S. (1981) *Extending Beginning Reading*, Heinemann Educational, London.

Spencer, M.M. (1976) Stories are for telling. *English in Education*, Vol. 10, no. 1, pp. 16–23.

Stanovich, K. (1980) Towards an interactive-compensatory model of individual reading differences in the development of reading fluency. *Reading Research Quarterly*, Vol 16, no. 1, pp. 32–71.

Stebbing, J. and Raban, B. (1982) Reading for meaning: an investigation of the effect of narrative in two reading books for seven year olds. *Reading*, Vol. 16, no. 3, pp. 153–61.

Stone, S. (1988) *Eid ul-Fitr*, A. & C. Black, London.

Stow, J. (1992) *The House that Jack Built*, Frances Lincoln, London.

Strickland, R. (1962) *The Language of Elementary School Children: Its relationship to the language of reading*, Bulletin, Indiana University, Bloomington.

Sutton, E. (1973) *My Cat Likes to Hide in Boxes*, Puffin Books, Harmondsworth.

Swann, J. (1992) *Girls, Boys and Language*, Blackwell, Oxford.

Swann, J. and Graddol, D. (1988) Gender inequalities in classroom talk. *English in Education*, Vol. 22, no. 1, pp. 48–65.

Sylva, K. and Hurry, J. (1995) *Early Intervention in Children with Reading Difficulties: An Evaluation of Reading Recovery and a Phonological Training*, SCAA, London.

Sylvester, R. (1991) *Start With A Story,* Development Education Centre, Birmingham.

Tanner, G. (1992) *Housework*, A. & C. Black, London.

Tansley, A.E. (1967) *Reading and Remedial Reading*, Routledge & Kegan Paul, London.

Teague, K. (1991) *Imran's Clinic*, Magi, Hayes.

Temple, C., Nathan, R., Burris, N. and Temple, F. (1988) *The Beginnings of Writing*, (2nd edn), Allyn & Bacon, London.

Tilbrook, B. and Grayson, B. (1990) What are writers made of? In National Writing Project, *What Are Writers Made Of? Issues of Gender*, Nelson, Walton-on-Thames.

Tizard, B. and Hughes, M. (1984) *Young Children Learning: Talking and Thinking at Home and at School*, Fontana, London.

Topping, K. (1985) Parental involvement in reading: theoretical and empirical background, in K. Topping and S. Wolfendale (eds) *Parental Involvement in Children's Reading*, Croom Helm, London.

Trelease, J. (1984) *The New Read-Aloud Handbook* (2nd edn), Penguin Books, Harmondsworth.

Trudgill, P. (1974) *Sociolinguistics*, Penguin Books, Harmondsworth.

Trushell, J. and Broderick, C. (1984) Primary observations of word processing, in D. Wray and F. Potter (eds) *Micro-Explorations (1) Using Language and Reading Software*, UKRA, Ormskirk.

Turner, M. (1990) *Sponsored Reading Failure: An Object Lesson*, IPSET Education Unit, Warlingham.

Verma, G.K. (1984) *Papers on Biliteracy and Bilingualism*, National Council for Mother Tongue Teaching, London.

Vygotsky, L.S. (1962) *Thought and Language*, MIT Press, Cambridge, MA.

Waddell, M. (1991) *Coming Home*, Simon & Schuster Young Books, London.

Wade, B. (1984) *Story at Home and School, Educational Review Occasional Publication*, 10, University of Birmingham, Birmingham.

Wade, B. (ed.) (1990) *Reading for Real*, Open University Press, Milton Keynes.

Wade, B. and Moore, M. (1987) *Special Children . . . Special Needs: Provision in the Ordinary Classroom*, Robert Royce, London.

Watanabe, S. (1977) *How Do I Put It On?* Puffin Books, Harmondsworth.

Waterland, L. (1988) *Read With Me: An Apprenticeship Approach to Reading* (2nd edn), The Thimble Press, Stroud.

Webster, S. (1994) *Inside My House*, Riverswift, London.

Weinberger, J., Hannon, P. and Nutbrown, C. (1990) *Ways of Working with Parents to Promote Literacy Development*, University of Sheffield Division of Education, Sheffield.

Weir, L. (ed.) (1988) *Telling the Tale: A Storytelling Guide*, Youth Libraries Group of the Library Association, Birmingham.

Wells, G. (1982) *Language, Learning and Education*, Bristol Centre for the Study of Language and Communication, University of Bristol, Bristol.

Wells, G. (1984) *Language Development in the Pre-School Years*, Cambridge University Press, Cambridge.

Wells, G. (1986) *The Meaning Makers*, Heinemann Educational, Portsmouth, NH.

White, J. (1990) On literacy and gender, in R. Carter (ed.) *Knowledge about Language and the Curriculum: The LINC Reader*, Hodder & Stoughton, London.

Whitehead, M. (1990) *Language and Literacy in the Early Years*, Paul Chapman Publishing, London.

Widlake, P. (ed.) (1989) *Special Children Handbook: Meeting Special Needs within the Mainstream School*, Hutchinson, London.

Wilkins, V.A. (1993) *A, B, C, I Can Be*, Tamarind, Camberley.

Williams, J. (1983) *The Practical Princess and Other Liberating Fairy Tales*, Scholastic, London.

Willig, C.J. (1990) *Children's Concepts and the Primary Curriculum*, Paul Chapman Publishing, London.

Wray, D. (1994) *Literacy and Awareness*, Hodder & Stoughton, London.

Wray, D., Bloom, W. and Hall, N. (1989) *Literacy in Action*, Falmer Press, London.

Wood, D.J., Bruner, J.S. and Ross, G. (1976) The role of tutoring in problem solving. *Journal of Child Psychology and Psychiatry*, Vol. 17, pp. 89–100.

Woods, T. (1989) *Postwoman*, Franklin Watts, London.

Zola, M. (1983) *Moving*, Hamish Hamilton, London.

Zolotow, C. (1972) *William's Doll*, Harper & Row, London.

Index